The
EVERYTHING
Homebuying Book

Dear Reader:

Welcome to an exciting and memorable part of your life: buying a new home. Certain life events come only once and have an important nature. Buying your first home is certainly a significant event, and it definitely falls into this category. Some readers will be reading this book as they prepare to purchase a second or third home because they didn't read or reference anything before, and to those readers I say welcome.

But to those who are first-time homebuyers, your acquisition of a first home will be a milestone, as was or is your graduation from college, your first love, your marriage, your first child, your very first car, and your first job. Goosebumps are the norm.

I sincerely wish that you will learn from what I've written on these pages. I urge you to be patient, to do what is right for you, and to be happy. Remember that if you make a mistake, that's only normal. Perfection is an abstract term and can never be achieved. Don't be too hard on yourself.

Enjoy the process, and have fun on the way. Learn the business of buying your home since you will most likely buy another, or even multiple homes, later on down the road.

Enjoy, and Good Luck,

The EVERYTHING® Series

Editorial

Publishing Director	Gary M. Krebs
Managing Editor	Kate McBride
Copy Chief	Laura MacLaughlin
Acquisitions Editor	Eric Hall
Development Editor	Karen Johnson Jacot
Production Editor	Khrysti Nazzaro

Production

Production Director	Susan Beale
Production Manager	Michelle Roy Kelly
Series Designers	Daria Perreault
	Colleen Cunningham
Cover Design	Paul Beatrice
	Frank Rivera
Layout and Graphics	Colleen Cunningham
	Rachael Eiben
	Michelle Roy Kelly
	Daria Perreault
	Erin Ring
Series Cover Artist	Barry Littmann

THE
EVERYTHING®
HOMEBUYING
BOOK

SECOND EDITION

All the ins and outs of making the
biggest purchase of your life

Mark B. Weiss, C.C.I.M., and Ruth Rejnis

Adams Media Corporation
Avon, Massachusetts

*I would like to dedicate this book to those who have supported
me with their love while I was continuing my education, career
advancement and diversification, and growth throughout the years.*

An Everything® Series Book.
Everything® is a registered trademark of Adams Media Corporation.

Published by Adams Media Corporation
57 Littlefield Street, Avon, MA 02322 U.S.A.
www.adamsmedia.com

ISBN: 1-58062-809-5
Printed in the United States of America.

J I H G F E D C B A

Library of Congress Cataloging-in-Publication Data
Weiss, Mark B.
The everything homebuying book / Mark B. Weiss and
Ruth Rejnis.—2nd ed.
p.   cm.
ISBN 1-58062-809-5
1. House buying—United States—Handbooks, manuals, etc.
I. Rejnis, Ruth. II. Title. III. Series: Everything series.
HD255 .W38 2003
643'.12—dc21
2002152394

This publication is designed to provide accurate and authoritative information with regard to
the subject matter covered. It is sold with the understanding that the publisher is not engaged
in rendering legal, accounting, or other professional advice. If legal advice or other expert
assistance is required, the services of a competent professional person should be sought.
—From a *Declaration of Principles* jointly adopted by a Committee of the
American Bar Association and a Committee of Publishers and Associations

Many of the designations used by manufacturers and sellers to distinguish their products
are claimed as trademarks. Where those designations appear in this book and Adams Media
was aware of a trademark claim, the designations have been printed in initial capital letters.

*This book is available at quantity discounts for bulk purchases.
For information, call 1-800-872-5627.*

Contents

11 Negotiating the Best Price / 167

12 Negotiating the Best Contract / 181

13 The House Inspection / 191

14 The Closing / 207

15 Building Your Own House / 219

Acknowledgments

I want to say thanks to Experience: Without your permission to travel your roads, I would not have been able to get here today. I would also like to say a special thanks to all the following people:

- Kathy Welton, who found me and who chipped away the surface, thus discovering the writer who now will be known as one forever.
- Daniel B. Weinberg believed in my ability to do business and trusted me with his confidence. Together we shared a family vision toward a business future when I was still a college freshman and only eighteen years old. Unfortunately, he died before we were able to share this vision. Thanks, Uncle Dan, for the short time we had together. I hope you are somehow aware of the thirty-year legacy I created in your name.
- Harriet and Hyman Bobrow, who lent me the start-up funds to begin in the business world. Somehow you trusted my dream and believed in me enough to take a risk on a nineteen-year-old with a vision. Thanks, Aunt Harriet and Uncle Hy.
- Marilyn, my wife and first love, who was with me thirty years ago when this all began and who continues today to be my guiding light and love of my life. It was you

who planted the idea of entering the real-estate field. It worked. I love you.

- Paul Egel, who was always a loving friend with a guiding hand. Dr. Egel, you supported my returning to complete my education, my business risk taking, and my entrée into real estate as a career. You have always been and continue to be interested in what I do. I have always valued our special relationship. I will never be able to express the full extent of the appreciation I have for you as my mentor.
- My son Daniel, thanks for hanging in there as I have had to take time from our special time together to work, as well as write this and the other books. We do have great vacations together though, don't we?

Thanks also for the assistance of those who helped with the research for the book: Kate Anderson, senior research editor and development liaison of the National Association of Realtors, provided valuable information and statistics throughout the book. Keith T. Gumbinger, vice president of HSH Associates, assisted with the mortgage information. Lorna Sisson of the Tolentino Agency assisted with the accuracy of the insurance information.

Thanks to you all,
Mark

Top Ten Things You Will Learn
From This Book

1. Doing your research can help you find the right home to fit your needs and those of your family.

2. Assessing your finances and knowing your limits will prepare you for the homebuying process.

3. Being happy with your new home is dependant on choosing a mortgage that makes sense for you.

4. Make the most of what's available by finding government programs for first-time homebuyers.

5. Choosing the right real estate agent will help you make informed decisions and maneuver the market wisely.

6. In some cases, it's smart to buy a house *without* an agent.

7. Savvy negotiating can ensure that you get more for your money.

8. You can save time and money by learning the importance of the house inspection process.

9. Closing on a house doesn't have to be a nail-biting experience.

10. Securing homeowner's insurance will help you protect your investment against the elements and the unknowns.

Introduction

▶MOST OF US START in the rental market first. This may be you right now. And you've started to think about taking a big step and purchasing your own home. But where do you start? It's easy to feel overwhelmed by all the new terminology you'll hear thrown around as soon as you mention "buying." And who's not at least a little bit afraid of plunking down such a huge chunk of money?

You probably already know more than you think you do about homebuying. And armed with the *Everything® Homebuying Book,* you will have all that you need to help you work through each step of the exciting process of buying a home. It explains everything from beginning to end—from choosing a real-estate agent and choosing a mortgage, to closing the deal and moving in. We will cover the ins and outs of what all the terminology means, discuss what to avoid, and pass along important tips that will help you save money and get the house you want.

In the 1950s, the people of the United States participated in the largest homebuying market the world has ever seen, due in part to the subsidizing of the G.I. Bill. That was the first time in American history that the rate of home ownership exceeded the number of people renting their homes. And today we've seen interest rates on mortgages drop so low that often the cost of a monthly mortgage payment is less than or equal to what it would cost you to rent!

For most of you, finding the right home will take about a year. You will want to see many properties in order to know what is *not* right for you. Only through looking will you know what to eliminate. You want to look and look in order to disqualify properties that you feel are not what you want to buy. Be comfortable in knowing what is not for you, and be picky, because buying a home is the largest investment you may make in your life.

The home you are looking for may not be on the market when you begin your search. Be patient—it will come on the market. You will reinvent your home in your mind many times during your search. Be flexible. By being flexible, you will create an opportunity. And aren't we all looking for a great opportunity?

You are entering a most exciting time in your life. You are, in essence, creating an estate! Congratulations. You will find *The Everything®Homebuying Book* fun and easy to learn from. With chapters on financing, mortgages, down payments and related costs, this book guides you through the initial steps of the home search. Then, chapters on different house styles, condos, fixer-uppers, and choosing a neighborhood cover the variety of options you will have once you begin the search for the perfect home. The book's subsequent chapters walk you through the negotiation process, the house inspection, and the closing process. Buying the right vacation home and building a home from scratch are also covered in detail here. No matter what your needs are, we will help demystify the house hunt and help you make this process smooth and efficient. So sit back, relax, and enjoy homebuying. Have fun! Ⓔ

Chapter 1

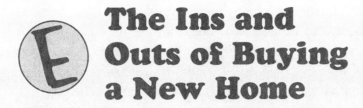

The Ins and Outs of Buying a New Home

Deciding to buy a home is a big step. A house is likely to be one of the biggest purchases you will make. But where do you start? There are many factors to consider before you make this important decision.

Renting vs. Owning

Many of you are probably renting right now, wondering if it's the right time for you to make the big move to buying your own home. There are several important differences between renting and owning a home.

When you rent, you are not as tied to your home, or at least you are not tied in the same way that you are when you own it. You leave choices about your home up to your landlord. It's easier to move, say if you have to move to another neighborhood or town on short notice, because all you have to do is wait until your lease is up (or break your lease). The dollar value of your home may increase—if you paint it (with your landlord's permission), for example—but it doesn't benefit you. It benefits the person from whom you're renting, financially speaking.

Owning a home gives you choices that you do not have as a renter. *You* are the one who chooses what new carpeting or flooring should go in when you need it. *You* choose when to water the lawn. *You* choose when it's time to replace the old dishwasher. You also have a lot more responsibility when you own, as you can see. With all of those choices also comes the responsibility to deal with problems when they arise— there is no landlord to complain to when the water heater breaks.

FACT

The U.S. home ownership rate reached 67 percent in the year 2000, the highest ever, according to the U.S. Department of Housing and Urban Development.

Owning can also make you feel more tied to a community than renting does. You are more "settled" there, even if you plan to stay only a few years. The value and appreciation of your home depends a lot on the neighborhood it is located in, as you will read about in Chapter 10. It will therefore be very important to you financially to take a strong interest in what's happening around you.

The financial difference between renting and owning is also significant. When you rent, your monthly housing cost goes out the door and doesn't benefit you (other than keeping you from being kicked out, of course!). When you move from your current rental, you'll have nothing more (financially speaking) than you started with. But when you own a home, each monthly mortgage payment builds equity (or, in other words, increases the amount you own of the property), increasing your net worth. Your home is likely to appreciate—or increase in value—over time, so when you are ready to move, you will be able to sell it for more than you bought it for. This is, of course, a great benefit to you financially.

The tax benefits of owning are also worth considering. You can deduct the cost of interest that you pay on a mortgage from your income taxes each year. And because, especially early on in a mortgage, the majority of the monthly payment is going toward interest, that means a substantial portion of your monthly housing payment can be deducted, reducing the amount of tax you owe by quite a bit. Renters can't deduct any of their rent, and so they end up paying more in taxes than they would if they owned their residences.

Overcoming Homebuying Fears

Buying a home may seem scary, especially if it is your first home. There are new terms being thrown around that you're unfamiliar with. It involves more money than you've ever spent. And it seems so *permanent!* But with good research you will gain a better understanding of the home-buying process, and you will also be able to approach it realistically and without feeling overwhelmed. Overcome your fears by knowing what to expect. Some people who are quite eligible to buy their own places have deep-seated fears that are keeping them from taking that important step. This is understandable. Whether you have been renting for several years and are a first-time buyer or you already own a home and want to understand the process better before making another purchase, you are entitled to be a little nervous about the whole homebuying process.

A home is, after all, likely to be the largest single purchase you ever make. Paying for it will take the better part of the rest of your life. So approaching the process with respect, even a little fear, is only natural. But don't let that fear get the better of you and keep you from knowing the joys of home ownership.

The following sections describe the most common fears about

homebuying and home ownership. By taking them apart one at a time, you'll see that buying a home is just another stage of life that you will get through. You may even enjoy the process.

Fear #1: I'm Worried About the Economy

What if I buy a home and then the economy collapses? Media and anti-administration (regardless of which administration is in power) critics continually forecast total economic collapse, but that has not happened yet—no matter how bad times have been, no matter how the stock market rumbles, and no matter how high unemployment rates get.

Also, homes are not subject to the high sensitivity that short-term investments such as stocks are. They do react to the overall economic climate—sales prices rise and fall—but not as quickly or radically as stocks.

By all means, you should keep an eye on the economy. Bad times often present excellent opportunities to buy. But don't let periodic downturns alarm you into thinking it's all going to tumble down, taking you and your home with it. If you buy wisely—and reading this book demonstrates your seriousness in learning about the real-estate market—your investment will be safe from the natural ebbs and flows of the economy.

Fear #2: I'm Confused About What to Buy

There seem to be so many different house styles to choose from. Yes, there are, and isn't that wonderful? The diversity and the wide range of prices are bringing home owning opportunities to many more Americans. Your decision whether to buy a house, a condo, a co-op, or any other style of shelter depends on your own situation.

Several factors go into selecting the right home for you. These factors include the price you can afford, the size of your family, your commuting time to work, and what the realty market around you has to offer.

Here are a few important points to remember:

- **Go with your instincts.** If you want a loft and it fits in with other areas of your life, then buy a loft.

- **Keep an open mind.** Consider all home styles and neighborhoods, even those that may not initially seem ideal. You may find that one of them is just right for your lifestyle and interests.
- **Think about what type of neighborhood you'd like to live in.** You say you would not be caught dead living in the city? Think the suburbs are too sedate for you? You may be surprised to find stable neighborhoods with vibrant communities in unexpected places.
- **Visit a variety of places for sale in your area, such as new condominiums and new single-family home developments.** Take in all that your area real-estate market has to offer. You will learn a lot about neighborhoods and house styles, and the confusion will eventually disappear.
- **Consider which homes you feel drawn to.** After conducting all of those various investigations, you should find yourself drifting back to one or two particular favorites. Perhaps it is a certain house style you especially like, or maybe your favorite style or neighborhood is the only one you can afford right now. But you will have made a decision. You will have narrowed your search, and you will have a good idea of what you want to focus on in your search for your new home.

Fear #3: I'm Afraid of Being Denied a Loan

Now that's a real fear. Here is some good news, though. Lenders say that some 85 percent of all mortgage applications are approved, so there's a good chance yours will be one of those. After all, lending institutions are in the business of lending money, and unless the country is sailing through some very troubled economic waters, making mortgage money available is their job.

If you have had credit problems in the past, and you're worried that they will work against you in trying to buy a home, you may well be wrong. Even if you have filed for bankruptcy, home ownership can still be within your grasp. Of course, it is wise not to go house hunting until you are back on solid financial footing. But with a stable financial situation, no matter what your past is, home ownership is still within your reach.

Fear #4: I Don't Have Enough Money for a Down Payment

What if I start this house-hunting process and find that I'm short of money? Down-payment requirements vary from one property to another. There is no blanket percentage of a purchase price that is required to buy a home, although the figure generally falls between 10 and 20 percent. A real-estate agent can acquaint you with the requirements in the area where you are looking. Large-display newspaper advertisements will usually show what local builders require as down payments for brand-new homes.

There are ways around down-payment requirements. If you can afford to carry the monthly payments on a home loan, being a few thousand dollars short should not deter you from buying.

Fear #5: I Don't Know Anything About Home Maintenance and Repair

There are three general types of homeowners: those who do all the work around a house themselves, those who do some and farm out the rest, and those who call in repair people for everything. You may think you belong to the last group, but when you buy, you will probably surprise yourself with your abilities—and your interest. When you are in your own home, puttering around can be enjoyable. After all, you are putting time and money into your own place.

Generally, buyers find they grow into becoming responsible home-owners in the same way one grows into other roles requiring responsible action and decision making. You do not have to learn everything at once, and you will be pleasantly surprised at how much help is out there—including help from relatives and friends, your new neighbors, the folks at the lumberyard, and the salespeople at the home center. They will gladly pass along tips on where to find craftspeople, how to repair widgets, and how to manage all the other complexities you will run into in your home. And, of course, there are dozens of books on the market about every aspect of home repair.

Just learn enough about your home to recognize a problem when it occurs and to know whether you can fix it yourself or must call in expert help.

ALERT!

You don't need to know the intricacies of what makes a heating or a plumbing system work. You can still be a good and intelligent driver without knowing exactly how your car operates, can't you? You only need to know when a job requires outside help.

If you are still concerned about maintenance, consider buying a condo or a co-op. Or how about sharing a two-family house with a relative or friend so that you can share concerns about a leaky roof?

Fear #6: I'm Afraid I'll Discover Too Late That I Can't Afford the Home I Buy

That is not likely to happen. Unlike a landlord, who generally does not care how much of your income you have to spend to pay the rent (as long as you pay it!), a mortgage lender has a vested interest in ensuring that you can make your monthly payments. (After all, it's their money.) They will ensure that the house you buy stays below a certain percentage of your income so that you don't get in over your head, financially.

In addition, reputable real-estate agents will not show you homes out of your price range. Before you see even one home, your lender and real-estate agent will have determined the price range you can afford. So as you search, you have two backups to keep you from getting carried away by a home you cannot afford.

Finally, if you have the home inspected by a professional before you buy it, you can avoid unexpected expenses. An inspector should give you a fairly clear idea of what is in good shape and what needs replacing immediately.

In sum, the homebuying process includes a number of checks that will help ensure that the house you purchase is one you will be able to afford.

The First-Time Buyer

Don't be scared the first time you take the plunge to home ownership; we've all been first-timers at one point or another.

There is a large emotional component that goes along with the change from renting to owning. You take on significantly more responsibilities, which can be intimidating. But you also enjoy all the benefits of making decisions yourself (and not waiting on a landlord to do it his way) and of being able to take pride in the results.

This is a serious process that requires research, time, dedication, and application; it's something that cannot be embarked upon lightly. As a first-time homebuyer, you must realize this is probably the largest investment you will make during your life. It can be a life-changing event, which now puts you in charge of home maintenance, repairs, and taxes. Paying your mortgage is a more serious financial obligation than paying rent has been. But paying on time is a huge step in establishing credit for yourself to use later in acquiring additional property in the future.

Perhaps you are still convinced that buying your own home is truly out of the question for you, at least in terms of the cost. On the one hand, you have noted that in the last several years, home prices have stabilized, and mortgage interests rates are as low as they have been in years. On the other hand, down-payment requirements still remain fairly high and can run as much as 20 percent of a home's purchase price. For a $125,000 home, that comes to $25,000!

QUESTION?

"How do I fit into this so-called booming market picture? Everyone is saying buy, buy, buy, but I honestly don't see how I can."
Even if you have saved only $4,000, chances are good that you can still find a way to buy a home.

Thousands of people who have the same fears as you have found that by considering some of the options below, they were able to afford a home of their own. You may be surprised to realize how many avenues there are to home ownership, even for those with limited means. Don't give up just because you don't have the $25,000 down payment for the house we mentioned above. The reward for persistence is home ownership!

Many renters could be homeowners today if they approached the house hunt with the same organization and determination that they bring to a job search—or even to shopping for a car! Because real estate is such unfamiliar terrain, however, they see figures and prices and sink back and sigh, "I just can't do it."

The biggest hurdle that prospective homebuyers have to face today—besides their own fears—is the down payment. Many can afford a monthly mortgage payment; it is likely to be about the same as, or not much higher than, the rent they are currently paying. But how can they come up with $10,000 or $15,000—or even more—for that money down? In Chapter 2, we cover some of the many sources for down payments.

If you are in your twenties or thirties, you may own several homes in your lifetime. Even if you are older, you will, in all likelihood, move three, four, or more times.

Another deterrent to homebuying for many renters has to do with tunnel vision. When you think of a home, do you imagine an attractive single-family house in a good neighborhood in your present community, perhaps on a half-acre lot? But you already know that those homes are out of your price range. That narrow view of what constitutes the perfect home could be holding you back from owning.

"First home" and "starter home" are terms you may have seen in real-estate articles. Consider closely those first words: "first" and "starter." You are at the beginning of a long period of ownership.

Homebuyer Beware—Why *Not* to Buy Now

The reasons not to buy a home are certainly fewer than those on the plus side of the ownership ledger. That's because, generally speaking, buying the place where you live is an excellent move. However, if you are in any of the following situations, you might want to put off buying, at least for the moment:

- **You do not plan to stay in a home at least three years.** If you sell too soon, all of the costs attached to selling one place, buying the next one, and then moving will mean that you take a loss. This is particularly true in times when annual housing appreciation is slight or nonexistent. If you are transferred frequently in your job, or you know that you will be leaving an area soon, you may want to continue renting until you can expect to stay in one spot for a while.

- **You are saving every bit of spare cash to start a business or to study for a graduate or undergraduate degree.** In these cases, it is best to put homebuying on the back burner until you can free up more money.

- **You regularly make significant and expensive purchases.** You may need to make some sacrifices to be able to afford a home. Not many house hunters have unlimited budgets. You may have to put off purchasing the expensive stereo equipment, hold down other credit-card purchases, and, in general, retrench and save. Careful spending is the key to home ownership.

- **You want to buy an expensive property fairly soon.** You should become even more serious about saving money. For example, forget the lavish wedding you had planned and have a smaller one, depositing the extra funds in your "house account." Planning a week's skiing trip 2,000 miles from home? Opt for a long weekend at a resort within driving distance instead. See how the money in that account will add up?

- **You truly do not have the money for a down payment and cannot carry a mortgage payment no matter how many tips on both are offered in these pages.** If this is the case, you should continue renting for now. A mortgage lender will be able to see that you are stretched pretty thin and, therefore, would be unlikely to grant you a loan in this case. Keep trying, though, and saving, and one day you will be handed the keys to your own place.

Be Objective

What should you look for your first time around? Don't get caught up in finding your dream house—that will come two or three homes down the road. First-time homebuyers usually must make sacrifices—sometimes a lot of them. Don't be discouraged if you can't afford a home like the one your parents live in when you're ready to buy your first home.

Keep your eyes on one objective: buying a solid home that you will be able to sell when you want, probably in the next few years. When you're ready to purchase your next home, you will likely be able to afford something more expensive, or larger, or in a better neighborhood. And from that home you may even move again, trading up just a little more.

The steps to becoming a homeowner may seem daunting, but taken one step at a time, you'll find they aren't so bad. The effort you put into buying your first home will pay off in countless ways. The financial and emotional benefits of owning a home are very rewarding.

ALERT!

Become an educated buyer and do your research. Understand the steps necessary before taking the homebuying plunge. Especially important is evaluating your credit rating—avoid paying credit cards or your rent late. If you need to make improvements, now is the time to do so!

A Home Is a Good Investment

Why do you want to buy a home? Perhaps your reasons are vague: "because that's what people do" or "because it seems like it's about time I did." Or maybe you know exactly why you want to take the step from renter to owner.

Let's look at some of the advantages of home ownership. These points will help you decide if it makes sense for you.

Investment Appreciation

A home is certainly a good financial investment, and most likely, the home you buy will appreciate. If you own it long enough, it is likely to rise in value, in some regions more rapidly than others. Even an annual rise that keeps pace with inflation is a savings for you.

The investment pays off when you move. If you can command even a little more money from the property you are selling than the amount you paid for it, you can use your equity in that home to buy a more expensive home than you were able to afford the first time. Gradually over the years, with buying and selling, you can build quite a nice investment for yourself. For many, that sizable amount of equity will contribute in a major way to a financially comfortable retirement.

Equity is the amount of a home that you own outright, not including the mortgage or any other debts against it. The more payments you make on your mortgage, the more equity you have in your home.

Of course, many people buy a home intending to stay in it for a very long time. You are looking for a place to live for many years, and it may be too early to think about when you might want to sell it. But even if you are not planning to sell your home in the foreseeable future, the appreciation of your home still makes your purchase a worthwhile investment.

Leverage

One of the greatest benefits of housing as an investment in this country is not completely understood by most of the people who use it. Real-estate professionals, however, understand it very well. It is called leverage. Leverage means investing as little as possible of your own money to make as large a purchase as possible. You gain leverage, in other words, when you use borrowed money (the mortgage loan) as a means to purchase your home investment. As a result, a small percentage of appreciation in home value can mean a large return on the cash you actually put into the purchase.

For example, let's say you are, because of a good income and credit history, allowed by a mortgage lender to make a $10,000 (10 percent) down payment on a $100,000 home. Your home appreciates at the rate of 5 percent the first year. At the end of that year, therefore, the house is worth $105,000. At the end of year two, it is worth $110,250, and so on. After three years, you are ready to move up to a larger house. Because you have taken good care of your property and kept up the interior, it sells for $119,000. When you have covered expenses related to selling, you net $110,000. After paying off the mortgage, which still has a balance of nearly $89,000, you have slightly more than $21,000 cash in hand. Your $10,000 investment has more than doubled in three years, all thanks to leverage. And those numbers are conservative. Some leveraged investments in homes bring their owners 200 percent or more in as little as three years.

Tax Benefits

Interest paid on a mortgage is deductible from your gross income on federal tax returns. So are real-estate taxes. The two together usually comprise the majority of the monthly payment made to the mortgage holder in the early years of home ownership. Thus, for the homeowner, housing becomes, in effect, a deductible expense. Tenants who pay rent have no such benefits.

Saving Money

Owning your own home can be a great way to save money. As you pay off your mortgage each month, you are gradually reducing the principal (amount of your loan), while your equity, or the amount of the home you actually own, grows. Your home is likely appreciating while you own it, but the amount of your mortgage remains the same. This works like a giant piggy bank, in a way. The money you accumulate in the home continues to increase, acting as a sort of high-interest savings account.

A fixed-rate, long-term mortgage is a popular form of home financing. (Other mortgage options are discussed in Chapter 3.) The amount of the interest you pay on the loan is fixed, which means you are assured of the same, constant base payment for your housing for the next twenty or thirty years. Inflation, or an increase in housing demand and its resulting rise in housing costs, will not change the payment. Even an adjustable-rate mortgage is likely to have a cap on possible increases in your monthly payments.

ALERT!

With a fixed-rate mortgage, your base mortgage payment will remain the same over the life of the loan. However, real-estate taxes and maintenance costs may increase as time goes by.

Can you say the same about rent? Of course not. Rents usually go up and up and up, especially when you look at a long-term leasing picture that covers the next twenty or thirty years.

More Space

You are likely to get more space for your money in your own place than in an apartment. Indeed, if your family is large, owning a home may be your only viable housing option. But it is more than a matter of bedrooms. With many homes, you also get storage space in the form of an attic, a basement, or a garage—sometimes all three. Closets are likely to be more plentiful and kitchens larger, even eat-in size.

Many people love the land, and to them, having a home means owning a bit of the good earth. Land buys distance from your neighbor—something that is hard to come by in apartment living. Land also brings the opportunity for gardening and growing your own vegetables. And usually, there is room for the kids to play.

Condos and co-ops do not usually include ownership of your own piece of land outside your unit. You may have only a patio or a small area for gardening. (However, you also don't have to mow the lawn!)

There is a feeling among homebuyers that they are ready to settle down. That does not necessarily mean they want to marry and raise families; it just means that they want to put down roots in a place of their own. They look forward to decorating or landscaping where the money and work they put into the place increase the value of their investment. Many also seek neighborhoods or communities that are stable and unlikely to change in the near future.

Buying a home makes you part of the community. You are likely to feel a stronger link to your town or city when you own property in it.

Security

Security means a variety of different things. To some homeowners, it means personal safety—being in a neighborhood with low crime rates, a good neighborhood watch program, and good lighting on the streets. Perhaps a living on a street with little traffic is important, an area where neighborhood kids can play safely in and around their homes. To others, the safe neighborhood represents security for their hard-earned investment dollars. They are certain that having chosen a home in a stable neighborhood, perhaps protected by strict zoning laws, their home will increase in value.

Pride of Ownership

Many homebuyers feel "pride of ownership" once they have purchased a home. A home becomes a status symbol, proof of your success and "coming up" in the world. Homeowners see their homes as extensions of themselves and are pleased that their hard work has resulted in their being able to have their own place.

Our society as a whole regards owning property as a positive status symbol. As a homeowner, for example, you will probably find that it is easier to get credit or a loan. And, truth be told, sometimes the "right address" can open doors for you, whether that's in terms of work or socially.

Patience Is a Virtue!

Do these reasons for buying a home resonate with you? Probably several of these reasons are on your list of why you want to become a homeowner. Be reasonable in your search. Give yourself enough time to find what is right for you, but know at the same time that you just might find the right property your very first time out. Straddling both sides of the fence is tough, but your good judgment must prevail—don't act hastily, yet move quickly if you see what you like. If you are buying a home for the first time, remember that the first time is always the hardest.

Armed with the knowledge you'll gain from this book, you'll find that it is easier and less intimidating than you thought.

Chapter 2

The Price of Home Ownership

The first place to start when you're interested in buying a home is with money. You'll need to evaluate your financial situation, consider the options for financing your home, and come up with a down payment. All of these things will determine the size, location, and style of house you are able to afford.

Examining Your Options

Using money you've saved up or obtaining gifts from your parents are wonderful ways to acquire your first home. The first thing to consider is the down payment. Most likely, you will need to spend anywhere from 3 to 20 percent of what the home costs for the down payment. You may use subsidized financing, like financing from the Federal Housing Authority (FHA) or a veteran's loan from the Department of Veterans' Affairs (VA). Subsidized financing that allows you to make a lower initial investment will include more restrictions than a standard bank mortgage. (These restrictions change and are updated frequently, so you should check out their respective Web sites or talk to your lender about what might be required.)

For those who don't want to deal with the stricter obligations of the FHA or VA, 5 percent of the cost of the home will be the absolute minimum down payment you can make in buying a home. The smaller the amount that you put down on your loan, the bigger the mortgage becomes. Anyone borrowing more than 90 percent of the price of their home is required to obtain private mortgage insurance, or PMI. This insurance guarantees the lending institution that it will be repaid the entire amount of the mortgage loan from you as the borrower. The PMI can add considerably to your monthly cost. If your mortgage payment is $500 per month, after you add the PMI to the payment, your monthly payment could go up to $575. Of course, the advantage of PMI is that it allows you to buy that first home with the most amount of leverage, so it is an option that is worth considering.

You're much better off putting more as a down payment rather than paying PMI, which only makes it more expensive for you in the long run and takes away from your equity buildup.

In addition to making a down payment, you must have the ability to borrow money. Remember, the home you buy is only as good as the money that you can borrow to buy it with. Certainly there are cash buyers in the marketplace, but in this day and age, when the average starter home in most urban areas can cost $200,000 to $300,000, paying cash for a house is fairly uncommon.

ALERT!

It's a good idea to meet with a mortgage company, your local bank, or a mortgage broker at a very early stage in the homebuying process. You need to find out specifically what is required of you and ensure that your credit report accurately reflects that you are a responsible individual with sufficient income and credit to buy a home.

Obtain a copy of your credit report—addresses and contact information can be found in Appendix C—to make sure that the information reported there is correct. Your mortgage lender will rely heavily on your credit history to determine if you qualify for a loan. If you've had financial problems, you will need time to eliminate that late payment penalty on your student loan, for instance, from your credit report. Having your credit history in order when you first approach a mortgage lender will help you ensure that the financing you need will be available to you. The most important aspect the lender looks for is whether or not you will be able to make those monthly mortgage payments. The ability to prove your financial capabilities is extremely important and needs to be looked on as the most essential item in buying your new home.

The Importance of the Down Payment

One of the biggest factors in your ability to purchase a home is the down payment.

By now, you have probably given some thought to the price you want to pay, can afford to pay, or have to pay for the home you want. Let's say you estimate the price of the home you want to buy at $110,000 to $125,000. Ten percent of that is at least $11,000. Most down-payment requirements are between 10 and 20 percent of the purchase price of a home. It sounds like a lot of money—it *is* a lot of money! But look at what you are getting.

Leverage has always been a key term in real estate. It means buying the most you can with the smallest investment of your own money. Applied to a home, it can translate into spending $15,000 to get a $125,000 house. How could you acquire so much for so little in another area of the marketplace? A house is something that will become more valuable over the years; it will not depreciate instantly like a car or furniture does.

TABLE 2.1	Median Sales Price of Existing Single-Family Homes			
Year	Total U.S.	Northeast	Midwest	South	West
1999	$133,300	$139,000	$119,000	$120,300	$173,900
2000	$139,000	$139,400	$123,600	$128,300	$183,000
2001	$147,800	$146,500	$130,200	$137,400	$194,500

Source: National Association of Realtors

Higher Down-Payment Requirements

There is both good and bad news here, however. You have just read the good. The other side of the equation is that over the last several years, some lenders have clamped down on the amount of money they are willing to extend for mortgages. They insist that mortgage applicants be prepared to invest more up front. If down payments are higher, lenders reason, homeowners in financial trouble will think twice about turning the key in the door and heading off down the interstate. They will stay and try to work through their problems, or they'll at least stay long enough to sell the house. Homeowners with bigger amounts invested in their property will be less likely to be willing to sacrifice their investment in times of trouble.

Lenders say there is a definite correlation between loan defaults and the amount of money a borrower has invested in the home. The lower the down payment, the greater the risk to the lender. Homes insured by the Veteran's Administration or the Federal Housing Authority—two agencies that provide sources of low down-payment financing—usually show twice the delinquencies of conventional mortgages.

Another reason for higher down-payment requirements is the existence of the secondary mortgage market. The secondary market is the market used to sell the loans. People don't realize that many lending institutions act as brokers for mortgages, rather than actually loaning the money for the long term to the homebuyer. As an example, you must realize that banks accumulate deposits to invest and then earn profit from the interest rate they lend at vs. the rate they pay out as interest. A bank that pays 3 percent on a savings account will earn big dollars in a 30-year mortgage because most of what is paid back to the bank in the first half of the life of the mortgage is interest. When banks have large deposits they look to invest their money, thus they look to purchase pools of loans that offer good rates of return. Banks that are looking for a quick return on their ability to place loans will lend money as mortgages, then sell the paper to other banks, get their capital back with a fee for acting as the originator of the loan, and start all over again.

These mortgages have to fit a profile when being offered on the secondary market. They must be no less than 80 percent of the value of the property. This insures the ultimate holder of the mortgage that if they foreclose, there is equity in the property that they may ultimately own.

These agencies have demanded that mortgage lenders scrutinize down payments far more closely than they have in the past. Here, too, the reason is protection against default.

Situations That May Demand Higher Down Payments

Putting down as little as you can is usually the best way to go. Still, if you are self-employed, if you have a poor credit record, or if you are very young—with no credit history and just starting your first real job—you may want to, or have to, come up with more than the minimum a lender is requiring. You may also have to come up with more if you want to buy a more expensive house than you can comfortably carry. A higher down payment can make lenders look more favorably on applicants who may have a poor credit history or other financial black marks against them. Consider the options that are listed in the following pages very carefully—and push hard to make one of them work for you.

Where Will the Money Come From?

Does this sound familiar? You build up $5,000 in savings and then pffft, out goes $800 for a car repair. How can you put together a down payment? Sometimes it seems that a down payment on a house is a hurdle too large to overcome. Is it hopeless? Of course not.

As the price of homes climbs each year, even by a little bit, you are likely to find your goal more and more elusive. By the time you have $6,000 saved up, you learn that you now need $9,000. When you inch your savings up to $8,000, what you are looking for now calls for $11,000.

Alternative Sources

Saving, while certainly a commendable practice, may not be the answer in this instance. You cannot save for the next ten years while home prices and down-payment requirements keep rising. You'll never catch up.

If you can afford the mortgage payments on a house once you own one, and you do have enough money for the 4 to 6 percent of the mortgage you will need for closing expenses, it makes sense to tap every source you can for a down payment and buy now.

The down payment is the one area of homebuying that is likely to prove particularly challenging. Still, you may well be able to buy a home even when you do not have enough up-front money.

Down payments often come from savings or from gifts. Your lender will want to verify where your initial down payment has come from. If the money was a gift, they will want to see check stubs or a letter from your parents (or whoever has given the money to you) indicating that this money was in fact a gift.

Look over your own resources that might be tapped. Maybe you are sitting on cash you had not considered. Do you have stocks you can sell? Do you have a life insurance policy you can borrow against? (Don't forget to budget the money you'll need in the future to bring its value back up again.) Do you have valuable silver or jewelry that you're willing to part with? What about tapping into retirement savings? Be careful here, though, of penalties and income taxes due on this money. Can you sell a car? One couple used their expensive foreign import, even though it was several years old, as an $18,000 down payment on a $50,000 condominium. The sellers, who were offering them a mortgage, were quite happy to take the car in lieu of cash.

In your eagerness to amass a sizable chunk of money, be careful not to leave yourself without emergency resources. Keep in mind that there are ways to buy a home with a low down payment (a process that is discussed later in this chapter). Don't use every last penny you have just to make the down payment.

If you decide to liquidate assets (that is, to sell them for cash), it is best to get the money into a savings account as quickly as you can. Don't wait until the day before you need a down payment to sell your Chevy!

TABLE 2.2   Sources of Down Payment

Source	All Buyers	First-Time Buyer	Repeat Buyer
Savings	57%	71%	48%
Equity from previous home	35	*	57
Gift from relatives/friends	13	22	8
Pension fund/401(k)	5	6	4
Loan from relatives/friends	4	5	3
IRA	3	4	2
Inheritance	3	3	3
Loan from financial institution	2	3	2
Sale of personal property	2	1	2
Sale of investment property	2	2	2
Credit from lease option to buy	1	1	1
Life insurance (cash value)	1	1	1
Equity from refinance of invest. prop.	1	*	1
Other	8	11	7

* Less than 1 percent
Source: *The 2000 National Association of Realtors Profile of Home Buyers and Sellers*

Don't Use Credit Cards for a Down Payment

It is not a good idea to borrow what you need as a cash advance on your credit card. Yes, you can get the money quickly without bothering relatives, and you can pay off the loan each month over a long period of time, but consider these negatives:

- Credit-card interest rates are usually the highest in the legitimate lending business.
- You cannot take tax deductions on the interest. (Remember that you can deduct the interest you pay on a mortgage, giving you a substantial savings in taxes.)
- Borrowing to your credit limit for a home will mean that you will not have any advance available in the event of an emergency.
- Credit-card borrowing will push up your debt load in relation to your gross monthly income. Lenders consider these figures carefully, and having too much credit-card debt might prevent you from getting the mortgage you want (or perhaps any mortgage at all).

According to the National Association of Realtors, in 1999, the average homebuyer had an income of $60,400.

FACT

Financing Options

Are you thinking about taking out a bank loan? Personal loans carry higher interest rates than mortgages. A personal loan will also increase your debt load in the same way borrowing on a credit card will. And a lender is likely to discover that you've taken out a loan to make a down payment, which will count against your total debt-to-income ratio as they calculate how much of a mortgage you qualify for.

Lenders often ask mortgage applicants to show proof that down-payment funds have been in a bank account for three to six months. (This is why you should liquidate assets as early as possible in your house hunting.) The lender wants to be assured that the funds have not been borrowed from another lender. They also want to know that the money you have for the house has come from a legitimate source, such as savings or the selling of some asset (another good reason to keep the receipts or statements handy).

Can Your Folks Help Out?

More than 20 percent of all first-time homebuyers get some financial help from their parents or other relatives. Parents mean well when they contribute to a down-payment fund, but be sure that you know that they have thought the matter through carefully. You don't want to let emotion get in the way of financial good sense. Be sure that Mom and Dad will not seriously miss that $10,000 for the short term. Does it hinder their own plans? Will the money be a loan or a gift? If a loan, how soon do you need to repay it? And over how long of a period?

If your parents help you with the down payment, the lender will probably ask them to sign a gift letter stating specifically that the money is a present and does not have to be repaid. The gift letter has to be accompanied by a document that shows Mom and Dad do indeed have the money to give, usually a bank statement showing that the donors have sufficient funds in their account.

ALERT!

If Mom and Dad's check represents a loan, lenders will factor in that repayment plan with your other financial obligations, and that is likely to reduce the size of the loan they are willing to offer. Indeed, some lenders will not make a loan if all of the buyer's down payment is borrowed.

If your folks do decide to help you, they ought to seek the advice of an accountant before writing a check. Gifts over $10,000 may incur additional taxes from the IRS. There may be ways your parents can structure gifts and loans to make them, if not advantageous, at least a little less painful for you at tax time.

Federal Government Programs

If you have exhausted your own resources and still don't have the money you need for a down payment, you may want to consider assistance from a government-backed home-buying program that calls for lower-than-normal down payments. The Federal Housing Administration (FHA) is a government agency that operates under the umbrella of the U.S. Department of Housing and Urban Development (HUD). (There is more about FHA-insured mortgages in Chapter 3. This section focuses on their down-payment requirements.)

With an FHA-backed loan, you can buy a home with a down payment of less than 3 percent. However, you will be required to pay their mortgage insurance, which will probably cost you 3.8 percent of the loan up front—it can be financed—and annual payments of 0.5 percent. These rates are designed to cut back on the number of problem loans to people who are likely to default on what they've borrowed. Private mortgage insurance with conventional loans (covered later in this chapter) also requires a monthly charge to the homebuyer, but there is no up-front fee. If you get a gift from a relative (or anyone else) that goes toward your down payment, under FHA rules that gift can even extend to covering your closing costs. For more information about FHA loans, call ✆ (800) 483-7342 or visit ✑ *www.hud.gov.*

Your real-estate agent can help you with all of these programs, although depending on where you live, he or she may not be familiar with the FmHA. You can also call those agencies direct. Remember, the FHA operates under HUD, which has regional offices (see Appendix C for listings); the VA has local and regional offices; and the FmHA operates under the U.S. Department of Agriculture.

If you qualify for a loan from the Department of Veterans' Affairs (VA), you do not have to make any down payment. These loans are available to veterans or widows or widowers of veterans who died of service-related injuries. Closing costs can be covered by a gift in this case, too.

The Federal Farmers Home Administration (FmHA) may not be a household name, but it can make a homeowner of you. If you are looking to buy a home in a rural area, the FmHA offers no-down-payment programs and lower-than-market interest rates. Here's the catch. The house you buy must meet their definition of rural, and it must be your principal residence (no second homes allowed here).

Look to Your State

Every state offers some type of home-buying program for first-time buyers that features low down-payment requirements and lower-than-market interest rates. Money is available through bond programs, which are handled by quasi-autonomous agencies known as mortgage finance agencies, housing finance authorities, or something similar.

There may be an income ceiling for those wishing to buy through this program, and you will likely to be restricted to certain areas of some towns—and even to certain blocks within those areas. The program is only for first-time buyers or those who have not owned a home for a specified number of years, usually three or five. But the program works! People who otherwise might not be able to come up with the financing to buy a home become proud homeowners with the help of their state agency.

However, this program regularly seems to be in danger of disappearing, for budgetary reasons (but it is still around); and also, when bond money appears for mortgage financing, it disappears quickly, so you'll want to keep an eye on the program and its disbursements. To learn more about this program, contact your governor's office for the name and phone number of the mortgage finance agency in your state.

The Five-Percent Solution

In addition to government-backed programs, there are a few lenders who will allow a mortgage with a 5 percent down payment—for those with assets and very clean credit. In addition, in tough economic times, some developers of new-home communities will advertise a 5 percent down payment. Sometimes that offer is made for only a short period of time, to help get a particular development off the ground, figuratively and literally. Developers will also sometimes, usually in certain tight economic markets, offer houses and condos under a lease/purchase plan.

Lease/Purchase Programs

A developer can offer a lease/purchase plan to a buyer, but more often it is the seller—not the buyer—who accepts this plan, which allows you to rent with the option to buy at the end of a specified period of time. Here is how the plan works, although there can be any number of variations. You rent a house or condominium, signing a contract that states that at the end of six, twelve, or eighteen months, you will be given the option to buy that property, at a price set at the signing of the contract. (But make sure that your lease/purchase contract stipulates whether you are *allowed* to buy the property or whether you *must* buy the property.) This contract protects you from ordinary price increases in the housing market each year. Additionally, the seller, who for the moment will be your landlord, allows you to apply some of your rent money toward the purchase. The rent you pay goes toward your down payment at the end of the rental period.

ALERT!

Try to negotiate as much as possible of that rent toward your down payment. If the owner offers 20 percent, try for 50 or even 100 percent of it. Naturally, there should be a written agreement between all parties to seal the pact and spell out specifics.

The lease/purchase plan can work well with new-home developers who are anxious to sell their properties and do not mind renting them initially, with the proviso that the tenant will eventually buy. You should know that your option money will not be refunded if you elect not to buy at the end of the specified time. Unless you can prove some sort of fraud on the part of the seller, you do not have any legal grounds for getting that money back. It must be applied toward the purchase of the house.

ESSENTIAL

Offer to pay six months' or a year's rent in advance as a way to entice the seller into a lease/purchase plan. That amount might be too little for a down payment but just right for a one-year rental.

If the real-estate market goes down, you can, of course, decline to exercise your option to buy, a move that could be wise over the long term, even though it will mean forfeiting the option money. As with every real-estate deal, everything in a lease/purchase plan is negotiable, from purchase price to such details as maintenance of the property while you are renting.

Renting that leads to buying can be an excellent path to home ownership, but do not waste your time trying to make such an arrangement work in a booming sellers' market. Sellers will not have any incentive to rent first to you, when they can sell right away to someone else. However, in an active buyers' market, where house hunters can pick and choose from a large pool of properties, sellers are likely to be more open to a lease/purchase plan. Sellers might also be interested in this plan if they are in a hurry to move and want to sell their property fast.

QUESTION?

Where do you find properties you can lease first?
Check the classified pages of the newspaper in the town where you are looking, under Houses for Rent and Houses for Sale. Contact the owners and, especially in a sluggish market, you may well come up with a home for yourself.

Equity Sharing

Equity sharing is a way to get help (from friends or family) with the up-front costs of buying a home that includes financial benefits for the investor. It is different from a gift or loan. Whether you will find equity sharing to be workable will depend on the state of the real-estate market where you intend to buy and on the national economy (and also on how familiar people in your area are with the concept of equity sharing). You will need an investor, and no outsider is likely to want to buy without knowing whether the value of your home will increase regularly. A family member may be willing to join you and risk a low return. Mom and Dad, for example, are more likely to tolerate little or no return on their investment.

Different Types of Shared Equity Deals

Shared equity deals can be arranged in a number of ways. Most commonly, an investor, known as the owner-investor, provides the down payment and possibly even the closing costs. The buyer (known as the owner-occupant) lives in the home, makes the monthly mortgage payments, and pays for taxes and maintenance. Both names are on the mortgage and on the deed.

At the end of a specified period, usually five years, the home is sold. The owner-investor receives the original down payment and any closing costs he or she paid from the proceeds of the sale. If there is a profit, the two split it. If the owner-occupant wants to continue living in that house, he or she can refinance the loan as sole buyer, reimbursing the owner-investor for the costs he originally contributed.

And what if there is no profit? Sometimes the agreement is then extended by both parties for another two or three years in the hope that property values will rise in that time.

Shared Equity Contract

There is no standard contract for equity sharing. Both owners should seek the advice of an attorney or a financial planner who can draw up the appropriate papers. Among other points, a contract should specify the following items:

- Title ownership by all of the parties involved.
- The percentage of the property owned by each buyer.
- A buy-out arrangement so that if one of you wants to sell, the other can buy out that share at a reasonable cost.
- How profits are to be split (most commonly in half after the sale of the property within a certain number of years).
- How disputes are to be resolved (perhaps through arbitration).
- Payment by the occupant of any capital improvements he or she wants, such as a pool or a porch.
- Cost splitting between both partners of expenses that exceed $1,000.
- A rental contract for the owner-occupant to rent the owner-investor's share of the house if the investor wants to deduct depreciation on his or her share of the property. (The IRS does not allow homeowners to depreciate a home, but if you are renting from yourself then you have an investment property, and investment property allows depreciation.)

How you work out these stipulations is between you and the other buyer. Naturally, you both should consult a lawyer, and the investor will want to consult an accountant as well.

Some lenders take a dim view of equity sharing. If they agree to the plan, they will probably demand a large down payment, perhaps even as high as 25 percent. Some will require that the owner-occupant's income be the only income used to qualify for the loan. Previously, many lenders had used the combined incomes of the investor and occupant to determine qualification. You may also find that you will be quoted a higher interest rate and might have to pay points on your loan (more about points in Chapter 3). In other words, you may incur higher total costs in an equity sharing plan, but it is one way to get your foot in the door, so to speak.

ALERT!

Some real-estate agents do not make equity sharing arrangements. Others might direct you to a company that will put together an equity-sharing program for you—at a cost of about $500.

Private Mortgage Insurance (PMI)

Private mortgage insurance, or PMI, is a common expense for first-time buyers. It protects the lender, not you, in case of default. Lenders usually require PMI of borrowers who need 90 percent financing, virtually always of those who want 95 percent, and sometimes even of those applying for 80 percent loans as well. PMI isn't terribly expensive—it can run about $25 per month for $100,000. PMI rates vary from one insurance lender to another. Your mortgage lender can tell you more about this type of coverage. More lenders today are getting into the PMI business themselves, sometimes undercutting outside PMI rates.

After you have owned your home for a few years and your equity reaches a certain percentage—usually 20 percent—you are entitled to cancel your PMI policy. However, you must initiate the cancellation with the lender. Many homeowners do not know this policy can be done away with at some point. They continue needlessly paying premiums well after the time that they no longer need that insurance. The easiest way to avoid PMI is by making a 20 percent down payment when you buy your home.

Low Down-Payment Options

Maybe you've seen the late-night television advertisements for buying a home with "no money down." These are often little better than scams, and you are smart to avoid them. As nice as it would be to buy a home without a down payment, the reality is that this is rare and will cost you significantly more money in other ways.

ALERT!

A few builders from time to time offer "no money down" programs, many of which come with higher-than-market interest rates and loan fees (or points). You are likely to have to pay private mortgage insurance (PMI), too. Also, the programs may be difficult to qualify for, calling for excellent credit and a large amount in savings.

Do some homework here. You can probably do far better with a low down-payment home and no loan fees or a better interest rate. Or you might want to wait a while and continue to save until you have more for a down payment. Remember, if it sounds too good to be true, it is. No one—neither a builder nor a lender—is going to be willing to take a chance with a "no down payment" program. The higher charges are their safety net—and your expense.

Be aware of the real-estate market, both nationally and locally, when you are ready to buy. That way, you will know whether you are operating from a position of strength in a buyers' market or whether at the moment the power is with the seller. The market will affect how much you will have to come up with for your home.

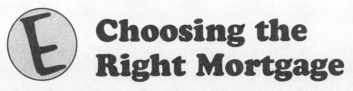

Chapter 3

Choosing the
Right Mortgage

It is wise not to begin serious house hunting until you are familiar with mortgages and, in fact, until you have been preapproved for a loan by a mortgage lender. Indeed, most real-estate agents will hustle you off to a lender before showing you homes. They do not want to waste their time with "browsers" who might not be able to secure a loan.

Getting Approved

You may be thinking, "Don't I find the house first and then think about the mortgage?" Actually, that would be working backward. If, for instance, you were purchasing a new television set, you would mentally go over your finances first, wouldn't you? You would have to think how you could pay for the set, weighing the credit card option against the reasons to pay by personal check.

Save money with adjustable mortgages. They will always feature interest rates lower than you can get on a thirty-year mortgage. There is usually no fee for these types of mortgages, so you can replace them annually if the adjustments head up.

In any case, although you might have researched television sets extensively, you cannot buy one until you know how you will pay for it. It's the same with a home. If you do not know, within a certain range, how much house or condo you can afford and how you plan to pay for it, how can you know to narrow down your search to certain homes? And once you find a home you like, how can you negotiate the price without knowing what you can afford?

TABLE 3.1	Type of First Mortgage by Region				
Type	Total U.S	Northeast	Midwest	South	West
Fixed-rate mortgage	86%	91%	85%	87%	82%
Adjustable-rate mortgage	11	7	10	11	14
Short-term mortgage w/balloon payment	2	1	3	2	1
Graduate payment	1	*	1	*	2
Land contract	*	*	*	*	*
Other	1	1	1	1	2

*Less than 1%
Source: *The 2000 National Association of Realtors Profile of Home Buyers and Sellers*

Preapproved vs. Prequalified

A few years ago, just being prequalified for a mortgage was considered novel and quite beneficial for home shopping. That's no longer the case. Now, real-estate agents prefer to deal with preapproved house hunters, and sellers are happier greeting those would-be buyers, too.

FACT

There are different types of mortgage options available. The most popular are fixed-rate loans that usually span either fifteen or thirty years. Other types include adjustable-rate mortgages (ARMs), FHA, VA, and balloon loans.

What's the difference between being prequalified and being preapproved? You can be prequalified simply by making a phone call to a mortgage lender. The loan officer asks to know your income and a general figure for the amount of your debt. He or she then quickly runs some numbers and tells you the amount that that institution would be likely to lend you for a mortgage, based on your replies. That's it. But it's not enough, certainly not these days.

To be preapproved requires a good deal more effort on both the borrower's and the lender's sides. You apply for a mortgage as if you have already chosen the house you want and are ready to make the purchase. The lender weighs your qualifications, checking your income, your debt, and your credit report.

ALERT!

Don't use any lending institution that wants to review your whole financial picture a second time before actually making the loan.

After reviewing your application, the lender will either approve or reject it. If they turn down your application, be sure you find out what you can do to improve your chances in the future. If you are approved, the lending institution will issue a letter or certificate saying that you have been preapproved for a loan of a certain amount. The only thing left at that point is an appraisal by the lender of the home that you eventually choose to buy. The lender will also want to confirm that your income situation has not changed since the time you were preapproved.

It makes sense to begin house-hunting after you either have a preapproved mortgage or are 99.9 percent certain of getting one. After your loan is preapproved, you will know what size mortgage you can get and, combined with your down payment, determine in what price range you should be looking.

Generally speaking, being preapproved does not guarantee that you will get a specific interest rate. If you are concerned about rates rising during the time you are house-hunting, look for a lender who will lock in a rate for at least sixty days.

Your First Preapproval

For someone buying a first home, a real-estate agent who has sold property to first-time buyers in the past is a good person to work with. The agent will use a formula to determine your ability to handle debt and price range for the loan you may be able to get, working with a mortgage company. He or she will ask you questions that may seem a little intrusive at first, but they are necessary for a lender to know. After all, the lender is potentially going to put up tens (or even hundreds) of thousands of dollars. They want to ensure that they aren't going to lose that money.

FACT

According to HSH Associates, the largest publisher of mortgage information, mortgage rates in the United States over the past ten years have averaged less than 8 percent.

Who Offers Mortgages?

You can walk into the bank where you have your checking account and take whatever mortgage terms they have to offer, but that wouldn't be the smartest way to go. It will pay you—perhaps thousands of dollars over the life of the loan—to shop around for mortgage terms. They are not the same with every institution. You could start with the bank where you keep your savings and checking accounts, since lenders often give preferential treatment to their long-time customers. But before you accept the first terms offered to you, check out what other institutions are offering.

A variety of sources lend mortgage money. These include savings banks and savings and loan associations, commercial banks, credit unions, mortgage bankers, mortgage brokers, government agencies, and sellers themselves.

Mortgage bankers are companies that qualify applicants, find the best available loans, fund the initial loan, and then sell or place that loan with another lender or investor. Mortgage brokers are persons (or companies) who, for a fee, will do the work to find house hunters a lender somewhere around the country.

Government agencies that lend mortgage money include the Federal Housing Administration (FHA); the Department of Veterans' Affairs (VA); the Farmers Home Administration (FmHA); and your state's mortgage finance agency.

In seller financing, home sellers offer mortgages to buyers, usually for a limited time of three to five years. After that time is up, the buyer secures more traditional, long-term financing. Seller financing works for buyers in a very slow sellers market, times in which properties remain unsold and on the market for months, perhaps years, or when a seller is particularly eager to move right away and cannot wait the few months it takes to sell his house through ordinary selling channels. This can be an excellent deal for the seller who does not need the proceeds from the house immediately and recognizes that quite a nice return can be realized by offering a loan to the buyer at 8 or 9 percent interest.

Your Loan Choices

Lenders may have several loan packages that vary in length of the loan, interest rate, and other particulars. The two most conventional loans are the fixed-rate mortgage (for fifteen, twenty, twenty-five, or thirty years) and the adjustable-rate mortgage (ARM). A fixed-rate mortgage, as the name suggests, has a fixed interest rate. ARMs are mortgages whose interest rates change over the life of the loan. They typically offer a "teaser" low-interest rate at the outset of the loan that can be three or more percentage points lower than a fixed-rate loan, but that figure can rise dramatically after the first year, and it usually continues to rise steadily thereafter.

TABLE 3.2 Length of First Mortgages					
Term of First Mortgage	Total U.S.	Northeast	Midwest	South	West
15 years	8%	10%	7%	9%	7%
30 years	86	83	86	86	88
Other	6	6	7	5	5

Source: *The 2000 National Association of Realtors Profile of Home Buyers and Sellers*

Fixed-Rate Mortgages

Fixed-rate mortgages are the most traditional of mortgages. They feature a fixed interest rate over a fixed term, making the monthly payments the same over the entire term of the loan. Fixed-rate mortgages are usually for either fifteen or thirty years. A variation on this mortgage type is the balloon mortgage. It will usually have a fixed rate and hence a fixed monthly payment. However, it spans a shorter time frame—usually three to ten years. While the payments may be based on a thirty-year term, at the end of the balloon term, you must either pay off the remaining debt or apply for another mortgage. Appendix B shows monthly payments, excluding property taxes and homeowner's insurance, for a variety of loans at different interest rates.

Adjustable-Rate Mortgages (ARMs)

Interest rates that lenders charge for ARMs are pegged to an independent financial index they select. There are many choices of index here, carrying a variety of components. To protect homebuyers from large rate increases, most lenders set limits on the amount rates may fluctuate at the time for a loan's interest rate to be determined. This is known as the adjustable-rate cap. With a lifetime cap, lenders set a ceiling and floor for rate increases and decreases over the life of an ARM. The lifetime cap is expressed either as a particular percentage rate or as five to seven percentage points over or under that initial rate. Be sure to ask about caps when you inquire about ARMs.

Some borrowers these days are opting for fifteen-year loans in place of the more traditional thirty-year term, both to build equity faster and to save thousands of dollars in finance charges. Fifteen-year loans may be a little harder to secure than the thirty-year terms because the monthly payments are higher, which means you'll need a higher income to qualify than you would to qualify for a thirty-year mortgage. However, your payments are not 50 percent higher than they would be with thirty-year mortgages. They are usually only 20 to 30 percent above that amount, because more of each monthly payment goes toward principal and less toward interest. Additionally, some lenders will allow you to convert an ARM to a fixed-rate plan at some point down the road. This is beneficial if interest rates drop significantly and you wish to lock in a low rate.

TABLE 3.3	National Rate and Points Fixed-Rate vs. ARM (Combined Averages)					
Annual Average	**30-Year FRM**		**15-Year FRM**		**1-Year ARM**	
	Rate	*Points*	*Rate*	*Points*	*Rate*	*Points*
1991	9.36	2.07	9.04	2.0	7.11	1.96
1992	8.51	1.84	8.07	1.77	5.65	1.73
1993	7.39	1.50	6.93	1.46	4.56	1.41
1994	8.53	1.35	8.05	1.32	5.43	1.26
1995	8.18	1.25	7.75	1.22	6.12	1.15
1996	8.05	1.13	7.60	1.11	5.88	1.07
1997	7.78	1.06	7.40	1.03	5.83	0.98
1998	7.06	1.05	6.72	1.01	5.74	1.02
1999	7.50	0.91	7.12	0.88	6.04	0.90
2000	8.21	0.78	7.89	0.74	7.11	0.82
2001	7.16	0.64	6.68	0.64	6.01	0.71

Source: HSH Associates, ✒ www.hsh.com

Other Mortgage Options

A slightly different variation of a loan is a balloon mortgage. When you take on a balloon loan, you agree to make a fixed monthly payment that will amortize (or repay) your loan over, say, thirty years. On a specified date—five, seven, ten, or any other predetermined number of years in the future—the entire unpaid balance of the loan becomes due and payable. At that point, you can either pay off the loan with your own money or refinance the home with another loan. Otherwise, you risk losing the property.

Which Type of Loan Is Best for You?

Each type of mortgage offers advantages and disadvantages. Choosing the one that makes the most sense for you will depend on your particular situation.

If you are buying a home that you expect to live in for a long time, and if interest rates are low (or if you can negotiate a lower interest rate), a fixed-rate mortgage is likely to be the best loan for you. Though your initial costs might be slightly higher with this mortgage than with another, higher interest-rate loan, you will pay significantly less in interest over the life of the loan with a fixed rate. The fixed-rate mortgage is a clear advantage if you expect to keep your house (and mortgage) for many years (and especially if you anticipate staying in one house until you've paid off the loan).

If you know you will be moving—because of a company transfer to another city, or because you anticipate buying a larger house to raise a family, for example—adjustable-rate mortgages can keep your monthly housing costs down. You are likely to have to pay less money up front, and you'll likely get an attractive low rate initially on the loan. Because you don't expect to keep the mortgage for the full fifteen or thirty years, you will not be hurt by any rise of interest rates that may affect this loan.

Likewise, if you are certain of a move within the period of the balloon, a balloon mortgage may make sense. You can find attractive rates that will help keep your monthly costs down. However, balloon mortgages will probably cost you more in the long run if you keep the loan through the end of the balloon period. If you expect to be in your home for a significant period of time, this should be your last choice in mortgages.

Points are fees charged by lenders for a mortgage. A point is calculated as 1 percent of the amount of the loan. Points (as well as interest rates) are negotiable. If you negotiate a lower interest rate, you may have to pay more points up front. If you choose to keep your initial outlay small, you may negotiate a higher interest rate and in return pay fewer points.

Choosing a Lender

Now that you are familiar with the different types of mortgages, you are ready to start calling mortgage lenders. Ask to speak to the mortgage department or a mortgage loan officer. When you call potential lenders, have a list of written questions in front of you. Use **WORKSHEET 3.1** (see page 44) to keep track of the information you learn. Some questions you should ask include the following:

- What types of financing does the institution have available now? Do they offer both fixed-rate and adjustable plans? Are FHA and VA mortgages available? What other plans does that particular institution have to offer?
- How long of a term are they willing to offer for each type of loan? Is the term of adjustable-rate loans fixed, or do they offer various lengths of terms? Is there is a lower interest rate for shorter-term loans?
- Can ARMs be converted to fixed-rate loans at some point? If so, what is the cost?
- What guidelines do you use for loan qualifications? (The next section, "How Much Can You Borrow?", goes into more detail about qualification guidelines.)
- What is the minimum down payment requirement for each type of loan?

- Does the institution charge points? How many points are charged for each type of loan?
- Is a loan origination fee charged to cover the cost of processing the mortgage?
- Is there an application fee? How much is it?
- Can the lender give you a rough estimate of closing costs in relation to the percentage of the home's sale price?
- Is there a prepayment penalty, or a fee for paying off a loan early, on any of the mortgages?
- Does the lender offer preferred-customer benefits for customers who use the lender's other services, such as checking or savings accounts?
- How long will a mortgage decision take after an application is made? (Three to five weeks is normal in a busy real-estate market.)
- How long will a mortgage commitment remain effective?
- Does the interest rate remain constant on the loan commitment?

FACT

The Federal Reserve Bank of New York offers many free booklets for the homebuyer, homebuilder, and anyone refinancing a home. Write to their Public Info Department, 33 Liberty Street, NY, NY 10045 for their free catalog, "Public Information Materials."

The last two questions are important ones to ask. You need to know how long a loan offer will be available to you at the rates you're first quoted. Some lenders will make a commitment for ninety days, with renewals available. Some will make commitments for up to six months, especially on homes that are new construction. Without a commitment to a particular interest rate, you may still be assured of a loan, but the loan will be written at the interest rate that is prevailing at the time of closing, which may be higher than rates were when you began your search. On the other hand, you may find a lender who will guarantee the interest rate on their mortgage offer. But be aware that if rates go down before you close, they will hold you to the original rate. To get a better rate, you would have to begin mortgage shopping all over again. Some lenders will guarantee the best rate. This is the best deal of all. If interest rates go up before you close on a house, the lender will leave your interest rate the same as it was when they made their commitment to you. And if rates are down by your closing, they will write your mortgage loan at the new, lower rate.

Getting an attractive interest rate locked in, as you can see, is a ticklish business, but it is an important one and certainly one that you must understand as you begin shopping for a loan.

Many lenders inaugurate, from time to time, special mortgage plans unique to their institutions. No doubt the officer you talk to will mention these programs, perhaps even open the conversation with them. If not, it cannot hurt to ask if that lender has any new mortgage programs on the horizon. Give the lender a chance to offer a mortgage that meets your needs. After all, they *do* want your business.

Talk with four to six lenders to help you analyze and compare effectively. A few may quote attractive rates over the phone; then, when you make an application, you find that the rates have risen. Overcome this problem by asking to lock in the rate you want.

Use **WORKSHEET 3.2** on page 45 to take notes on your loan options as you talk to prospective lenders. Be sure you are getting quotes on comparable loans. There are simply too many possible variations on rates and loans for us to cover them all in these pages. However, here is one example of how offers that sound similar at first may be quite different in reality. You might be given one quote on a thirty-year, fixed-rate loan. But what this could really mean is that the lender offers a thirty-year loan with a fixed rate for the first seven years, at a low interest rate for those seven years, but with a balloon payment or refinancing at prevailing rates due at the end of that time for the final twenty-three years. Programs can be very narrowly defined, as you can see, and there are sometimes programs within programs.

Lender   Phone

Address   Fax

Types of financing

Current interest rates

Term

Minimum down payment

Limit on loan amount

Loan qualification guidelines

Points

Loan origination fee

Application fee

Appraisal fee

Credit check fee

Other fees (list)

Prepayment penalty

Preferred customer benefits

Time needed for lender's decision

Length of loan commitment (number of days)

Renewable?

Rate guarantee on commitment (if any)

Late payment penalty

Notes:

The best offering for us seems to be:

Cost of obtaining the loan (add all the fees payable at the closing): $_____

Monthly cost of carrying the loan: $_____

(Use mortgage tables to find the principal and interest payment at the named rate of interest for the named term. Or enter the lender's figure for fixed payments on an adjustable loan. Add mortgage insurance premiums, if any.)

	Cost of Securing Loan	Monthly Carrying Costs
Lender 1_____		
Loan_____	$_____	$_____
Loan_____	$_____	$_____
Loan_____	$_____	$_____
Lender 2_____		
Loan_____	$_____	$_____
Loan_____	$_____	$_____
Loan_____	$_____	$_____
Lender 3_____		
Loan_____	$_____	$_____
Loan_____	$_____	$_____
Loan_____	$_____	$_____
Lender 4_____		
Loan_____	$_____	$_____
Loan_____	$_____	$_____
Loan_____	$_____	$_____
Lender 5_____		
Loan_____	$_____	$_____
Loan_____	$_____	$_____
Loan_____	$_____	$_____

How Much Can You Borrow?

Typically, renters allot 25 to 30 percent of their income to rent. However, if they are paying a higher percentage, their landlords generally don't care, just as long as the rent is paid every month.

That is not the case with mortgage lenders. They will make sure that your mortgage is no greater than what you can reasonably afford. For example, if they are willing to offer you a mortgage for $110,000 and the home you want costs $130,000, you will have to make up the difference by coming up with another $20,000 for the down payment.

Ten or fifteen years ago, most lenders used the gross annual income formula to determine mortgage amounts. If you made $30,000 a year, you could get a mortgage loan of $60,000. Today, lenders who still use that formula—and they are mostly small, hometown institutions—allow two and one half or even three times gross annual income.

There is also the income-to-housing-costs formula. In this qualification procedure, the lender computes anticipated housing expenses and factors these into the equation as they determine the size of the loan they'll offer. These expenses include mortgage payment, real-estate taxes, fire and catastrophe insurance, and mortgage insurance, if any. To qualify with many lenders, your total monthly figure for housing expenses must not exceed 28 percent of your gross monthly income. Some lenders will go slightly higher. FHA loans will not go above 29 percent of your monthly income. **TABLE 3.4** lists the 29 percent ratio for different annual and monthly incomes.

To qualify with most lenders, your total monthly payment for housing expenses and long-term debts must not exceed 33 to 36 percent of your gross monthly income.

Another criterion is the formula that determines the ratio of income to long-term debt payments. Rather than monthly housing costs alone, here all of the borrower's long-term (ten months or more) debt payments are calculated. Included are car payments, large outstanding charge account balances, child support, and college loans.

As you work the numbers to see how much you can probably afford, keep in mind that a mortgage lender is not concerned with the fact that you may need a new car or are planning to return to school for graduate work or that you have no furniture to fill the home you buy. Mortgage lenders are going to look at your current financial situation to ensure that their investment is protected. If you anticipate having large expenses in the near future, *you* will have to decide how much of your income you can really commit to housing.

TABLE 3.4 Mortgage Qualification Worksheet		
Annual Gross Income	**Monthly Gross Income**	**29% of Gross Income**
$15,000	$1,250	$363
$20,000	$1,667	$483
$25,000	$2,083	$604
$30,000	$2,500	$725
$35,000	$2,917	$846
$40,000	$3,333	$967
$45,000	$3,750	$1,088
$50,000	$4,167	$1,208

Source: U.S. Department of Housing and Urban Development

But just a moment! Are those ratios carved in stone? Are lenders totally inflexible? Interestingly, in the last few years there has been a drift toward approving applicants with a considerably higher debt load than 36 percent. While it's becoming more common to qualify with a 40 percent debt load, some borrowers have been approved with figures as high as 50 or 60 percent, or even beyond. Borrowers with such high debt loads who are approved for mortgages are not irresponsible; lenders are not reckless to grant loans to them.

Those borrowers have good credit. They pay their bills on time, and they have never, never "maxed out" their credit cards.

If you fit that profile, you might want to push the debt-ratio envelope yourself. Just be careful not to leave yourself only $50 a month to live on after your mortgage and other expenses have been paid!

Applying for a Loan

Applying for a loan can be one of life's more dramatic—and even traumatic—moments. You may feel like lenders are trying to make it harder than it should be. But remember, mortgage lenders are in the business of loaning you money for a home. They want to help you.

Pay down your mortgage as quickly as possible. There is nothing sensible about paying interest. If and when you can pay more than your required payment amount, pay more. This will not reduce the amount of your monthly payments, but it reduces the principal (or the total amount you owe), which means you will pay it off sooner and pay less interest in the long run.

Having a document from a lender stating that the institution will offer you a mortgage of X dollars will make you look like the serious buyer you are. It is a good negotiating tool as well. No eager seller is going to turn away a qualified buyer too quickly. There are many factors, as you will see, that go into the approval process.

The Paper Chase

Get ready for a lot of paperwork. Papers, documents, files, numbers—whew! It may seem like a lot of work, but knowing what will be needed will help you get organized and be prepared for the mortgage application.

Income, debt, down payment, and a good credit report are the prime components that lenders use as a gauge of creditworthiness. Based on that information, they will determine what amount they are willing to lend you. You might learn that you need to pay off some old bills, clean up your credit, or save still more money. But whatever information lenders pass on to you in the way of tips will help move you along through the mortgage approval process.

It is a good idea to take the mortgage application form home to fill it out when you can give it your full attention, rather than trying to complete it in the lender's office. Ask for a few copies. Use one as a rough draft, making all of the changes you need on that form. Then transfer your answers neatly to the final copy, so it will be as neat and correction-free as possible. Don't let the lender see a form with scratched-out figures or huge dabs of correction fluid here and there. Besides looking messy, it could cause the lender to wonder about the truthfulness of the information you've written down.

Information You Will Need to Provide

It's a good idea to do a little research and find the following information for the mortgage application:

- **Recent address(es).** List the places where you have lived for the past two years.
- **List of assets.** Assets include holdings such as stocks and bonds (if you have an account with a stock brokerage firm, include the most recent statement), IRAs, vested amounts in retirement plans, surrender value of life insurance policies, cars, and so on. Include current balances, names and addresses of institutions, and account numbers for each item. Remember that if you're planning to sell assets, such as jewelry or a car, to help get the money for your down payment, you should do it as soon as possible so that your bank balance reflects as long a history of savings as possible. Lenders don't just want to know your current bank balance; they also ask for the average balance for the last three to six months.
- **List of debts.** Make a list of your credit cards, auto loans, school loans, and any other debts you currently have. Show the names of the organizations that have extended credit to you, the addresses, your account numbers, the amounts owed, and the monthly payments. You're probably keeping a tight reign on your money now, in preparation to buy a home. Still, if you can, pay off as many bills as possible, to reduce your debt load. Debt will count against you in the loan process.
- **Divorce papers, if applicable, along with child support agreements.** If you *receive* child support, you may choose to have this income considered to help you get the mortgage you want.

- **Extra income.** If you have regular sources of extra income, include these on your application. That does not mean occasional overtime; it means, for example, a second job.
- **Foreclosure and bankruptcy status.** If you experienced either within the previous ten years, you must report that information to the lender. (They'll probably find out anyway.) Neither has to keep you from buying a home. Sometimes bankrupt house-hunters can qualify for a home as soon as a year or two after a bankruptcy is discharged.
- **Gift letter.** If Mom and Dad are helping you with the down payment, get a letter from them attesting to that, noting that the money is indeed a gift and that they do not expect to be repaid.
- **Income and employment records.** Collect W-2 statements for the last two years and pay stubs from the previous month. Incidentally, this is not a good time to change jobs, unless your new position will be in the same line of work and you will be earning more. A lender will be skeptical of too much job-hopping, especially if the changes were not really promotions or if they involved a total career switch. If you are self-employed, you will need to show your federal tax returns for the previous two years, as verification of income.
- **Social security number.** List your number and that of anyone buying with you.
- **VA documentation.** If you are applying for a VA-backed loan, you will need a certificate of eligibility. To obtain that form, contact your local VA office six to eight weeks before applying for a loan.

Your Credit Report

A vitally important part of your loan approval is your credit report. It is wise to send for a copy now, before a lender sees it, so that if there are any errors on it, you have time to clear them up. Typically it will cost you about $9 for a single copy of your report. (Residents of Colorado, Georgia, Maryland, Massachusetts, New Jersey, and Vermont are entitled to a free copy periodically, as determined by each state.) You can contact the following national credit bureaus to get a report.

- **Equifax:** ▤ P.O. Box 740241, Atlanta, GA 30348
  ✆ (888) 685-1111
  ✎ *www.equifax.com*

- **Experian:** ▤ P.O. Box 2104, Allen, TX 75013
  ✆ (888) 397-3742
  ✎ *www.experian.com*

- **Trans Union:** ▤ P.O. Box 1000, Chester, PA 19022
  ✆ (800) 888-4213
  ✎ *www.transunion.com*

In the credit report, you will find your personal credit history, including information on every credit card or loan you have had, when and how promptly you made payments, department store charges, auto loans, and the like. This is not, as many consumers mistakenly believe, a rating service. Credit bureaus attach no rating to those they list; they merely collect data and pass it on upon request.

Go over everything in that report carefully. If you see an account in which a payment has not been recorded and you don't have time to clear up the report before meeting with your mortgage loan officer, bring a copy of your canceled check showing you did pay that store or credit card company.

QUESTION?

What if you find an outright mistake in your report?
Write to the source of the erroneous data and clear up the matter with them. Work with the credit bureau until you are satisfied that the mistake has been corrected. Give yourself plenty of time. Credit bureaus can work slowly.

Dealing with a Poor Credit History

Maybe you already know that your credit report is a little messy. Delinquencies, for example, have been recorded, and as much as you hate to admit it, they are correct. Now what do you do?

Be prepared. Were you delinquent in paying bills for four months last year because you were laid off? Because you had serious surgery? Was there a death in the family? A divorce? Send a letter of explanation to the credit bureau and ask them to affix it to your report to serve as an explanation for anyone requesting your file. Be ready to explain your reasons to the mortgage loan officer as well. Copies of doctors' bills can help document long illnesses. If you had a dispute with a credit card company over a payment that is still being worked out in correspondence, bring copies of those letters with you to the lender.

FACT

A copy of your credit report is free in some cases, including the following: if you have been denied credit, employment, or insurance within the past sixty days; are unemployed or on welfare; or if you suspect credit fraud.

If you have no good explanation for the six months or even two years of late payments, you will just have to work around that black mark. Explain to the mortgage loan officer that you are more responsible now about your debts; be willing, if possible, to make a larger down payment than would normally be required. A lender will be more willing to take a risk loaning you money if you can demonstrate that you have changed your ways.

Another way around a poor credit history is to use a pledged account. This means the lending institution keeps extra collateral available in a third-party escrow account in case of your nonpayment. You supply funds equal to three or four months of your mortgage payment in an account managed by some third party. This could be the seller, a title company, or even your employer. You can use cash or another type of collateral, such as stocks, bonds, or certificates of deposit, for this fund.

The escrow instructions will state that this money is to be used only for any delinquent loan payments and late fees for the first three years of the loan. If the loan is in good standing at the end of that time, the funds, plus any interest accrued, are returned to you.

Bankruptcy

Bankruptcy is more serious than late payments. If you can afford to buy a home now, however, do not let that blot on your credit keep you from approaching mortgage loan officers. There are, legally, no time limits on how soon you can secure a conventional mortgage after a bankruptcy is discharged, although some lenders will turn you down no matter how long ago the bankruptcy occurred. With FHA-insured loans, a bankruptcy must be discharged for at least one year; the Department of Veterans' Affairs insists on a two-year wait with VA loans. When applying for a home loan in this instance, you must anticipate the following:

- A good deal of shopping around among lenders.
- Telling the truth about your situation and appearing remorseful and apologetic, not cavalier or casual.
- Giving an explanation of what caused the bankruptcy.
- The need for a scrupulously clean credit report since the bankruptcy.
- Paying a sizable down payment, perhaps 20 percent or more.
- Utilizing some less conventional sources for funding.

ALERT!

Keep in mind that if you have not used credit since a bankruptcy, you will need to build up a credit record by charging inexpensive items or taking out small loans and then repaying them promptly. If there is no repayment record since the bankruptcy, the lender will not know if you can now handle debt.

In dealing with lenders after you have had credit problems, keep in mind the words of one mortgage loan officer: "The important thing is to be honest and open with us and to have a good explanation for what happened. We don't like surprises." Focus on the last four words. Banks and other lenders are ultraconservative institutions. The unexpected makes them very nervous.

You are striving to show as much in savings as you can muster and as few debts as possible. Pay off as many bills as you can before applying for a loan. And, as mentioned earlier, convert as many assets to cash as you can to build up a sizeable savings account. Put off major purchases until you have that mortgage nailed down.

ALERT!

Have answers ready for any point that does not look good on your application. If you have changed jobs frequently, for instance, prepare to explain to the lender that each was a move up—in terms of higher salary or expanded experience. If there are snags in your credit history, be prepared to explain them.

Sources for Homebuyers with Poor Credit

If you have trouble finding a lender because of your credit history, you may need to consider some less conventional methods of securing mortgages. They may not be as common as a "standard" loan from a bank, but these resources may be less stringent about qualifications. You have several options:

- **Mortgage brokers.** A mortgage broker will know a variety of lending institutions across the country and will be able to find a lender willing to work with buyers with less-than-perfect credit histories.
- **Seller's mortgage.** This is offered by the seller of the home for a term of three years or so, after which you secure a mortgage.
- **Assumable loans.** You can take over someone else's mortgage, such as one offered by the FHA or VA, often with no need to qualify on your own. Adjustable-rate loans can be assumed, but, in general, fixed-rate loans cannot be assumed.
- **Lease/purchase.** Renting with the option to buy at the end of a specified period is discussed in Chapter 2.
- **Cosigner.** Parents or another family member might cosign your mortgage, thereby increasing the likelihood that your application will be approved (but also making them responsible for the mortgage if you cannot make the payments).

Mortgage Insurance

There are two kinds of mortgage insurance you may hear about during your house hunt: mortgage payment insurance, and mortgage life insurance. (Don't confuse these with private mortgage insurance, or PMI, which insures lenders in cases where a buyer puts down only a small percentage of the mortgage cost.)

Mortgage payment insurance covers monthly mortgage payments if the homeowner is forced out of his or her house because of a disaster, such as a fire. There is really no need for this type of insurance. Your homeowner's policy should cover the cost of any rebuilding necessary, and often, if you must live elsewhere during that time, that expense is covered, too. So you are unlikely to have significant additional expenses that aren't already covered. And you were already expecting to make those mortgage payments, so insurance that covers these is an unnecessary expense.

Mortgage life insurance provides funds to pay off a mortgage if the principal wage-earner dies before the loan is repaid. However, if you are at all concerned about such a possibility, look into purchasing term life insurance instead. Mortgage insurance is more costly, and the money from that insurance must be used to pay off your loan, whereas the proceeds from term life insurance can be used for any purpose you choose.

Chapter 4

Working with a Real-Estate Agent

Now that you've got the down payment and mortgage figured out, it's time to start looking for your new home. But where do you start? Consider taking advantage of the many services offered by real-estate agencies. They will cost you nothing because it is usually the seller of a house who pays an agent's fee. A knowledgeable realty agent can direct you to a pool of properties likely to interest you and away from houses that don't meet your needs, saving you time and energy.

How Can an Agent Help You?

If you are following our advice, you have already been preapproved by a mortgage lender by the time you begin the house hunt, and you can approach a realty agent with the offer from your mortgage lender in hand. But some house hunters go straight to the real-estate agent for the number crunching. In some instances, the real-estate agent might be plugged into a lending institution you did not already contact. Maybe the agent can steer you to a good financing package, if you do not already have a commitment.

ALERT!

Be open with your agent about what's in your mortgage application—your bad credit report, your mere two months at your present job, or any other fact in your past or present that could work against you in buying. Agents will listen—they have heard it all before—and try to turn negative data into a positive buyer profile. They want the sale.

A word here about who's who in this field. A real-estate *broker* is any person, firm, or corporation that, for a fee or commission, seeks to sell, buy, exchange, or lease real property. Every state has strict laws for licensing brokers. Only a licensed broker can enter into a contract to act as an agent in handling real property. The real-estate office you visit is owned by a broker.

FACT

According to the National Association of Realtors, real-estate agents continue to be the leading information source used by homebuyers.

A person licensed by the state to work in real estate is the real-estate *salesperson,* more commonly called an *associate* or an *agent.* Salespersons cannot enter into a contract to sell property, act in any agency capacity, or collect a commission for their work. Those roles are reserved for the broker, under whose supervision they work. In practice, most of the people who will show you homes are salespersons. (Because agent is the more frequently used term for folks selling real estate, that term will be used throughout this book.)

FIGURE 4.1 Information Sources Used in the Home Search	
Source	**Percent**
Real-estate agent	80%
Newspaper advertisement	43
Internet	37
Yard sign	36
Home book/magazine	29
Open house	28
Friends/neighbors/relatives	24
Builders	10
Television	5
Knew the seller	5
Real-estate phone hotline	3
Relocation company	2
Yellow pages	1
Other	4

Source: *The 2000 National Association of Realtors Profile of Home Buyers and Sellers*

Supplying Local Information

Is there Little League in this town? A major bookstore? A theater? A fishing hole nearby? Each real-estate agent will know his or her geographical territory extremely well. An agent can provide information on property taxes, schools, neighborhoods, recreation facilities, and so on. Use their knowledge to help you choose among towns and from one neighborhood to another within a town. (See Chapter 10 for more on choosing a neighborhood.)

Offering Maps and Printed Information

If you ask, most agents will give you a street map of the local area. That will be invaluable for drive-by tours without the agent and for poking around surrounding regions. Many local nonprofit organizations (like the Newcomers Club, the library, or the League of Women Voters) leave flyers and newsletters in real-estate offices. Take them home and read them. They will give you a more personal insight into the area that interests you.

Using Multiple Listing Service Tools

The orderly arrangement of listing sheets on nearly all the property that is for sale in a given community, by price, with pictures and all pertinent sales information, is the hallmark of multiple listing services across the country. If you work with a real-estate office that belongs to such a service—and most do—your house hunt will be less tiring and a lot more thorough. Ask the agent to see the listing books. Go through the listings. You may see something that interests you that the agent may not have thought would, but most of all you will be sure you have not missed anything.

Offering Comparables

One of the best services an agent can provide is knowing prices of similar properties that have sold recently. Most real-estate agencies have such information on file. Ask to see the comparables book or comparables file as you begin to narrow down your search to one particular neighborhood. These listings of houses that sold in the previous year, with both their asking and selling price shown on the page, should help you make smart decisions in the negotiating process and prevent you from overpaying.

Evaluating Properties

You can expect your agent to have inspected a property before showing it to you, although that is not always possible with brand-new houses or with one that came on the market half an hour before you walked into the agency office. The agent will be able to answer your questions about the neighborhood, the lot, the floor plan, and so on. After he or she has been working with you for a while, the agent will know your preferences and will be able to eliminate undesirable properties without dragging you out to see them.

Hand-Holding

Your agent will be there to answer all of your seemingly endless questions about the buying process. He or she is your one constant contact during the homebuying process, and you are likely to turn to him or her far more often than, say, to your lawyer. The agent has helped many people before you—many of them probably even more nervous than you are—through sales, and he or she is accustomed to smoothly handling the stumbling blocks that can sometimes crop up along the way.

Real-estate agents are a great resource for information on services from home inspectors, mortgage lenders, and land surveyors to attorneys, homeowner's insurance, and home improvement companies.

Finding the Right Agent

Finding the right agent could take some time. If you are seriously considering several towns in your region, you should probably find a different agent for each—an agent's knowledge of his or her turf is one of the major benefits of the service. (In heavily populated areas with contiguous towns, one agent may handle a strip of two or three communities, knowing all of them well.)

Where to Start Looking

How do you find a top-notch agent? The best method is through personal referral. Ask for recommendations from friends who have recently purchased homes. Read the large-display advertisements in your local paper or the paper for the town where you would like to move. That is where real-estate offices congratulate their top performers. Call one of those stars, and make an appointment for an interview. You should also find someone with whom you feel comfortable. You want someone who knows the market and works hard.

Once you have chosen an agent, stick with him or her. In areas where a multiple listing service is commonly used, your agent can show you any property advertised by any other member office.

You may have attended a few open houses by now. Talking with the agent stationed there for the day incurs no obligation on your part and may yield an agent with whom you can work.

Two of the chancier methods of finding an agent are to call an office in response to an ad you have seen and to walk into a realty office with no appointment and say you want to buy a home. Most realty offices assign their agents floor time. Any prospective buyer who calls in response to advertising or who walks in the door with no appointment is assigned to the agent who has drawn floor time that day. Unfortunately, floor time is not assigned by competence, just by rote. A slight improvement on that poor strategy is asking for the listing agent for the property in the ad you have noted. That will at least direct you to the person who is most familiar with the home that interests you.

You don't need more than one agent (unless perhaps you are searching for homes in multiple towns that are not located near each other). You are not restricted to only the properties listed with your particular agent. When you see another realty office's ad in the paper for a property you think you might be interested in, tell your agent, and he or she can find out more about it for you. Even when a property is not listed on a multiple listing service, most realty offices are happy to cobroke—that is, allow another agent to show their listing for a split commission if the house-hunter buys that property.

By remaining loyal to your agent, you will save yourself countless phone calls from every agent who gets your name. You can also save yourself a lawsuit. This is rare, of course, and certainly drastic, but here is how one could happen. Agent X shows you a home; you decide that it is not right for you. Three weeks later, Agent Y convinces you to look at it again. Well, now it looks better somehow. You buy it. The first agent sues. The legal question is whether the first agent deserves part of the commission. The answer is often yes, but each case is decided individually, and court time can delay a sale. Do you want the aggravation?

ALERT!

Avoid working with relatives, unless perhaps they are award-winning salespeople. Also, skip part-time agents. You want someone who works full time, who is there when listings come in, and who is always "plugged in."

Loyalty, however, does not make sense if you feel your agent is not doing the best job for you. If that is the case, find another agent. This is a major and important purchase, and you need the best.

How to Evaluate Real-Estate Agents

Evaluating real-estate agents is an art, not a science. An agent you might not like could rate a "terrific" from another house hunter. You can compare agents by answering the questions in **WORKSHEET 4.1,** giving each agent one point for each of the factors listed there and then adding up the points. Remember that five points on the plus column is the highest grade, and five points on the minus side is the lowest. Zero signifies either no opinion or no information.

What You Need to Know about "Disclosure"

There are two major areas of homebuying where the word "disclosure" has been cropping up in recent years. The first is real-estate agents' disclosing to would-be buyers that they represent the seller. Many buyers do not know that extremely important fact about the buying process. The seller pays the agent's commission out of proceeds from the sale of the home. Agents' loyalties are with the seller, although they may very well be genuinely helpful to you and sincerely interested in helping you find a home you like.

Because of this relationship with the seller—and given that you should certainly tell the real-estate agent all you can about your financial situation, your mortgage application, and what you need and want in a home—you should *not* disclose exactly how much you will pay for a home.

WORKSHEET 4.1   Rating Real-Estate Agents

Factor	Plus Points	Minus Points
Community	Local resident for two years or more	Lives outside the community; new to the area
Professional	Three or more years' experience in residential real-estate sales	Fewer than three years' residential work; primary involvement is in commercial or other real-estate field
Commitment	Full-time agent; earns his or her living through real estate	Part-time agent; sells only on nights and weekends
Competence	Takes time to qualify buyers; shows properties in their price range	Does not qualify buyers; shows properties above buyers' stated range
	Plans showing routes carefully; has pre-inspected most properties	Has not seen properties prior to showing
	Thorough knowledge of financing options and local lender policies	Cannot answer buyer's questions about financing
Ethics	Alerts buyers to problems in location or condition of the property	Neglects to mention known problems—for example, the proposed highway one hundred yards behind the house or the water stains on the basement walls

If you have been approved for a mortgage, both you and the agent know the price range in which you are shopping. Do not be any more specific than "I want to look at something costing no less than about $120,000 and no more than $150,000." Don't give away your bargaining hand by telling the seller (or the agent working for him) the specific dollar amount that you are willing to spend.

The second use of the term "disclosure" refers to an agent and seller bringing any problems with the house to the attention of buyers, hiding nothing. Disclosure can also apply to a seller's or agent's knowledge of plans for the community or the street on which the house stands, plans that may turn off a prospective buyer.

Just how much an agent—and to a greater extent the seller—should disclose is still being weighed, both in the profession and in courts. (Some cases have cropped up in courts, so this is likely to be an ongoing concern for buyer, seller, and agent.)

In any event, you cannot afford to accept passively what agents say—or do not say. Rely on them for information, but research and poke around on your own to get satisfactory answers to the many questions you'll find raised in these chapters.

The Buyer's Broker

Buyer's brokers are real-estate agents who represent the buyer rather than the seller. Buyer's brokers can be especially effective when acting for you in "for sale by owner" home sales. (These appear in print as "FSBO," pronounced "fizzbo.")

FACT

Buyer's Homefinding Network provides a free service to match consumers with buyer agents. You can contact them at ✆ (800) 500-3569 or visit them at ✍ www.finderhome.com.

If you are interested in this concept, there are a couple of points to ponder. First, you should not have to sign a contract with a buyer's broker. But if you must, make it for no longer than thirty or sixty days.

A snag could arise when you are looking at homes in towns fifteen to thirty miles from one another. Unlike the traditional realty agents, a buyer's broker may represent only one area, meaning you would need another individual for the town fifteen miles away. That is a needless complication for you.

Second, fees for this service can vary. Sometimes a FSBO seller will pay half a buyer broker's fee. If you are charged $150 or so for a broker's service in finding you the home you buy, do not pay that sum up front, at the beginning of your house hunt. You should not have to pay anything initially to get a broker to work for you.

Buyer's brokers are still fairly uncommon in many parts of the country.

Discrimination by Agents

Discrimination does still exist, of course, despite governmental, professional, and civic efforts. Race is the most obvious basis for discrimination, but religion, national origin, sex, marital status, and children in the family all may predispose an agent to show or not show certain properties to certain people. Such activity is called steering, and it is against the law.

ALERT!

If you are not satisfied with the local board's response to your complaint, you might contact the National Association of Realtors (NAR) at 430 N. Michigan Avenue, Chicago, IL 60611. Their phone number is ✆ (312) 329-8200, ✆ (800) 874-6500, *www.realtors.org*. An investigation will follow.

If you feel you are being steered, for a reason other than your ability to afford the home in question, you can change the situation. If the agent in question is a member of the National Association of Realtors (NAR), call or write your local realtor board first. You can find that group listed in the white pages of the phone book or in the yellow pages where real-estate agents run advertisements. In the corner of some of the larger ads, there is likely to be a line such as "Member, Upstate County Board of

Realtors." You can find that board's office usually in the town where the county seat is located or in the largest community in the county.

If you wish to take this action against discriminatory practices further, you can notify your state real-estate commission. Proven cases of discrimination can result in suspension or loss of license for the agent involved. Sometimes just the threat of reporting discriminatory practices will put an end to them. Another source of advice is your local community housing resources board.

Making the House Hunt Easier

Even if you work with a real-estate agent, you will want a system to organize your search to keep you from being overwhelmed by information after all you will see and hear. First, be sure the agent knows the type of home you want, the price range, and the architectural style. Specify absolute needs—such as four bedrooms, a two-car garage, or being close to the parkway—that you consider essential.

You cannot turn over to a real-estate agent, even a buyer's broker, the responsibility for finding you a perfect home. It is you who must watch out for your money and your happiness and you who must make the right decisions each step of the way.

Second, limit yourself to viewing no more than six to eight properties a day. Beyond that number, features blur in your mind and fatigue affects your perceptions. Similarly, give a day to each town, if you are interested in several. Do not keep crisscrossing back and forth from, say, Pleasantville to Pleasant Cove. By concentrating on separate towns on different days, you will get a good idea of comparative value.

Third, take advantage of having the agent drive you to properties. Chauffeuring is also his or her business. While the agent is driving, you can take notes, mark your street map, or just take in the view. Following the agent in your own car is not a good idea. Being in the car next to the agent allows you to ask questions as you think of them. You can always talk privately—if you are house-hunting with a partner—back at home or on the drive home.

House-Hunting Without Your Agent

While you are out with an agent, look for "For Sale by Owner" signs in front of properties that might be of interest to you. There is no harm in calling those sellers and arranging to see the homes on your own.

There is a lot of paperwork involved in a real-estate transaction. Things move quickly. Mistakes can be—and often are—made in one area of a property transfer or another, from stupendous blunders to trivial oversights. Remember, you are in charge here!

Your real-estate agent can be an invaluable help to you, but it is up to you to continue working with your lender, house inspector, and everyone else involved to get answers to your questions, to double-check documents, and to run figures through the calculator yet again.

House-Hunting Online

Most real-estate agents these days have Web sites that feature their real-estate listings, including photos, prices, and in some cases virtual tours of homes for sale. You can get a good idea of the price ranges by city, state, and even zip code.

Billed as the "world's largest database of homes for sale," ✍ *www.realtor.com* provides information on millions of listings around the country.

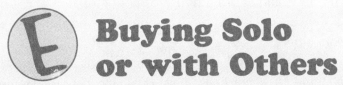

Chapter 5

Buying Solo or with Others

Are you buying a home by yourself? Or are you planning to share the expense with your spouse, or even a friend or brother or sister? There are important legal distinctions in each case that you should consider. How you buy your home—how you hold title to that house or apartment—is important to your enjoyment of that property and to your financial life, too, as you will see in reading on.

Single and House-Hunting

There is an irony here that—if you are old enough—may not have escaped you. Thirty years or so ago, in the early 1970s, young single people began to purchase homes. They did not wait until they married. They did not wait to buy with a "significant other," and they did not wait until they turned forty. If they could afford a house or condominium and it made good financial sense for them to buy, they did so, even if they were twenty-five years old.

However, in the space of that thirty years, the price of homes has risen drastically, and so, accordingly, have down-payment requirements. Now, many single would-be buyers find themselves unable to buy a home. But it is not their single status that is hurting them. It's their need for a second income to make them able to afford the expense. While many single buyers might well be able to carry a mortgage payment, the giant hurdle of the down payment can be hard to overcome without the help of a second income.

All Together Now

There are single parents who join forces and buy together, brothers and sisters who buy and share houses, and former college roommates who take the plunge and sign for mortgages not long after graduating and starting their first jobs. Each of these new homeowners has been imaginative enough to see beyond the traditional, to say "Why not?" and begin carving out his or her own interpretation of home owning.

A Sharing Situation

Michelle and Don are both single and work for nonprofit agencies in a midsize city. They were in their late twenties a few years ago when they purchased a three-story row house in a revival neighborhood of their city. They were not involved romantically; they were merely work buddies.

She loved her community and wanted the privacy of a house over that of a condominium. But she was not handy and was more than a little overwhelmed at the thought of rattling around in so many rooms.

She could afford a down payment and the monthly mortgage.

Don presented the flip side of that situation. He could not come up with a down payment, but he certainly knew his way around a tool box. He had a reasonably well-paying job and could carry a monthly mortgage payment.

The two joined together to buy, with Michelle making the full down payment and Don repaying her gradually by handling much of the renovation work that was needed. The two put a dollar value on Don's rehabbing. All of this was spelled out in a written contract.

Michelle took the top floor, which they converted into a full apartment; Don chose the floor just below that. The ground floor, which was half below and half above the ground, was converted to another apartment. They rented that unit, depositing the rental money into a joint checking account to pay for other renovations.

Michelle and Don consulted a lawyer to work out all of the details of their arrangement. And it works. If one of them decides to sell—either to the other or to an agreed-upon outsider—that new half-owner will continue the smooth working relationship.

Ways to Share

Financially you are probably better off owning a home than renting, even if you can't own a house entirely by yourself yet. Sharing a house today can get your foot in the door to home ownership. Stretch your thinking and this might work for you. Following are some additional points to consider.

Why *not* buy half a house? That shared-housing style is solid and well conceived, and it is not just for those twenty-five-year-olds. Many strapped renters can enter into a shared buying arrangement at any age and can enjoy the privacy, freedom, investment potential, and tax advantages of ownership.

You and another buyer could purchase a two-family house, each inhabiting one apartment. Or you could buy a single-family house, sharing it equally or spending money to convert it into two complete dwelling units. Yes, you will essentially be living in an apartment, but remember that this is a starter home, not the house of your dreams. Or think of it this way.

You may not be able to afford a $225,000 house in the neighborhood you like, but half that house, at $112,500, could be within your means.

In the early and mid-1980s, there was a home style built by a few developers known as "mingles" housing. These were homes built specifically for sharing and were often constructed in high-priced areas, particularly resorts, where the cost of a single-family home would be prohibitive to many buyers. There was a common living/dining area, a kitchen, and then separate bedrooms and baths at each end of the dwelling. For whatever reason, mingles housing did not exactly grow at a furious pace. But if you find some of these homes in your area, it might pay to investigate them. Call your local or state builders' association and ask where there might be some developments like these.

"Put it in writing" is the cardinal rule for sharing ownership of a house. Have a lawyer draw up an agreement for the two (or three or four) of you, covering every aspect of your buying, maintaining, and selling that home.

If you cannot find any, look for a home design that lends itself nicely to sharing. These homes will have a kitchen, a large living/dining area, a master bedroom/bath at one side of that area, and another bedroom and bath or two at the opposite end. That design works better for unrelated sharers than having all of the bedrooms clustered at one end of the house.

The Legal Options in Shared Ownership

Owning a house, as you already know, is an enormous responsibility. The key word here is *owning*. The names on the deed to a property are accountable for that piece of real estate—to the mortgage holder, to the insurance company, to the local tax office and utilities, and to some degree, even to the neighbors, for keeping up the appearance of the place. Despite that burden, the house is an asset—an important part of one's estate—that you will have to pass on in the case of your death. This is usually done through a will.

If you are single and buying solo, you are likely to have that house in *sole ownership,* which means you are the only title holder. (You could also take title in a living trust. This is discussed later in the chapter.) When there is more than one owner involved, even when they are married to each other, there can be questions about inheritance and tax consequences of the ownership style they have chosen.

ALERT!

Do not buy with others without knowing fully the financial situation of your prospective house sharer(s). These arrangements work best if everyone involved has similar incomes and assets. You do not want to end up shouldering most of the financial load because your sharer loses his minimum-wage job and your higher, professional income has to carry the house.

At this stage, everyone involved in a joint purchase should be deciding how they want to buy so that any problems that come to the surface can be worked out. Let's start with the most common shared buying style—marriage.

Thinking about Probate

Probate is a legal term describing a court process when a will or the authenticity of a will is in question. Probate provides that the estate is left to the court to settle. One wants to avoid probate by having a will witnessed by two parties in place so the specific instructions of the deceased can be followed through and influence of third parties is then eliminated. In a partnership situation, this is critical if the intent of deceased is to leave his share of ownership to a partner.

Married Couples

"Well, naturally, we're buying together," you say. "We'll own the house equally." Of course, what could be simpler? When one spouse dies, the property automatically passes to the other, without having to go through probate.

This ownership style is known as *joint tenants with right of survivorship.* When one party dies, usually only a certified copy of the death certificate and an affidavit of survivorship need to be recorded, and then the name of the deceased is cleared from the title to that property.

FACT

An affidavit of survivorship is a legal term for an official statement that the person who has died is the person whom the joint tenant knew and shared property with. It is used to pass the title to the surviving party.

But just a minute. While that is the usual way a husband and wife own property, it is not necessarily their best choice. By holding a property jointly, some couples are likely to be required to pay larger amounts in estate taxes than they might otherwise owe. Also, in cases where a buyer wants to leave his share of the house to someone other than his current spouse—for example, to children from a previous marriage—owning as joint tenants is probably not the best choice.

There is an alternative to the joint tenants buying style. *Tenants in common* allows each spouse to co-own property, but each can leave his or her share to anyone he or she chooses, not necessarily the spouse. In community property states (Arizona, California, Idaho, Louisiana, Nevada, New Mexico, Texas, Washington, and Wisconsin), spouses can hold title as community property. Each then owns one-half of the property, and that half can be passed upon death by will.

ALERT!

A very important point to keep in mind is that joint tenancy with right of survivorship *overrides* both a will and a prenuptial agreement. So, if Karen marries Joe, and the two have a prenuptial agreement in which Karen leaves her share of the house to the children from her first marriage, but the two buy property in joint tenancy, then upon Karen's death, her share of the house automatically becomes Joe's.

Couples Living Together

Opposite sex couples who purchase a home together will face more complex issues, such as who will maintain the property, what happens when one party wants to sell, and who will inherit a co-owner's share upon his or her death. This situation calls for a contract, along with deciding on an ownership style.

There is no law requiring unmarried sharers to have a written agreement, but it is a wise step to take. A written contract is different than a prenuptial agreement. It does not cover all financial aspects of the sharers' lives, only that of shared housing.

The legal system sometimes has its hands full with couples living together. Cohabitation is still illegal in a handful of states, although those particular laws are rarely enforced. However, there is little uniformity among the other states regarding the legal status of the millions of couples who live together. This legal area continues to change. Such relationships are governed by contract law. When problems arise, they might be decided by a jury in civil court rather than by a family-court judge.

The phrase "living together" usually applies to opposite sex couples. But same-sex couples who live together have similar concerns in owning property. Single people in any long-term relationship may want to pass the property they co-own to each other. Or they might want to will their share to a designated family member.

Besides having a strong contract, you should also keep careful records of all major expenditures and purchases that either of you make while you are together. This may seem unromantic or petty, but you never know what may happen in the future, and money, assets, and estates are sensitive and significant issues.

Buying with Family or Friends

If you choose to buy a home with friends or relatives, such as brothers, sisters, or cousins, you will almost certainly want to purchase a home as tenants in common. You might also consider forming a partnership, particularly if there are more than two of you who want to co-own a property. An accountant can help you choose what makes the most sense for all of you.

The Contract among Cobuyers

Most unmarried couples and cobuyers own their home, in equal or unequal interests, as tenants in common. But this can sometimes cause complications. Consider an example in which two men, Frank and Jeff, own a home together. Frank wills his share of the house to his twenty-four-year-old daughter Kate, who lives 2,000 miles away. When he dies, Kate is left with half of a house on the other side of the country. What is Kate to do with the house? She hardly knows the forty-two-year-old Jeff. Her options are to sell her share to Jeff; to rent her share, with Jeff approving of the tenant; or to sell the house with Jeff, with the two splitting any profit. Here is a perfect example of the need for a contract between co-owners, spelling out every possibility as it applies to them and the property.

ALERT!

Naturally, any contract should be in writing. Courts refuse to assume partners' understandings by their words or actions. The written agreement can be worked out just between partners or with the help of a lawyer.

As we've seen, the contract should cover how the home is owned in the legal sense, what will happen in the event the co-owners separate—whether the house will be sold then or at any other specified time—and how the proceeds from a sale will be split. There can be clauses covering any decision about the termination of the agreement—such as upon the death of one partner, upon marriage to each other, or upon marriage to someone else—or just a mutual agreement in writing about termination. A contract can contain as many stipulations as the parties choose, regarding any aspect of owning and maintaining the property.

Finally, you might also specify in a contract that any disputes you both (or all) cannot resolve will be turned over to the American Arbitration Association for settlement. Sometimes only a qualified outsider can come up with a solution to a heated disagreement.

QUESTION?

Are these contracts enforceable?
Contracts can always be challenged, but a well-written agreement can protect partners. Anything in writing is stronger than a verbal promise that you relay in court, like, "He promised me we'd sell the condo in four years."

Living Trusts

A growing number of Americans, seeking to avoid probate and its attendant costs, have instituted a living trust instead of a will (sometimes in addition to a will). Both sole owners and co-owners can hold title to a home in a living trust. Among other provisions, this allows for automatic property disposition upon death, according to the trust terms, without delays or probate costs.

ALERT!

Whether you are no-strings unattached, married, or in a committed relationship, you will no doubt want to see a lawyer and/or an accountant to discuss the ramifications of various types of property ownership as they affect your estate.

Until death, the property owner retains complete control over the living trust property, as its trustor, trustee, and beneficiary. When that trustor dies, the trust assets automatically pass according to its terms to the person(s) designated. During the trustor's life, the living trust can be changed and the properties (including, naturally, real estate) in that trust can be bought, sold, and refinanced the way they would be if there were no trust.

Chapter 6

Which House Is Right for You?

Now that you have made some major decisions about financing and paying for a home, it's time to get to the fun part! Choosing your new home! Before choosing a house style, you need to think about and examine your present lifestyle, as well as possible changes in the future. What would you like in a home? What must you absolutely have? Do you want to live in an adult-only community? Are you interested in living behind protective gates?

Understanding Your Lifestyle

Perhaps this is your first home. If so, then all of this is new to you. If it has been some years since you have been house-hunting, circumstances in your life might have changed. Certainly real estate has changed, as you will see.

Finding the right home will require objectivity. You may be surprised to find that what you think you want might not be all it's cracked up to be. Don't expect to find the perfect home immediately—be diligent in your search, and give it time.

Your preferences in housing style are likely to be dictated, at least in part, by the circumstances of your household. This may be the most important factor in the buying decision. Who will be living with you, not just now but in the immediate future?

If your life situation changes in a way that alters your housing needs in the near future, you may not be able to sell your home quickly. Indeed, you may not want to sell. But adapting that house to fit your new needs could be costly and inconvenient. So it is best to look ahead now, to be sure the home you buy will lend itself—as much as you can foresee without a crystal ball—to your potential future needs. Here are some things to think about:

- If you have preteens or teenagers, they could be off to college in the blink of an eye, perhaps never to live at home again. If you plan to look for a large home now, will you need (or want) all that space in five or so years? Or do you still want to buy big and then downsize when the time comes?
- If you are moving to a resort area, you can almost bet you will have houseguests galore. They will want to see you, of course, but have a nice little vacation, too. Do you want to have extra space for a guest room? Or, rather than spend the money for room that will not be used full-time, will you have guests make do with a pull-out sofa in the living room or maybe in your home office?

- What about visits from grown children? Is this the time to give them their own room?

- Consider your parents and/or your spouse's mom or dad. How long will they continue to live on their own? Is it possible that someday an older parent will come to live with you? Should you buy a home with extra space or—if not existing space—the possibility of a bedroom/bath addition?

- If you are single and want a fairly sizable house, do you think you might want—or financially need—a sharer at some point?

- Are you in a precarious job or self-employed? You might want to consider a two-family house that you can rent half of to a tenant to take some of the burden off making those monthly mortgage payments.

- Are you approaching retirement and expecting the home you buy now to become your retirement place? If so, then you have other considerations. For example, you might opt for a ranch or a patio home, all on one floor, in the event that you or your spouse eventually finds it difficult to climb stairs.

     If you do buy a two-story house, keep in mind how, if need be, you might be able to convert some space on the ground floor to sleeping quarters someday.

- Do you plan to start a home-based business one day soon? Be sure the home you buy is zoned for that kind of activity, if your business will draw customers to your home. If you will need space for a product you want to sell, look for an adequate basement or a garage.

You can see how your current lifestyle is not the only thing to think about when looking at homes. People do not move annually to accommodate their changing needs and wishes. Thus, it is necessary to anticipate future needs.

The City or the Suburbs?

If you are living in an apartment downtown and thinking about buying a home, your first thought might be that a home means the suburbs.

However, that is not the case. In the same vein, living in a suburban rental house or apartment complex does not mean you have to stay in the suburbs when you buy.

In most parts of the country, you are likely to have a choice among the city, suburbs, or country. Most of that decision will be made based on your personal choice. You just want to be in one place or the other. There are some other factors that could enter into your decision, however.

If you are now in the city and hold a city job, residing within those metropolitan borders may be required by law. If you think that may be the case, investigate before you go house-hunting in the suburbs. In fact, if you work for any regional government entity, you should investigate possible residency requirements.

TABLE 6.1 Location of Home Purchased					
	Total U.S.	Northeast	Midwest	South	West
Suburban neighborhood	46%	52%	44%	52%	37%
City neighborhood	41	26	42	36	53
Rural	11	18	12	9	8
Resort property	1	2	1	2	1
Other	1	2	1	1	1

Source: *The 2000 National Association of Realtors Profile of Home Buyers and Sellers*

Travel Time

Commuting time is bound to be a primary factor in any home you buy. Consider, too, commuting costs. Will you have to buy a second car, because you and your sharer each need transportation? If you will take a train, check the monthly commuting fare before you buy the house you like. It could make a sizable dent in your monthly budget. Will you be on a public transit line—bus or subway?

Have you considered reverse commuting? Perhaps you like the idea of living in the city, but suburban office parks have the jobs you want. Commuting from the city to work in the suburbs is likely to be far less of a hassle for you than for those who are heading in the opposite direction.

Working in the suburbs does not have to mean living there as well.

Consider how far you want your kids to travel to school. The country home of your dreams may mean that Jason must get up at 5:30 A.M. to catch the school bus. And what about Samantha's dance class and the swim team she is currently involved with? If she is able to pick up those activities in the new locale, how much chauffeuring will you have to do?

If you are at or close to retirement age or have chronic health concerns, you might want to be fairly close to a hospital for convenient access to emergency room services. If you have small children, you'll want to keep that in mind, too.

Other Considerations

Also, if you are older and or if you have potential health problems, consider the alternative modes of transportation available if you are not able to drive for a brief time because of an accident or illness. Is there a bus that runs downtown or to the shopping mall? Is there special seniors' transportation, such as a van or minibus? How will you get to the supermarket if you are unable to drive?

If you think that the suburbs are only for the children/minivan/big-shaggy-dog set, you should know that many single persons live quite happily in bedroom communities and small towns. In fact, in towns around larger cities, singles form a sizable minority of residents!

ALERT!

Remember that, if you do opt for the suburbs, you should look for an area in which you will feel comfortable and one that offers clubs and other activities you can take part in.

At Home in the Country

Are you a country mouse? Do a fast mental check of your family's health. Do you need to be close to a hospital? How about their interests? There may not be many organizations that they are interested in joining in the country. However, if your interests are, for example, growing a vegetable garden, hiking, skiing, or fishing, you will fare very well indeed in the outback. But it is important to picture yourself there before you buy.

What about commuting? Are you too far from the city to commute? If your work is very near your country home of choice, then good for you!

Homeowners' Associations

Whatever part of town you are interested in, you should know that there are sometimes rules about the types of households to live in certain communities. Some types of single-family homes, like condominiums, require owners to belong to a homeowners' association, abide by its bylaws, and pay a monthly maintenance fee. You will want to consider these associations carefully as you contemplate what neighborhood you will move into.

There was a time—not so long ago—when a new development of, say, fifty-five single-family homes would be given a name, like "Wood Hollow." An entrance to the development proclaimed the name, but buying a house within the development was no different than buying one on any other suburban (or even city) street.

FACT

The homeowners' association charges dues, which are usually paid annually but are sometimes charged on a monthly basis. These fees can range from $75 to $150 a month or more and are used for maintaining the entrance, landscaping, perhaps building up a savings fund for certain purchases and common repairs, some entertainment programs, and possibly a newsletter.

That is less common today. Now, many single-family developments around the country, and some communities of other house styles such as co-ops and condos, operate with homeowners' associations that are established by the developer of the property. Everyone buying into that development must join. The association is bound together by covenants that owners are required to honor. These can cover just about any issue, including the colors you can use to paint your house, the roofing materials you must use for repair, whether you can operate a business from home, and, often, how many cats or dogs you can have and the maximum weight of those pets.

The Pros of Homeowners' Associations

The major plus to a homeowners' association is that you know your property values will be maintained in that community. No one can get away with leaving old, beat-up cars in the driveway, allowing his or her grass to become as high as an elephant's eye, or creating other neighborhood eyesores.

The association fosters a sense of neighborliness, too. Besides meetings to which all residents are invited, many developments have community-wide garage sales and holiday parties for residents.

The Cons of Homeowners' Associations

So what is the downside of moving into a neighborhood controlled by covenant? Well, no one is going to make an exception for you, allowing you to keep a recreational vehicle (an RV) in your driveway because you are a nice guy, for example. And no one's going to let you put up a basketball hoop in front of your home if the covenants say no. *Everyone* sticks to the fine print here.

ALERT!

Whether you want a development with these strictures or you want to steer clear of one, be sure to tell your real-estate agent and keep your eyes open yourself while house-hunting.

Not every community with its name at the entrance has a homeowners' association, but many do. Ask to see the bylaws of any development you are seriously considering. The rules can vary from one complex to another. In most of them you will not be able to keep an RV in the driveway for more than two or three days, and most have fairly universal restrictions on, for example, the color you can paint the exterior of your house or where you can place a satellite dish (not on your front lawn!). Some rules and regulations vary from one community to the next, so do not assume that if you have seen one community's covenants, you have seen them all.

A Choice in Associations

Finally, there is another type of homeowners' association—one that is established by the residents of a community. Membership is not mandatory, nor are the rules and regulations, aside from those that parallel the municipal laws that apply to every resident of the town, such as keeping the grass mowed and, perhaps, not parking a large truck regularly in the driveway. In these communities, you are invited, even urged, to join, but you do not legally have to hand over a check for membership just because you own a home there.

Gated Communities

One of the newest trends in neighborhoods are developments that have a gate or some other design to keep nonresidents from driving through. Do you like that concept?

On one hand, you will have privacy, with no through traffic. That could mean that it's safer playing outdoors for your children. You will never have outsiders—such as salespeople—ring your doorbell unexpectedly. And you will have as much security in your home and neighborhood as is possible.

Remember to have an open mind when looking at homes. Use your imagination and understand that while a home may not be decorated to your tastes, walls can be painted, carpeting can be changed, and kitchens and bathrooms can be updated.

On the other hand, you might find it a nuisance having to pull out your card or other identifying item to get through the gate once or twice or more a day. You will have to leave messages with the gatehouse when you are expecting visitors or packages. Your monthly or annual service fee will be higher to cover the gatehouse and salaries for its staff, who may be there as much as twenty-four hours a day. The community may not be as secure as it seems. It may be possible for someone to enter from one part of the community or another, away from the entrance, and there are those who say once the first pizza delivery is allowed in, the security is compromised.

Some gated communities come complete with a full gatehouse and a staff of guards. Other communities may have a railroad-like gate that rises only when residents—or their expected guests—punch in a personal security code. The latter is likely to be far less costly than paying a staff, of course, although probably not as effective in keeping out unwelcome visitors.

No Children Allowed

Be very careful in looking at single-family developments that are advertised as adults-only communities if you have children, want to have children, might be marrying someone with children, or are a grandparent who could be raising a minor grandchild sometime soon. Adults-only communities are often found in resort areas. These developments, too, are controlled by covenants, and along with the restrictions on house colors and the like, they include a significant rule that says no children under the age of eighteen can live there on a full-time basis.

The associations are very inflexible about this stipulation. There is no pity here, so be *very* sure of your life situation and your willingness to abide by its bylaws.

ALERT!

Keep in mind that these are not senior-citizen communities; rather, they are for adults only.

Naturally, minor children are allowed to visit—even every day, if you like—and, according to individual community bylaws, a child or grandchild (or unrelated youngster, for that matter) can spend perhaps two or three weeks a year, staying overnight, at your place. Maybe that is all you have planned anyway. Still, do read those covenants carefully before making a decision.

Incidentally, it is legal to discriminate against children in certain housing communities, providing they follow federal guidelines that require at least one owner in a minimum of 80 percent of the community's homes to be at or above the minimum age for entry. That age can vary according to developments, from forty-seven to fifty-five to sixty-two or more. (The age for entry into adult-only communities has been dropping over the years and may in fact be as low as forty-seven in some complexes.)

What do you think? Do you like the idea of like-minded folks living in harmony and following the rules, at the expense of some freedom of choice, to help ensure security and an increase in property values? Or does that rub against your free-spirit grain? It is certainly best to know in advance if the house you like comes with quite a few strings attached.

Your Dream House

While you are thinking about what areas might be best for you, and before you get bogged down by all the options in home styles (discussed in the following chapters), consider what you want in a home.

Would you like an eat-in kitchen? How about a room on the first floor that can become your office? Is a garage on your list of must-haves? Think about how many bedrooms you may need, and what kind of storage space you want. Of course, you may not find (or be able to afford it if you do find) the house or condominium that has everything you want this time out, but you certainly should be able to get some of your ideal features.

What is important to you? Use **WORKSHEET 6.1** on the following page to help you clarify what you want. Make several photocopies. You should fill in the blanks on one copy and then give a blank copy to each member of your household so that he or she can jot down responses, too. Then use all those responses to create one master sheet. Give a copy of the master sheet to your real-estate agent so that he or she has a clear idea of what you are looking for. Remember, without this information, your agent will not be able to steer you toward homes that have the things you want. And take a copy with you as you go through the homes for sale.

Here is a sample of a completed worksheet:

Must Have	Would Be Nice	Do Not Want
Three bedrooms	Fireplace	Busy street
Eat-in-kitchen	Two-car garage	Split-level style
Basement	Formal dining room	Sloping lot

Now it's your turn. Make the list as long as you like.

WORKSHEET 6.1	Dream-Home Worksheet: Needs and Wants	
Must Have	**Would Be Nice**	**Do Not Want**
_____	_____	_____
_____	_____	_____
_____	_____	_____
_____	_____	_____
_____	_____	_____
_____	_____	_____
_____	_____	_____
_____	_____	_____

Keep the Resale Value in Mind

When you buy a home to raise your family in and plan to stay for the long term, resale is something way off in the unimaginable future.

It used to be that grandchildren visited their grandparents in the home that their parents grew up in. This situation is often no longer the norm. Statistics now show that 20 percent of the population moves each year. People move for job opportunities or because of divorces more than ever before. Baby boomers are reaching retirement age in large numbers each year as well and are moving into smaller homes or retirement communities. It is likely that you, too, will move out of the home you are now buying, and even though that day may be far off, it is worthwhile to consider the resale value of your home when you are buying it.

Many first-time buyers will purchase a starter home, knowing that this is only their first and that others will follow. Many buyers calculate the resale value in anticipation of the acquisition of the next home, treating the home as an investment on which they want a good return. The buyer likely will have projected the resale price based upon the anticipated or historical increase in value in the neighborhood or area.

The variable is that markets change. You may find your starter home increases more or less than you anticipated as the economy and employment rate of the country changes. Nothing guarantees that your home will appreciate at the same rate that others like it have in the past. So while you should consider resale value as you are looking for a home, keep in mind that its future value is dependent on the work you put into it as well.

ALERT!

You will always be best off taking good care of and maintaining your property. Whether you purchase the property for the short or the long run, not taking care of your property will cost you more when it's time to sell.

A roof problem gets worse with time. A sewage problem doesn't cure itself, and tuck pointing does not regrow. You must spend money to maintain your property. This does not include redecorating, however. The interior decor will not increase the resale value of the home—new buyers will naturally want to decorate to their tastes. Somewhere in your future there is likely going to be a resale of your home. Buy with an eye to what will appeal to other buyers in the future, and maintain your property during the time you live there. The results will be worth it.

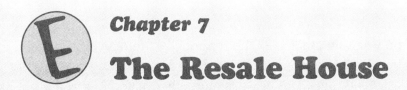

Chapter 7

The Resale House

Aresale house is any dwelling that has been lived in by another owner, even if that owner is moving out after only six months in a brand-new home. A resale house is more affordable, generally speaking, than a brand-new one, and it can carry a price tag competitive with condos, while still allowing you the opportunity to buy a whole house.

The Benefits of a Resale Home

In 2001, the median price of an existing home was $147,800, while the median price of a *new* home was $174,100, according to the National Association of Home Builders.

Besides price, there are other pluses in the resale home column:

- The neighborhoods in which they are situated are usually "finished." You won't find that stark, barren look of the new development.
- Houses of a certain vintage were sturdily constructed, with solid basements, thick plaster walls, and other materials that are not likely to be used these days because they are prohibitively expensive or just not available anymore.
- Older houses, especially *old* homes, also have architectural and design features that are not incorporated in most of today's new houses, again because of cost.

There is, of course, a flip side to all the charm of the old house. Who needs an ancient heating system? Who wants the design that may seem dated rather than charming? Or what about the expense of replacing old windows? Or bringing a 1950s kitchen into the twenty-first century? Or upgrading electrical service?

Despite these issues, two-thirds of homebuyers choose to buy a resale home rather than a new one. You may be looking at a resale home because you cannot afford the new house you would otherwise prefer. Or maybe you prefer the proximity to the city center of older homes in established communities, whereas a brand-new house would mean a long commute. Or you may be aiming at the resale market because you just like the character of lived-in houses.

Choosing the Right Neighborhood

Location, location, location—you can't beat it in determining the value of a home. The homes around yours will have a substantial effect on what your home is worth. If you purchase the most modest house in a high-priced community, you can do very well indeed for yourself, in terms of your investment. The more expensive houses will raise yours to a higher value than it would command in lesser neighborhoods. You have an equally sound investment if your home is in the same price range as the ones around it. But if you buy what you consider an attractive house that happens to be in a bad neighborhood, you might just as well toss your potential investment out in a plastic trash bag. Location is that important.

Pay close attention to the homes on the streets around the house you are interested in. You don't want to buy on a street that is fading fast or that has already become off limits to sensible investors. There are neighborhoods in many cities and towns that are making a comeback from decay and decline. If you do not know where those enclaves of revitalization are, you can discover them by reading the news articles in the real-estate section of a local paper, by going on house tours (most community associations sponsor one each year), by attending open houses, and, of course, by driving by. When you see three run-down houses, then one prettied up—perhaps sporting a window box of seasonal flowers—then another being renovated a few doors down, and an overall air of busyness and repair, you will know that you have come across your area's newest revival neighborhood.

Real-estate agents and everyone else engaged in buying and selling homes agree that new homes are not necessarily better buys than older houses. What determines the value of each, they say, is that all-important factor: location.

These communities offer some fine bargains for the novice who feels priced out of just about everything else. The trick here, of course, is to move in before renovation is completed and the community becomes red-hot for buyers. Prices are likely to climb steadily, and it may quickly become an area too expensive for many house hunters. The biggest problem you might encounter here is in fixing up the house—many houses in once run-down neighborhoods will need substantial rehabilitation.

Here are a few tips to keep in mind as you look at resale homes:

- Stay away from a community with too many "For Sale" signs. Do all those home sellers know something you do not? Is there a master plan for the area that shows some new undesirable construction is moving in soon? Perhaps the only corporation in the area is relocating. Too much competition, with too many houses on the market at the same time, drives down the value of each property. If you can see no apparent reason for so many signs, it would be wise to head for the town hall to see what is on the books, planning-wise, for that part of town.

- Avoid the house that has been overimproved for its block. You do not want the highest priced house in the neighborhood. You will most likely not get your money back when it is your turn to sell.

- Look for a house whose style fits in with the others in its neighborhood. A California-style, ultracontemporary home in a community of two-story colonials may seem fun now, but the different style could make the house difficult to sell when the time comes, if you cannot find others who share your enthusiasm for alternative architecture.

- If you expect to move again in just a few years, buy the most ordinary home you can find, one that can easily satisfy the greatest number of houseseekers when you do decide to sell. This has long been a successful buying strategy for corporate transferees and military families.

- Check into commuting time, schools, houses of worship, and nearby shopping.

- Be very sure, if you want to make any major changes to the appearance of the house, that the zoning laws will permit you to do so. Zoning laws could apply to your building a sunroom or a greenhouse, constructing an extra bedroom or a garage, putting in an in-ground pool, and even building a sturdy tool shed. Don't laugh at the latter. Some towns have made owners take down children's tree houses because they violated zoning laws!

Location is not the only factor that determines satisfaction and investment appreciation. "Features" should be considered. Some features are good, and some are a detriment to a house.

Every home is different. Even resale houses in a development of seemingly look-alike homes have owners who have made improvements over the years. Look at the houses in New York's Levittown, Long Island, now forty-plus years old, and notice how years of different owners and remodeling/improvements have changed those once nearly uniform exteriors.

QUESTION?

During your home walking tours, ask yourself two questions: **"Will I enjoy living here?"** and **"Will I be able to sell when I want to, with at least a small profit?"**

As you go through homes you will, understandably, be caught up in the look of each one and how it is decorated. But you are choosing your future home, and so you must remember to evaluate it in terms of your own lifestyle, needs, and goals, not those of the current owner. A checklist will help. The one that follows, in **WORKSHEET 7.1**, is merely a suggestion. Change it to suit you and your family. Make photocopies of the worksheet, and use one for each different home that you are interested in. It will remind you to notice each feature specifically, and it can serve as your notes later, after you've seen so many houses that they are starting to run together in your mind!

Features to Look For

You will want to look for features such as architectural details, window style, kitchen plan, a basement, a garage, bathrooms, and so forth. Some features add to the enjoyment of the home. Others add to its resale value, and some add to both. And of course there are some features that are negative qualities to some buyers and positive to others.

Address_____

	YOUR IDEAL	ACTUAL FEATURES
❏ View		
❏ Landscaping		
❏ Siting		
❏ Style		
❏ Construction materials		
❏ Driveway		
❏ Garage		
❏ Deck, porch, patio		
❏ Windows		
❏ Entranceways		
Front		
Back		
Other		
❏ Floor plan and traffic pattern		

	YOUR IDEAL	ACTUAL FEATURES
☐ Kitchen		
☐ Bathroom		
☐ Laundry facilities		
☐ Closets		
Bedroom		
Linen		
Utility		
Coat		
☐ Bedrooms		
☐ Family room		
☐ Living room		
☐ Dining room or area		
☐ Attic		
☐ Basement		

To buy wisely, you must know what to look for. If you plan to stay in a home for a long time—twenty or so years—then you are likely to consider comfort paramount. But most of those who buy intending to move within five to seven years make investment potential their first priority.

ALERT!

A house that is totally different from its neighbors is often difficult to sell. It stands out like a sore thumb, and few buyers have the courage to say, "I'll take that one."

Once you establish your priorities, the next step is to recognize which features will add resale value and which will detract from it, as well as which features will add to your living comfort and which will cause inconvenience. This is an art and not a science, so it is impossible to give an exact list of good and bad features. Every buyer and every situation is unique. It *is* possible, however, to give you a general idea of the most common homebuyer and homeowner responses to the most (and least) desirable features. Let's start outside and then move indoors.

Style

A stone-and-glass California-style contemporary may be just your style, but it will be difficult to resell if it is located in a neighborhood of clapboard Cape Cods. Similarly, Spanish-style ranch houses do not sell well in the Northeast; a colonial saltbox style house would probably remain on the market a while in Florida, and a present-day replica of a Victorian farmhouse is not likely to be anyone's preference in Phoenix.

Usually, style positively affects investment potential when it harmonizes with the area, and it negatively affects investment potential when the style is jarring to look at. If resale value and speed are unimportant to you, you can feel free to choose the unusual or offbeat. If investment appreciation and resale are essential to your purchase, stick with the prevailing styles in a particular area.

Construction Materials

Brick houses are considered desirable all across the country. Wood is also acceptable everywhere, although it is somewhat less desirable in areas where termites are abundant.

Vinyl or aluminum siding over a wood frame may or may not add to resale value, but it will probably save you maintenance time and money. However—and this is an important point—vinyl or aluminum siding over a house that's in a historic district is considered an abomination. Usually such siding is prohibited in those neighborhoods, but some houses may have been covered before the designation.

Stucco is an attractive and widely used material throughout the South, with good buyer acceptance. In the North, however, stucco houses can be hard to sell because their unjointed surfaces are subject to cracking from the changeable weather. Stone and granite facades, on the other hand, have expansion space and rarely cause problems. They are usually attractive, too, which is a selling plus.

Driveways

Blacktop or concrete driveways are most preferred and add to resale speed and value as well as to owner convenience. Crushed bluestone is acceptable, especially in tract developments where blacktopping the driveway is not included in the price of the house. Gravel driveways, however, are usually a resale and convenience minus. They are muddy in wet weather and dusty in dry. They are also more difficult to clear in the winter and require time each spring for picking the stray stones from the lawn near the driveway.

The large turnaround area of a circular driveway certainly adds to owner convenience, not to mention safety, but rarely affects selling price. A particularly long or steep driveway may not significantly affect resale value, but it will usually increase the length of time needed to sell the property.

Garages

The attached two-car garage is preferred by buyers everywhere. Usually, a garage located to the side of a house brings the best buyer response. If it is eight or ten feet wider than the size needed for two cars, that is better yet. That additional space can be used to store the lawn mower, garden equipment, bicycles, and other gear.

Garages located under the house are less desirable. Many owners complain about drafts in the rooms above and about higher heating and cooling costs. And many object to the fact that getting into the house means climbing a flight of stairs. Think about unloading a car full of groceries from the garage to the kitchen, and you will understand why that complaint is common. You might prefer having your car on the same level as the house.

Consider, too, the number of cars in your family. Is there room to park all of them? Will the parking spots be convenient to all of the residents of the house?

Detached garages are unpopular in the North because no one wants to shovel through a foot of snow to get to the car. And carports do not offer a penny extra in offering price. In the South, however, carports are acceptable for the family car, and detached garages are just fine.

View and Landscaping

Is a view—the mountains, the ocean, or perhaps the city lights— valuable? Views are one of those features that turn property appraisal from a job to an art. No one can be certain exactly what a given buyer might be willing to pay for a view until that buyer makes an offer. Sometimes a house with a view sells quickly—the view was valuable. But sometimes a house-and-view package stays on the market until the owners reduce the price to a level comparable to other houses of approximately the same size—the view was not valuable.

View doesn't have to mean something on the distant horizon— sweeping mountain landscapes, or ocean or lake views. Your windows may look out on beauty close at hand. What is a stream or a pond worth? A forest that will always remain natural? The beauty of what you are buying is a known quality, but the investment potential will always be something of a question. Therefore, always try to buy property with unusual landscape features as though it were an ordinary lot. If you must pay extra for the beauty, raise your price gradually until the view becomes more painful to your purse than pleasing to the eye.

If you should fall in love with a house with a view, try to buy it without paying for the view. Get comparables, and make your first offer at a price slightly below the market value for a similar house with no view. If the sellers hold firm on their price, however, you will then have to decide exactly how much that view is worth to you.

Siting

Which way is east? North? The answers will affect your heating bill and maybe even your disposition. Which rooms will have morning light? Which will bask in the afternoon sun? Are there rooms that will remain dark most of the day?

Decks, Patios, Porches, and Pools

Any place to sit or eat outdoors is almost always a plus for both comfort and resale.

The value of a pool will depend on the climate where you're house hunting. Many buyers in the North do not want the work involved in maintaining an in-ground pool that can be used only a few weeks a year. However, in the South a pool is a plus. In any region, buyers with small children might be concerned about safety issues around a pool.

Windows

Self-insulating windows and sliding glass doors are often considered such positive features that they are specifically mentioned by brand name in advertisements. However, some homeowners claim that old-fashioned storm windows are better at keeping out the elements.

In some very cold areas, or on the northern exposure of some houses, some owners have installed conventional storm windows over self-insulating windows, and most buyers consider the installation a positive feature.

In the North, houses with neither self-insulating windows nor storm windows lose points with buyers. In the warm climate of the South, though, screen windows without the extra storm protection are acceptable. Southern oceanfront properties often feature hurricane shutters to protect both the window glass and the interior of the house or apartment. They are a plus for buyers, but they do not raise the property's value.

Entranceways

A nice front entry is, well, nice. Many owners, after the first few weeks in a new house, begin using the back door almost exclusively. Still, that front entranceway is an important factor in the salability of a house. It is, after all, a potential buyer's first impression, and first impressions are hard to dispel.

ALERT!

Aluminum doors in an entry are a fashion faux pas. Heavy wood or steel are better choices.

Back entranceways do not have much effect on salability, but they certainly play an important role in owners' enjoyment and comfort, especially if there are children or pets in the household. The "ideal" back door opens into a mud room, a back hallway, or cubicle where there is space to hang coats, remove wet boots, or wipe dirty paws. In the best-planned houses, this back hall is adjacent to or combined with the laundry room, which saves carrying the dirty cloths, rugs, and rags very far.

Back doors that open directly into the kitchen can be bothersome because of the increased traffic and clutter that they generate, but they are preferable to family-room back doors, especially if a patio or outside eating area is serviced by the door. Sliding glass doors are popular and will not hurt resale.

Kitchens

Most homebuyers have eat-in kitchens on their list of must-haves. In contrast, long, narrow "pullman-style" kitchens are least popular and will often keep a house on the market a long time.

Center islands are positives, as are sinks (especially double sinks) under a window. Counter space is important, and gourmet cooks often look for a minimum of 4 unbroken feet of work space. And plenty of cabinet space is always mentioned in a sales pitch.

And what of the old-fashioned kitchen, in the older, perhaps very old, home? Sellers are advised not to spend the time and money renovating an old kitchen in search of a buyer. Buyers generally can expect to spend that money themselves if they want an updated kitchen.

Many buyers forget to look for a broom closet, and many houses do not have one. Ask yourself where mops, buckets, brooms, and the vacuum cleaner will be kept. Some substitutes for the broom closet are the back-hall coat closet, the laundry room, the garage, and the pantry.

Bathrooms

The days of a desirable one-bath house are long over. Today's sellers, it seems, must offer, if not two full baths (or two and a half baths), then at least one bath and a powder room. Bathrooms with outside windows are far more appealing to buyers than interior baths with vent fans—but better an extra bathroom in the interior than none at all.

Walk-in shower stalls are preferable to shower-over-tub arrangements, but most people want at least one bathtub in the house. Bathroom vanities are becoming a must in today's new homes. Double sinks are a plus, too, as are full-wall mirrors behind the sink/vanity. Wallpaper is preferred over paint.

Closets

There are never enough of them. Large bedroom closets are a selling point and a better-living feature. A walk-in closet in the master bedroom is on most buyers' must-have lists. But while going through homes, look for these closet features too:

- A foyer or front-hall closet where you can hang guests' coats.
- A linen closet (ideally, one closet—perhaps in a hallway—for sheets and blankets and another in the bathroom for towels).

- A broom or utility closet, preferably near the kitchen.
- A back door closet or at least some place to hang family coats, store boots, and the like.

Bedrooms

Well, we would all like large bedrooms—three large ones in a three-bedroom house and four large ones in a four-bedroom house. Unfortunately, generously sized rooms seem to rank on the luxury level when it comes to home construction, and it is rare to find more than one large bedroom per house. If some of the bedrooms are small, look at least for good wall space for furniture arrangement and easy access to a bathroom.

Attic additions or Cape Cod–style bedrooms with sloping ceilings and dormer windows are not buyer favorites. But they do rank higher in appeal than basement bedrooms, which no one seems to want.

Family Rooms

Today, family rooms are more important than living rooms and sometimes larger. In the South and West, family rooms are being combined with kitchen and eating areas into great rooms that most buyers seem to like. In contrast, basement family rooms are out of style and almost a detriment to a sale. In the North, family-room fireplaces are a major plus.

Paneling is still popular, but some homeowners prefer conventional wallboard that can be painted or papered. Others choose slats (actual boards cut thin for application to walls with bonding cement), artificial brick, or even vinyl panels. More important than any of that is enough room for furniture.

Fireplace

There are no negatives to this feature. Fireplaces are popular with buyers even if they never light a fire, using the hearth simply as a decorative focal point in a room.

Living Rooms

In a house without a family room, the living room should be as large as possible. But in houses with family rooms, most buyers are more concerned with the location of the living room than with its size. They prefer the living room to be formal and out of the path of day-to-day traffic. Living-room fireplaces are fine, but they rarely bring a penny more in offering price.

Dining Rooms

Articles have been written over the last few years on the theme of "Whither the Dining Room?" Some folks do want a formal dining room, but others think just an eat-in kitchen is fine. They may turn a part of the dining room into formal dining when the occasion calls for it but keep the rest of the space as a sort of secondary living room, with books and easy chairs and lamps. When company arrives, out comes the folding dining table, around which are chairs from that room, with more added from other living spaces, if needed.

If there is a formal dining room, it should have a direct doorway to the kitchen and another to the foyer or the living room. If it is separated from the kitchen by stairs or a hallway, as is often found in rehabilitated brownstones, for example, some buyers will turn away from the house.

Attics

The old-fashioned attic, with real stairs, is certainly the most useful kind of home storage space. Such a space often comes only with an older home. Today's modern attics are far less accessible. Pull-down stairs in a hallway are acceptable to most buyers, and they do provide a means of getting to the holiday decorations each year. Less appealing to buyers, and downright inconvenient to homeowners, is attic access through a trap door in the ceiling of a bedroom closet.

Basements

Where they are commonly found (primarily in the North), basements are high on a buyer's demand list and high on the homeowner's convenience list. Above all, they should be dry; good lighting is an added plus. Also very desirable is a direct exit from the basement to the outdoors.

In homes without basements, a utility room for the furnace, water heater, air conditioner, and so forth is usually located on a lower level or in a back corner.

In poking around basements, you'll want to know about heat. You can't always get gas heat, which might be your first choice because of its low maintenance requirements. Oil heat requires periodic delivery to your home. Electric is the most expensive heating style, although it, too, is low maintenance. Beware of heat pumps in the North, which don't seem to provide quite enough warmth for residents in that part of the country. Heat pumps are fine in the warmer South, though.

When going through homes for sale, you may get caught up in admiring other people's furnishings. That is understandable. But once you are at the point of actually choosing your future home, try to evaluate it in terms of what will work for *you* and not the current owner.

When it comes to radiators versus forced air, the disadvantage of radiators or baseboard heat is that you'll need a separate system if you want central air conditioning one day. However, heat is moister with circulating hot water, which is better for those with allergies. With forced air, you can use the same duct for heat and air conditioning, and you'll have either quickly—within five minutes of flipping a switch. Radiators take longer to heat up a room.

Laundry Facilities

A washer and dryer hookup in the basement is better than no facilities at all, but it will not help a resale. And you, the owner, will not enjoy carrying the laundry up and down the cellar stairs. The most requested laundry facility is a separate room near the kitchen. If that area is large enough to accommodate an ironing board or a sewing machine, it becomes a major selling point for the house.

Laundry facilities in the kitchen behind sliding or folding doors do not seem to hurt resale value, but most homeowners don't like having dirty laundry in the kitchen on wash day.

Evaluating Floor Plans

If you have looked at brand-new homes, you have probably seen floor plans. They can be found on builders' office walls, and you may even have brought home a set for your "house" file. However, if you are considering an older home, a floor plan may not be available. Therefore, mentally walk your way through any older house that interests you. Imagine both your daily routine and a special situation, such as a party. Where will you come in from work? Where will you hang your coat? Where can you read quietly while the kids are playing video games?

You will have to make your own notations, in lieu of a set of plans, of where walls, windows, doorways, and so forth are situated in the house. You do not have to make a fancy drawing, but it is smart to scribble some kind of floor plan, even though you can actually walk through the rooms of the house. This will help jog your memory later, and it will be useful for answering questions that you may have forgotten to think about the first time you walked through.

Few people really try out a house when they first inspect it. Most just glance around as observers and guests. That is fine for the initial "just looking" stage, but it is not adequate for a house that one is seriously considering.

If you draw and take home a floor plan, no matter how primitive, you can live in the house mentally. Questions will almost certainly pop into your head as you look at that plan.

Here are some of the most important traffic pattern questions:

- **Are there rooms that must be walked through in order to reach other rooms?** Only the kitchen is an acceptable walk-through room, and it is often located at or near the activity center of the house. All other walk-through rooms are a detriment to a sale. You will want to be especially careful to avoid floor plans where you must walk through one bedroom to get to another bedroom. Such houses are very difficult to sell.

- **How do you get from the kitchen to the backyard?** This is especially important for families with young children who need to be monitored. But anyone will find it handy to be able to go from the lawn chairs to the refrigerator easily.
- **Where will guests enter the home?** Most buyers prefer some kind of foyer or front entrance hall in which to greet guests. From there, movement into the living room should be natural and easy. Then think about how a guest will get from the living room to the dining room. And where is the powder room or guest bathroom? If entertaining is your style, you might also consider where guests are likely to mix during a party.
- **What is the traffic pattern between the family living area (the kitchen or family room) and the most often used bathroom?** Some bathrooms are located off the foyer, which is convenient for guests but inappropriate for the family, especially when muddy children are told to wash up and must walk through the dining room to the bathroom.

Before you read this book, the traffic pattern of your future home probably was not on your list of things to consider when house hunting. Was it? But you can see how important the layout of rooms can be—and how frustrated you can become after moving into a poorly laid out place.

- **What is the traffic pattern for bringing groceries and other merchandise into the house?** As we mentioned earlier, it can be inconvenient to have to lug bags up from a downstairs garage. Check the stairs that must be climbed and the distance that must be walked to perform this task.
- **What is the distance and traffic pattern between the family room and the kitchen?** Often, buyers like them to be adjacent or for one room to serve both functions; others prefer a separation.
- **Are any of the hallways particularly long or dark?** Many buyers

object to long hallways. Lighting from a skylight can eliminate that objection, at a cost to the buyer of about $1,000.

• **How are the bedrooms laid out?** Many buyers prefer the "split" bedroom layout, where the master bedroom and bath are on one side of the house and the other two or three bedrooms and one or two baths are on the other. This works particularly well for unrelated single buyers and for couples with older children; it gives everyone some distance.

Historic Houses

Perhaps the resale home that interests you is not a 3-year-old preowned ranch but a 110-year-old Victorian or a 126-year-old farmhouse—in other words, not just an older house but an *old* house. Especially in a newer town, homes that date back to the 1930s are also old enough to consider "old."

It is certainly true that not all old houses are glorious examples of their particular architectural style. Some do not appear to have any particular style. However, one thing you can say for even nondescript oldies is that they are solid. After all, they are still here, aren't they, after all these years? And while not all of them have stained-glass windows, medallion ceilings, and other grand touches, many of even the simpler ones have little nooks and crannies and design features that are just not that common in newer houses.

Some houses are just old; others are officially designated "historic." In the latter case, the house may have been named to the National Register of Historic Places, which comes under the U.S. Department of the Interior. Such houses have architectural or historic significance. Frequently, they do not stand by themselves but are part of a historic district—Brooklyn Heights in New York and part of Charleston, South Carolina, are two well-known examples. Some old houses have state historic status, and others are local landmarks.

Do these homes intrigue you? Do you want one of your own? If so, there are some important points to consider. For example, don't let your love for old houses lead you to buy a withering but charming wreck of a structure that is far beyond your financial capabilities for "fixing it up." Mortgage payments, real-estate taxes, fuel bills, plus a hefty home-improvement loan could be far too much debt for you to handle, especially if you are a first-time buyer and home ownership is new to you. Better look for a home that is old but in need of a smaller infusion of funds. Find a house inspector familiar with old, possibly historic, house construction. That should not be difficult in a town with a sizable inventory of older residential properties.

Be very sure you know if the house that interests you has any historic designation—local, state, or federal. That can affect how much, or how little, hacking away you will be able to do with repairs or installations. This designation affects how you can treat the outside of the house— setback, paint colors, surface materials, and so forth. Inside, you are on your own, although an addition or bumping out a wall to create a bay window may have to be approved by the state or regional historic district commission.

Contact your state historical society or local landmarks preservation commission for more information. These offices are likely to offer preservation project guidelines that you can apply to your old house. In the main, they will help show you what is worth preserving and what can be seriously altered. You will find, and learn as you go along, that distinctive stylistic features should be treated carefully and sensitively.

ALERT!

Probably the most important point to take away from a discussion of buying an old or a historic house is this: Be sure that you and any workers you engage know exactly what is to be done, before any irreversible attacks are made.

Give yourself time to get acquainted with your house before you start any serious work on it. Most homeowners find that they change their minds several times about how they want the kitchen remodeled or whether they want that dining room wall knocked out. One of the advantages of not being able to afford to do everything at once is that you can alter plans mentally without making serious financial and/or design mistakes by moving too quickly.

You should think not only of remodeling or preservation but also of the market value of your place. Future buyers will not appreciate a dropped ceiling, for example, no matter how much you spent to put it in. However, they will appreciate the house's original eleven-foot-high ceiling with handsome moldings. You would be wise to keep the older ceiling, repairing the plasterwork if necessary. (Yes, it is costly to heat those high-ceilinged rooms, but you need to protect your investment in that house. "Wear sweaters" is the advice from old-house mavens!)

If there is a historic district near you or a neighborhood that has seen a revival of interest in buying and fixing up old houses, you might contact their civic association or one of the homeowners directly. They are likely to have names and addresses of artisans they recommend, as well as those they suggest you avoid.

A Word of Warning

Unlike a used car, a home has few moving parts. There may be components that require replacement, but they can easily be replaced if necessary. Please remember to carefully read the disclosure list required to be supplied to you by the seller and spend the money to have the home inspected by a professional. Look for structural defects, as these are serious, but they can also be remedied if properly addressed. (E)

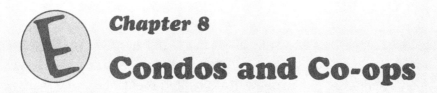

Chapter 8

Condos and Co-ops

Are you thinking about shopping for a condo? You can frequently enjoy a swimming pool, tennis courts, fitness center, and clubhouse right on the grounds of your complex. There are not too many residential communities, certainly not of older homes, likely to offer all that!

The Growth of Condominiums

If you are a first-time buyer, you will probably be able to afford to live in a better location by buying a condo than you would if you purchased a traditional single-family house. That is because you share the expenses—for example, of the landscaping and other amenities—with the entire condo community. You also share the high property taxes!

For the more than thirty or so years of its growth in this country, the condominium has been considered the starter home for the first-time homebuyer. Indeed, retirees and first-timers form the principal makeup of many complexes. For retirees, the attraction is smaller, more manageable living space, the amenities, and, to a lesser extent, lower costs than those of a house. After cost, the appeal to the first-timer is minimal upkeep. Many first-time buyers say they are busy with careers and do not want to spend their little free time keeping up with the demands of a house. They want fun, and if a condo community comes with a pool and other special features, so much the better. Young empty-nesters are flocking to condos, too, also looking for a low-maintenance, more amenities-packed lifestyle.

The condo can free its owner from that "rent-check-down-the-drain" living style. It can give buyers a chance to buy something without sacrificing location, for example in a large urban area, where there may not be single-family houses located on the subway but where the buyer may not want to give up his convenient city lifestyle. It can be a reasonably sound investment, too, allowing a unit owner to later trade up to a house, if he or she chooses, or perhaps to a more expensive condo complex or location. However, if chosen for the wrong reasons or without sufficient thought, the condo lifestyle can prove to be unsatisfactory.

TABLE 8.1	Median Sales Price of Existing Apartment Condos and Co-ops				
Year	Total U.S.	Northeast	Midwest	South	West
1999	$108,000	$112,500	$114,600	$84,100	$132,100
2000	$111,800	$111,200	$121,700	$87,700	$136,800
2001	$123,200	$124,200	$134,900	$97,100	$141,900

Source: National Association of Realtors. Used with permission.

Is Every Owned Apartment a Condo?

Various types of homes are often incorrectly called condos. Clarification of some terms used is in order here:

- A *condominium* is a housing style in which the buyers own their apartment units outright, plus an undivided share in the common areas of the community, which include their front and back lawn, if considered part of the design of the complex. Maintenance is handled by the complex or homeowners' association.
- *Town homes* are two-story attached units that feature the sleeping quarters upstairs. They can be run in a joint-ownership style, the way the condo is, with residents joining an owners' association and paying a monthly maintenance fee to the governing entity. Or residents can own the ground under their unit. The owners' association, maintenance fees, and so forth still apply.
- *Patio homes* are almost always one-floor houses with a patio or deck in the rear. But these are indeed houses, not apartments. Patio homeowners buy their own place, including the land under and around it (the front and back lawns). They are responsible for the outdoor maintenance. Membership in the owners' association can cover maintenance of the entrance to the community, publication of a newsletter, some social activities, and the like.
- *Cooperatives* are a form of legal ownership and not an architectural style. In a co-op, tenants own their building by purchasing shares in it and forming a corporation to pay maintenance and repairs. New buyers must have approval of the co-op board.

The most popular of these joined housing styles is the condominium. Virtually all of this chapter is concerned with buying and living in a condo. If, however, you prefer town homes or patio homes, the advice here—on choosing a location, plowing through bylaws, and the like—will apply to you, too.

How a Condo Works

Condos date back to ancient Rome and have been in existence in Europe far longer than they have in this country. It is the legal system of ownership that determines what is a condo, not a particular building style. Indeed, a condo community can be a high-rise tower in the city or a sprawling garden complex in the suburbs. It can be a single-family home community at a lakefront resort, too.

A condominium complex, regardless of how it is laid out, is a shared-ownership community. Residents own their own apartments, or "units"; rather, they own what is within the exterior walls but not what is outside those walls. They also own a proportional share of what is known as the common areas. Those areas include the apartments' outside walls, driveways and roads inside the complex, garages or carports, and all of the land within the complex's boundaries, including the landscaping around each unit. If there is a pool, tennis court, or clubhouse, those, too, are held jointly by all owners.

The Purchase

A condo is purchased the same way as a house. You can work with a realty agent, or you can find units on your own that are for sale by owner. You apply for a mortgage the same way you do for a new or resale house. Price negotiation, the closing—in fact, all of the steps toward ownership—follow the same lines as any other property transaction.

Your mortgage interest is tax deductible, and so are the real-estate taxes for your unit. You are also allowed a tax deduction for your share of real-estate taxes on the common areas. A statement sent to you by the owners' association will inform you of the amount. The monthly maintenance fee is *not* tax deductible.

	Co-op Corp. or Condo Owners' Assn.	Apartment Owner
Repairing damage to a wall or landscaping after a storm	☒	☐
Pumping out a flooded basement	Depends on whether the basement is shared space	
Sweeping a patio reserved for the use of one unit	☐	☒
Repairing cracked or heaved concrete on one unit's patio	☒	☐
Removing graffiti from the blacktop of one parking space	☒	☐
Repairing damage from a small fire inside one unit's garage	☐	☒
Landscaping in front of one unit	Could be either	
Landscaping near the entrance gate	☒	☐
Keeping the hallways clean	☒	☐
Landscaping in an interior surrounded completely by one unit	☐	☒
Repairing damage when the dishwasher breaks and floods an owner's kitchen and dining area	☐	☒
Repairing damage when a tree is struck by lightning and crashes through an owner's window, causing rain damage inside	Probably both, to different degrees	
Raking leaves, cutting grass, shoveling snow	☒	☐
Redecorating the interior	☐	☒
Painting the exterior	☒	☐

Everyday Life

There is more to living in a condo than knowing the legal workings. If you are moving from an apartment building, you will probably pick up the condo lifestyle quite easily. If you have been living on a military base or a college campus, you, too, will quickly grasp the condo lifestyle. But if you are buying a condo after living in a single-family home, you may need a bit of orientation. You may feel just fine and accepting of the restrictions that come with condo living. Or you might say, "No way," and move on to the next housing possibility.

For one thing, every new condo buyer must join the association that "runs" the community. You will be required to join, say, the Brierwood Community Association, which represents the 350-unit complex and its owners and is run by a volunteer board of directors elected from residents. Your monthly maintenance fee is, say, $265 a month. That fee covers your share of the community's real-estate taxes, insurance on the common areas, the cost of landscaping, pool maintenance, perhaps monthly extermination calls on each unit, and any employee salaries—for example, for someone to run a front office. Some of the money collected may also go into a fund to cover upcoming expenses at the complex. These expenses might include replacing roofing over two or three units or buying play equipment for land within the development that residents voted for use as a playground.

Maintenance Fees

Maintenance fees vary according to the size of the complex and the number of auxiliary features, buildings, or amenities that form the total expense for running the place. The fancier it looks, the more it costs to run, and the more you will have to pay each month to keep it going. Complex size affects maintenance costs as well. Because there are more of them sharing expenses, residents of a luxurious 400-unit complex are likely to pay less for niceties in their complex than those living in an equally posh community with half the units.

The money collecting, bill paying, and purchasing might be handled by the board of directors, or it might be under the jurisdiction of a local property management company that the owners' association has hired.

If there is such a company, its fee also is also included in the monthly maintenance charge.

The owners' association holds an annual meeting, to which all residents are invited, and perhaps a few other sessions throughout the year. There might be a regularly published newsletter as well.

Bylaws and Other Legal Stuff

There is a lot in writing to plow through when purchasing a condo. You can be a loner and still adapt to this lifestyle, but you must be willing to conform to the rules of the condo complex. Each condo association has its own rulings that govern virtually every aspect of life within the community outside your own four walls. All of these do's and don'ts are designed to keep up the appearance of the development and, by extension, the property values.

Do I need a lawyer if I am buying a condo?
Yes, you should have a lawyer represent you when buying a condo. Read everything, or have your lawyer read all the material you are given, and ask him or her to check special points that will be of concern to you.

Sometimes, the number and size of your pets can be restricted. You might even be unable to plunk on your front lawn that birdbath you have had your eye on at the home center. And don't even think about a satellite dish! If you run a business out of your home, you might have a problem if it means having a number of people (and their cars) coming into the complex at one time. Understandably, condo residents dislike lots of people coming in with cars and taking their parking spaces.

These bans may not bother you. But they do annoy some folks, particularly those who have owned a home and are not at all used to being told that their front door can't be any color but white.

What If Something Breaks?

You are responsible for fixing the things that break. That can be one of the major adjustments for those who come from apartment life. If you are used to calling the building superintendent when there is a problem in your apartment, you will have to adjust to the fact that it might *look* like an apartment, but it's all yours. There is no building manager or managing agent you can call when a faucet drips. It is up to you to have it repaired, just as it is your problem to deal with in a single-family house.

FACT

> Generally speaking, with a condo, you are responsible for the things inside, and the association is responsible for the things outside.

All of this can be a tricky area, however, which is why your community's bylaws are likely to be such a hefty packet. Take, for example, a burst pipe. It is the responsibility of the association to repair a malfunction if it is caused by a problem in the main or branch pipes serving your unit. What occurs within your own four walls—for example, that leaky faucet—is yours to repair.

However, if you notified the association of a plumbing problem within the common walls, and they failed to repair it before a pipe burst and ruined your carpeting, the association is then likely to be responsible for the damage. You must also allow access to your apartment in order to get that leak fixed. If you refuse, you could be responsible for the cost of repairs to all of the apartments involved! If the workers must break through a wall in your unit to get to some defective pipes that are staining someone else's walls, you must allow them access. After the plumber leaves, the association is required to repair your walls and leave the area clean. The question of whether it's them or you who foots the bill to redecorate (things like paint or wallpaper) is debatable.

Your responsibilities are not exactly those of a tenant or of a totally free owner, either. As owners, you are all mutually dependent on one another. You cannot simply call someone and have a repair taken care of if it affects any common areas. On the other hand, you do not have to shovel your way from the front door to the street and beyond with each snowfall or mow the grass and trim the hedges around your unit, or paint its exterior.

Maintenance-Free Living

A condo, co-op, or town home will provide you with a more maintenance-free environment than a single-family home. The condo complex will take care of much of the maintenance and upkeep that can become time-suckers for individual owners. Watering and mowing the lawn, trimming trees, shoveling snow, and tending to the pool are all the responsibility of the association. You can enjoy having a lawn without the fuss of cutting the grass when you'd rather be doing something else.

This can be a big plus if you are making the leap from renter to owner and do not feel quite ready to deal with the new responsibilities that would come with owning a house on a lot. Or perhaps you travel a lot on business and worry that you might not be around often enough to do a good job keeping up with the maintenance. Whatever your reason, a condo or town home may be more adaptable at different times of your life.

Beware of Overbuilding!

Condominiums are popular—sometimes too popular. The most important point you can take away from this discussion is that while condo buying can be quite successful, it can be almost disastrous in some situations. The huge amount of overbuilding of condo complexes in some parts of the country—and in some parts of any town or city, for that matter—has brought a glut of units to the market. You should be very careful not to buy in a saturated neighborhood, where it may be difficult to sell later because of a proliferation of other apartments for sale. Too many other units for sale in an area might cause your purchase price to drop over the years, so that when you're ready to sell, you have to take less for your home than you paid for it.

Selecting the Right Condo

Most condominium complexes do look, well, nice. Is that enough? Unfortunately, no.

You may notice that in some communities, maintenance could be better. There is nothing outrageously wrong, but the trim around the exterior doors and windows needs a coat of paint. Or some of the mortar between the outside bricks is crumbling. Does that mean the association is lax about maintenance? It could be, although it is more likely that there are no funds for repairs!

Reading Between the Financial Lines

Major repairs and improvements in a condo must be paid for by special assessments to the unit owners. It is important that a healthy condo community have a contingency fund for emergency expenses and a reserve for future improvements or repairs. A portion of each unit owner's maintenance fee should be put into those funds.

Read through the financial statement to see if there have been any recent special assessments. Ask members of the board and the management company, if there is one, if any major changes or repairs are being contemplated. How much are they likely to cost? What sum is being held in reserve for them? How much more will be raised through assessments?

While some communities do not have funds for repairs, others may have the money but may not spend it for repairs. There could be disagreements over how money is to be spent, or the association may just be slow to respond to needs. Be on the lookout for such poorly managed associations, and avoid them where you find them.

You may want to hire an accountant to explain to you these and all other financial details for the community that interests you. Or perhaps your lawyer can translate documents for you. This is a very, very important consideration. Be sure the community spends money wisely, both for your enjoyment in living there now and for resale value when you want to sell.

About Tenants

Condo units are frequently bought for investment purposes, rather than as primary residences for the owners. In most condo communities, there are a number of rental tenants. That is particularly true in overbuilt areas in which owners cannot sell and so must rent their homes when they move. Indeed, some communities have a high percentage of renters. Owners make the best occupants, however, because it is their money, their pride, and their hope for future appreciation of the unit that is on the line.

At unit owners' meetings, owner-investors may be less likely to vote for major improvements to the community, because they are not living there and may not see the need. While they do want to protect their investment, they may be hesitant to vote for measures that will cost them additional money. If the complex has a high percentage of owner-investors who do not live on the property, control of community improvements may, as a result, be controlled by nonresidents, which could be very frustrating to you as an owner living in the complex. It can also be more difficult to get the members together for projects, social programs, and the like. Tenants sometimes do not care what is going on in the community.

ALERT!

A common complaint made by condo owners concerns poor soundproofing between units. Be aware of that potential problem when you are going through apartments. If there is no one upstairs or next door during your calls, come back in the evening, when there are television sets and stereos going. If you can hear noises from adjacent units, you would be wise to keep on shopping.

Checking Out the Complex

Once you have narrowed your condo choice down to two or three communities, visit them often. Drive around at night to check lighting and then again in the morning to have a look at rush-hour traffic. Walk around the grounds, and talk to at least three residents. They are usually happy to chat about the good points of their community and about any problems and looming expenses. Is there a community newsletter on a countertop in the laundry room or on a clubhouse table? Help yourself. Read about the residents to get some idea of whether you could feel at home in this place.

Buying into a Brand-New Community

There are a few additional things you'll want to be on the lookout for if you are considering buying a condo in a brand-new complex. Again, be certain that the new complex you are interested in is not located in an already saturated neighborhood. When the time comes, it may be difficult to sell, and the value of your unit could drop over the years.

Another major consideration is maintenance fees. Developers sometimes lowball maintenance charges initially, not only to attract buyers but also because at that stage, they do not know exactly what maintenance will cost each owner. The builder may guarantee no maintenance fee for two years, but how will you know what those charges will be at the end of that time and whether you can afford them? While there are no guarantees, you might check the maintenance fees at similar condo communities in the same town or county.

Ask at what point the developer will turn over the community to unit owners. If he holds on to too many unsold units for too long, the condo association cannot become an independent entity. If he continues to own more than a few condos after the turnover to residents, he can still influence the board of directors, with his voice being far louder than that of the individual unit owners.

Recreational facilities are almost always the last part of a complex to be constructed. Sometimes things happen that cause the developer to not get around to them. Are you sure this builder will put in the pool he mentioned? Will you have to pay a special fee for its use? That happens sometimes to buyers who think their monthly maintenance fee covers the use of the pool, tennis courts, and even the clubhouse (for parties and so forth). Then they are hit with a $500 annual fee to join a "club" so that they can use those facilities. There is nothing illegal about this fee, but naturally you will want to know it exists before you commit yourself to buying.

The Cooperative Lifestyle

Cooperatives are not as common as condominiums, and they are run differently. In some states, a cooperative apartment is considered real estate, but in others, it is considered intangible personal property. (It is defined as "intangible" because stock certificates show you own shares in the corporation that owns the building. You do not own the building itself.)

All of the unit owners in a cooperative building purchase shares in the corporation that owns and runs the co-op. How many shares you buy is likely to depend on the size of your apartment. When you buy a unit, you automatically become a co-owner and have a proprietary lease on that unit; the lease runs as long as you live there.

There is a monthly maintenance fee that includes the same general charges that a condo owner pays, but co-op owners also pay their proportionate share of the building's mortgage, if there still is one. That part of the monthly maintenance is tax deductible for owners.

To buy a co-op apartment, you must be approved by the board of directors of that building. Accordingly, when you sell, your buyer has to be given a green light by that board.

Financing is acquired through a co-op loan, secured by the certificates of your stock in the corporation. You can shop around for the best fixed- and adjustable-rate packages. The interest on a co-op loan is tax deductible.

The Nonprofit Co-op

Occasionally you will come across a cooperative run on a not-for-profit basis, with government or private association backing. These are generally reserved for people or families with lower-than-average incomes. In these apartments, if you are approved for residency according to the income ceiling, you make a nominal down payment—perhaps several hundred dollars—and your monthly maintenance fee is reasonably low.

When you are ready to sell, the down payment is returned to you, along with some fair market interest, and that is that.

The nonprofit co-op can be a step toward having your own home in that it does offer a sense of ownership. It could also allow you to save toward a down payment on your next place, including in that sum your co-op down payment plus interest. But by definition, nonprofit co-ops are not going to return you very much money on your investment, no matter how long you stay and no matter how popular these apartments are in your area.

Condo or Co-op?

Both condos and co-ops can be wise housing choices if they are selected after careful deliberation and preparation. The condo, however, because it is real estate and is owned free and clear without the strings of a corporation, comes out ahead. However, the region of the country you are in will play a big part in this choice. In New York City, for example, there are far more cooperatives than condominiums. There are a number of them in Washington, D.C., too, where no one blinks at buying a co-op. Nevertheless, for the best investment appreciation and greatest ease of selling, depending on that all-important factor of location, both come out behind the single-family house.

Chapter 9

Special Home Choices

There are a few choices other than buying a resale home or a condo. You may want to consider some of these options—one might be just right for you! Maybe you are eager to get into a brand-new house. Or perhaps buying either a loft or a "fixer-upper" are choices that are more truly "you." Or perhaps a manufactured, modular, or mobile home is your choice.

New Housing Developments

New houses are, as you might expect, more expensive than resale homes, all other things being equal. Still, with a new home you can have all the space you need. It can be as light and bright as you want. New means cutting-edge technologies, too.

You might want to consider purchasing a new house in a development. With some careful shopping, you might even be able to strike a price deal for yourself.

How to Find These New Affordables

Start by looking beyond the city limits and most likely beyond the suburbs. You will get a better deal on homes way, way out, where the developer has not paid astronomical rates for land. Where such homes are situated is vitally important. Part of the attraction of such developments is their price. And they are likely to grow into larger communities over time. But you will probably want a reasonable number of existing services there now. Are there schools, stores, houses of worship, and recreational amenities, or will you truly be a trailblazer?

You may be in for a long commute to work if you buy in these areas. Does the area have easy access to highways? With new developments, too, you are less likely to have large trees for shade and privacy.

ALERT!

Don't buy the flashiest house on the street, even in a new development.

Keep in mind that it is not just the house itself, all new and shiny, but the total picture that makes for a successful home purchase. Look at your lifestyle to see if you might be sacrificing too much just to own a new house.

Here's another suggestion for finding affordables. Look for the innovative builders in your area who specialize in quality, medium-cost construction. A call to your statewide builders association can bring you their names, as well as some addresses for you to check out.

When looking at new construction, beware—just as you would in a traditional neighborhood—of buying the largest, most expensive house in a development. Look instead at the mid-priced or lower-end models. The value of the lower- and mid-priced homes will be pulled up by the splashier ones around them. The only exception would be a community that stresses recreational amenities, where being right on the golf course, say, or on the lake makes for the top-of-the-line location, and one future buyers would be willing to spend extra money to acquire. Pick the home with the best view of what the community has to offer.

Owners' Associations

Many new single-family home communities these days open with formal homeowners' associations in place. New residents must join the association and pay annual dues. The dues go toward maintaining the entrance and any other product or service residents want.

Negotiating to Sweeten the Deal

Developers do not usually like to lower the sales prices of their homes. However, the state of the economy (both national and local), the developer's finances, and other factors could make any developer more amenable to "talking."

The trick here is to keep cool. As with other types of negotiating, it is not a good idea to seem too excited about what someone is trying to sell you. "Oooh" and "Aaah" too much, and the builder or the on-site sales agent is going to think, "This one is hooked," and there go your bargaining chips.

When a community is essentially finished and running smoothly, a developer may well want to "close out" that complex as quickly as possible. If there are two or three houses that remain stubbornly unsold, a developer might lower their prices. Occasionally, the model home might be sold that way, although it could also be sold early, with the deal not formally enacted until the developer is prepared to close down sales. The developer who has many unsold homes is also likely to be amenable to some negotiating. It costs money to carry empty houses.

In the off season for homebuying—generally, October through January or February—when developers are drumming their fingers on desktops in sales offices, you will also be very welcome, and all of the stops might be pulled out to keep you from looking elsewhere.

More likely than a price cut is negotiation over what will be included in a sales price, which will stay firm. All the little extras can add up, and it is up to you to ask for them. Perhaps a house is selling for $125,000, and you know you want to spend another, say, $6,000 for the decorating features you want. If you get $3,000 from the developer in the form of extras, that is $3,000 you won't have to spend.

Analyze all concessions that the developer offers you. Some may be a good value; others may not stand up to the figures run up on your pocket calculator. Perhaps you can secure a commitment from the developer to pay your first year's real-estate taxes or part of the closing costs. Always ask. You cannot expect goodies to be offered to you out of the blue.

Be careful, though, with frills. If the builder says, "I'll cut the price by $5,000 or give you $5,000 in credit that you can use to buy the things you want from our design center," take the price cut. There is usually quite a markup on developers' upgrades.

Lofts

A house is not a home to you. You want to live in a trendy neighborhood as a resident of . . . a hat factory? Well, at one time it was a hat factory. Right now, it is perhaps more evidence of a strong back-to-the-city movement in one urban section of your metropolitan area.

You may find lofts in a former factory or any other industrial building where the company closed or moved to newer facilities, leaving behind a vacant structure. Over the last two decades, those handsome buildings, usually found downtown and/or along a community's waterfront, have been rescued from abandonment or a mishmash of other uses to become attractive and—in the beginning, anyway—affordable housing.

Lofts can offer many pluses to the house hunter of any age, including the following:

ALERT!

> Though lofts may be affordable, their locations often make them highly desirable, driving up the prices over time. This can be a good thing if you buy when they are still relatively "undiscovered." But you may find that a loft downtown or along the waterfront costs more than you're willing to spend.

- You'll be living in a home with a history, sometimes of a century or more.
- It's affordable housing, at least in some cities where housing is not sky-high and the loft movement is still new. (However, recently, in some areas lofts have changed from the Bohemian type of cheap living to an expensive alternative to a conventional condominium dwelling.)
- Space! There's often a lot of it.
- Light! These are not dark, dreary factory homes. Many lofts boast huge floor-to-ceiling—and high ceilings, at that—windows that will let in a lot of natural light. They'll often give you marvelous downtown views, too.
- You'll be close to city life, with its excitement and fast pace.
- Fellow building residents, because of their housing choice, often become more than just neighbors. You're likely to develop a close-knit community with people who share your love of the loft lifestyle.
- Since the loft is likely to have been only recently renovated, appliances, flooring, ceramic tile, and other features are practically brand-new.

Is there a downside to all this enthusiasm over lofts? There are some negatives, including the following:

- Lofts could be quite pricey. In New York's SoHo, the district in Manhattan in which the loft movement began in that city, the artists who originally settled there before the area became trendy in the 1970s have given way to high-income residents living in lofts costing well into six figures. Affluent buyers now dominate the loft market there. (To be sure, there are some concessions made to loft renters who are artists, thanks to protection from Manhattan's so-called loft law, which imposes limits on rent increases by landlords.) All around that city, there are lofts carrying $1-million-plus price tags.

- Some lofts that are affordable may be raw space. That is, you buy your 2,000 square feet, and then you put in electricity, plumbing, walls, appliances, fixtures, and so on. It's expensive and *a lot of work.*

- In manufacturing areas, residents of a loft building may have nowhere to go even for such basic services as food shopping. Heading for a supermarket, dry cleaner, and so forth may involve a bus or car ride of some distance.

- Some loft buildings skirt local regulations and codes. Sometimes the building has to be brought up to building and safety code compliance, at the expense of loft dwellers. There may not be adequate rear yards, for example, to meet a city's fire, safety, and air requirements. The answer? In that instance, it could be necessary to actually remove parts of the building.

Ah, but to you the positives of this living experience far outweigh the few negatives, you say? So, how do you choose which loft to buy?

ALERT!

Watch out for possible contaminants in a loft from its days as an industrial factory. Ask the developer and the city about possible contamination *before* you buy.

Your best bet is to hang around, literally, the loft area that interests you. Talk to residents. Read real-estate ads. See what the prices are and what is going on in that neighborhood. What are residents angry about? What are they doing about it? How is city hall treating loft dwellers? Gather as much information as you can before stopping in at a realty office to loft-shop.

Fixer-Uppers

If the idea of rolling up your sleeves and working on your home after you move in excites you, a fixer-upper may be your answer to home ownership. You can often find a house in need of repairs in a good location. A fixer-upper will cost less than a similar house in good shape would cost. And you'll have control over the quality and look of the repairs and updates you make to the house.

Be realistic when looking at fixer-uppers. Know how much repair work you can actually take on and complete once the initial wave of rehabbing enthusiasm passes.

Additionally, avoid houses in which major repairs are needed. Stay away from houses with serious defects in the foundation or working systems (such as heating, electrical, or plumbing) or in which a major reshuffling of rooms is necessary to create a workable traffic pattern. All of this work is expensive, and you may not see much of your financial investment returned when you sell. A buyer will *expect* workable plumbing and heating, adequate wiring, and so on. Even adding a new roof comes under the heading of a major repair, though this can add to value because it improves the appearance of the home.

If you have the ability to virtually build a house yourself or if you have family engaged in one phase or another of the construction trades, these cautionary words might not apply. Broadly speaking, however, truly run-down houses—houses that are little more than shells—are just too far gone for the novice homebuyer, who is merely a little clever and handy.

There are two exceptions to these caveats. One is the professional renovator who buys a tumbledown house, renovates it, and sells it for a profit. The other is the fixer-upper enthusiast who buys a distressed property in a new restoration area, where there are dilapidated houses that with enough care (and funds) can eventually be worth a lot of money.

Can You Handle It?

Neophytes should stick to houses that need painting, landscaping, minor to medium-size repairs, carpeting, and other cosmetic improvements. Upgrading the kitchen and bathroom(s) can also be profitable when it comes to resale, and so will adding a second bathroom. The house should look untended and slightly shabby, not like a bombed-out shell.

There are a number of things to keep in mind while shopping for the least expensive yet potentially most salvageable and profitable fixer-upper. Prices for shabby properties might be almost as high as prices for houses in better condition. It is important not to overpay for any house, but it is particularly important for you not to spend all of your money on a house that will need still more money—and big bucks at that—to make it look good.

Location, Location, Location

Remember location, of course. A run-down house in a solid or even a pretty darned attractive neighborhood can be a good investment. Alas, too many of those dwellings are in equally run-down blocks, where no amount of renovating will increase their value.

Creative Solutions

If the fixer-upper you are considering has been on the market for a long time, ask yourself why. Location aside, it might be that it needs a lot of work, but there could be other reasons. Suppose the house is very dark and dreary inside. That defect could be remedied by installing a skylight or two, an idea that might not have occurred to other house shoppers. Be creative as you go through these homes. Knowing how to fix flaws that might put off other buyers to a basically sound property could bring you an excellent deal. (Be sure, too, that the seller is not asking too high a price for the house.)

Estimate Repairs

As you walk through fixer-uppers, make notes on repairs needed, remembering that a house inspector will do a more thorough job later on. Then take out your calculator when you return home and figure roughly how much you will need to spend in upgrading costs. If you cannot estimate costs to fix some malfunction or other, at least list the problem, with a repair figure to be filled in later. Seeing a sizable list of wrongs could well change your mind about buying a particular property.

Use your own judgment in determining how much fixing up you can undertake, both emotionally and financially.

Speaking of work, consider who will do the repairs in the house you buy. It is most cost-effective if the owners do most of the work themselves. Labor costs are high. In the ideal situation, the pros are called on only for highly specialized areas such as electrical work, heating, some plumbing, and the like. You should be willing to do as much as possible of the other jobs, with a little guidance from the folks at the local home decorating center.

Zoning Restrictions

Look into local zoning restrictions when you find a house that interests you. Be sure that you can renovate the way you want, particularly if you are interested in adding an extension or second floor to the house. Perhaps you will not be permitted to do so, or perhaps you will require a variance. Are you sure you can win one? Do you want to go to that trouble?

Your Living Quarters

Is the renovation work going to be so drastic, or so messy, that you will be unable to live in the house until most of the work is complete? If so, where will you live? Can you afford to carry a mortgage payment and pay the rent on the place where you are now, perhaps along with a home repair loan payment each month?

If you feel you can—or must—live there while work is in progress, try to organize yourself to settling in for the long haul. Be certain your family, or your marriage, can stand the strain of the always-present odor of sawdust and paint, the constant walking around of ladders and planks of wood, and the sense that life at home is always going to be messy, dirty, and incomplete.

How Long Will This Take?

How much time are you going to be able to devote to a renovation project with your work schedule? Do you travel in your job? Do you put in ten-hour days at the office? Is your spouse equally busy in a demanding career? Are you single, with no one to share the rehab burden? Consider all of this in determining just how grand a rehab project you can undertake. If you think, "Well, I'll work on the house weekends," you may be surprised at how soon you will begin to tire of that weekend agenda. It ceases being fun and challenging for many people after, say, three months.

Special Concerns

Buying a house in a designated historic district brings special concerns. You could be restricted from making the types of changes you envision to the property that interests you. Exterior alterations will, in all likelihood, have to be approved by a local commission. Exterior surfacing and paint colors will probably be regulated. However, you will be allowed to do anything you want inside the house.

ALERT!

Always have a fixer-upper—or any house, really—inspected by a professional before you commit to it. See Chapter 13 for more on inspections.

Learn all you can about the district that interests you before you make an offer on any property inside its boundaries. Homes in these enclaves usually retain their value and cachet because of the uniform appearance of the neighborhoods. Still, some house-hunters do not like the restrictions or curbs on their own artistic expressions.

Paying for a Fixer-Upper

When considering what to offer, take the market value of the house, deduct what you think repairs will cost, add a little extra in the event your repair estimates are low, and you will come up with a fair offer. Another formula that works is to consider how much the house would be worth if it were in top-grade condition. You should buy at 20 to 30 percent below what the house would cost if it were not a fixer-upper.

In the sales contract, include this phrase: *subject to the buyer obtaining a satisfactory inspection report and satisfactory repair bids within ten business days.* The inspection is standard these days; the "repair bids" phrase should be incorporated in fixer-upper bids. If you are not satisfied with the reports and recommendations you receive from the house inspector and from the repair people you bring in for estimates, you can cancel the agreement to purchase and have your earnest money deposit refunded.

If a house needs extensive work, many buyers skip calling in a house inspector and instead call a contractor—the person they will engage later to do the repair work—to look at the property. Naturally, they stick close to that individual as he goes through the property, jotting down his comments to familiarize themselves with, and remember, the house's problems.

The National Association of the Remodeling Industry (NARI) offers a ton of material, including design ideas, remodeling plans, a library of resources, and consumer tips to help avoid scams in this industry. You can contact them at 780 Lee Street, Suite 200, Des Plaines, IL 60016, ✆ (847) 298-9200 or visit them at ✍ *www.nari.org.*

If You Need a Home-Improvement Loan

If the home you buy needs repairs or improvements, you will have to come up with the money for that renovation. It may take a little—maybe only a couple thousand dollars—or a lot to make your home the way you envision it.

Keep in mind that loans cost money, no matter how advantageous the borrowing terms. It is better to pay cash for repairs if you can.

An exception might be if you are using a government-backed low-interest loan, maybe one at 5 or 6 percent. Then you might leave your savings alone, especially if they are drawing a higher rate of return from interest.

Naturally, if you are making substantial repairs to a fixer-upper, you are not likely to be able to pay for the work in cash. But if you are doing a small job of, perhaps, $5,000 or so, you might be better off waiting until you have saved that money to make the repair.

Where to Find Additional Loans

Look at your own resources first. Do you have a life insurance policy you might be able to borrow against? The face value of the policy is, of course, reduced by the amount of the loan, but you can make up that amount by increasing your regular premium payments.

If you own securities, you might ask your broker about borrowing against some of the paper you hold. That could result in a better deal for you than heading for a commercial lender.

Credit unions are excellent loan resources. If you don't belong to one through work, look for other "ins" you might have to a credit union. Some credit unions exist for members of particular professions. Perhaps you can find one for your religious group or your community. Does your special interest or hobby association have a credit union?

Be aware that in the always-growing world of home-improvement scams, financing can be one of the ways contractors fleece customers. Consider carefully before taking out a loan from your contractor.

You can also look to unsecured personal loans, where your home is not put up as security, that you can find offered by commercial lenders. The terms and amounts vary from one lender to another, but essentially you can expect to be able to borrow $15,000 to $20,000 for five or ten years at a rate of interest likely to be around 15 percent, which is pretty high and will be fairly costly to you in the long run.

You are judged for eligibility the same way you would be for any loan: based on your income, employment record, and credit history. You will need to get three written estimates for the work you want done; this is a requirement of lenders to make sure you are not overpaying for the improvement. The lender will want to see those estimates, but as long as they are considered reasonable by the institution loaning you money, you are free to choose the contractor you want from among them. The lender also requires an outline or plan for the project and the name of the contractor you have chosen. The interest on these loans is not tax deductible.

The lowest bid is not necessarily the bid you should take. Consider also the quality of work for the money. Many folks tend to go with the middle estimate.

Some Other Sources to Try

There is more good borrowing news. Besides the tried-and-true lender we all know so well, there are steady loan sources that may not be familiar to many or most people. These sources sometimes offer good borrowing terms, especially if they are federal or state government programs.

The 203(k) program, offered by the federal government through the Federal Housing Authority, or FHA, enables the buyer of a one- to four-family house to borrow both the sale price for the house and its renovation loan. The loan amount offered is based on the estimated post-refurbishment value of the house.

The maximum amount you can borrow for renovations is subject to FHA lending guidelines for that particular geographic area. (There are no income caps for buyers, however.) Financing is based on an estimate of the value of the home after renovations, with the mortgage and renovation loan created for that total amount. Interest rates are slightly higher than conventional mortgage rates, but they are lower than rates for conventional renovation loans.

The minimum you can borrow is $5,000, but with a fixer-upper, and sometimes with any old house, you will find that you have at least this much work to be done. The money can even be used for paint, sod, and appliances. Call your local HUD office for information about area lenders and this program.

Another popular federal government loan source is the FHA Title 1 program, in which the FHA insures loans made by private lenders for as much as $25,000. The payback period can be as long as twenty years. Interest charged might be higher than with a home equity loan (discussed in the next section) but lower than with a home-improvement loan from a commercial lender. The interest is tax deductible.

Here are some of the advantages of the Title 1 program:

- You do not have to live in any particular area to secure one of these loans.
- You seldom need any security for loans under $7,500, other than your signature on the note, and you do not need a cosigner.
- You do not have to disturb any mortgage or deed of trust you have on your home.
- You need only to own the property (or have a long-term lease on it), fill out a loan application that shows you are a good credit risk, and execute a note agreeing to repay the loan.
- Your loan can cover architectural and engineering costs, building permit fees, title examination costs, appraisal fees, and inspection fees.

FACT

If you are sixty-five years of age or older, you may qualify for loans geared just toward you. Check with your local utility company, community development agency, regional HUD office, or other government agencies for programs for seniors.

Check with your local utility if you are planning any energy-saving improvement, such as the installation of storm windows or added insulation. Some utilities work with local lenders to allow homeowners to make energy-efficient improvements at as little cost to them as possible. For example, families with incomes of up to $30,000 a year can qualify for interest-free loans of from $500 to $4,000. Those with higher incomes are eligible for loans at a low 5-percent interest rate.

What about Home Equity Loans?

You might have another choice when looking for funds. You could draw on the equity in your home. You may have heard about this borrowing style. Home equity can be borrowed in two different ways: through a home equity line of credit, which you can draw on as you need the money, or through a home equity loan, which comes as a lump sum, similar to a second mortgage.

With the line of credit, you need only draw on your equity by writing a check or using a credit card as you need it. You pay interest only on the amount you borrow. But since a loan comes to you in a lump sum, you pay interest on all of it.

One advantage to each is that the interest is tax deductible (most other loan programs are considered consumer debt, with no tax deductions allowed). The disadvantage is that your house is collateral. If you miss payments, you can lose your home.

This last point of caution is particularly important to the first-time buyer. If you do qualify for a home equity loan, be absolutely sure that you can carry the new burden of a mortgage before taking on another home-related one. It is easy to become overwhelmed by the debt.

If you are a first-time buyer, you might have had to scramble to put together a minimum down payment. So where is your equity? Hmm, that's a good question. Usually lenders offer 70 to 80 percent of equity in a home—usually, not always. These days there are programs that offer borrowers not only 100 percent equity but also more money than their home is worth! When lenders have money to lend, and the buyer has good credit, then 100 percent financing is often available. Not all lenders offer 100% financing, but in every major market in the U.S. this 100% financing is available. Needless to say, interest rates are high, and the previously mentioned cautions about possibly losing your home also apply.

Credit Cards: Skip This Option

Paying for a home renovation with credit cards is a good deal more costly than the more traditional borrowing methods you have read about here. With credit cards carrying interest rates of 17 to 19 percent, you will be paying off that loan forever, even if you shift your account from one lender to another, taking advantage of low introductory interest rates. They almost all eventually rise. Do some shopping around, and you will find far more agreeable terms.

Using Contractors

If you decide to use the services of a contractor, take care to choose one with a reputation for honesty and good workmanship. There are several ways to check on a contractor, according to the U.S. Department of Housing and Urban Development:

- Consult your local chamber of commerce, the Better Business Bureau, your state attorney general, or your local consumer protection agency.
- Talk with people for whom the contractor has done work.
- Ask your lender about him, if you plan to finance the project with a loan.
- Check his place of business to see that he is not a fly-by-night operator.
- Find out, if you can, how he rates with known building-product distributors and wholesale suppliers.
- Ask friends and relatives for names of firms they could recommend.

ALERT!

Understand what you sign. The contract both you and the contractor sign should state clearly the type and extent of improvements to be made and the materials to be used.

Before you sign a contract, get the contractor to spell out the following in exact terms:

- How much the entire job will cost you.
- How much interest you will pay on his loan (if you choose to use his financing).
- How much you will pay in service charges.
- How many payments you must make to pay off the loan, and how much each of those payments will be.

After the entire job is finished in the manner set forth in your contract, you sign a completion certificate. By signing this paper, you certify that you approve the work and materials, and you authorize the lender to pay the contractor the money you borrowed.

Manufactured or Modular Homes

Manufactured or modular homes are produced in sections—that may include even carpeting—and then shipped to the building site, where the parts are assembled to form a house. Some houses are very plush and are virtually indistinguishable from site-built (or in-the-ground) homes. Others are quite large but simpler in style.

Manufactured homes used to be called mobile homes, but now, because they are permanent residences, the term is no longer used. That fact was recognized by Congress in 1980, when it changed the word *mobile* to *manufactured* in all of its federal laws and publications. However, you might still see the word "mobile" around in some older parks, and it is used by some retailers who feel buyers continue to relate to the word. Manufactured homes must comply with federal standards set by HUD.

Modular houses are also constructed in a factory and then shipped to the building site to be assembled. However, modular homes must adhere to state and local standards (rather than federal ones).

Homebuyers (and developers) choose these homes for one simple reason. They are usually less costly than site-built homes of similar size. An average three-bedroom, two-bath house, with amenities, can cost under $50,000, including setup or installation (but not including the cost of land where the house will be located). Larger homes can carry $100,000-plus price tags. Manufacturers usually offer a variety of architectural styles. Carports and garages cost extra.

You have three options for these homes.

1. You can have one assembled on your lot in the area you have in mind. (Be careful. Some communities do not allow manufactured homes that meet federal, rather than local, standards.)

2. You can purchase an already-built manufactured or modular home by itself or as part of a new- or resale-home community.

3. You can buy a house from a dealer and have it put in a planned community that you choose.

A fourth, and less common, option does exist. You can buy a manufactured home and place it in a rental community, where you lease the land beneath the house. You should look into this move very carefully before committing, and ask a number of questions of the owner or manager of the community. For example, will you have a written lease for the land? For how long? How will the financing of your home work? How much are utility hookup charges in that community? Can you afford that expense? Who handles maintenance there? What if the owner of the community wants to sell his land? Will you then have to move your home?

The Consumer Information Center offers a free catalog (available at most libraries) as well as many good government pamphlets of settlement costs, manufactured homes, and GI loans. Write to them at P.O. Box 100, Pueblo, CO 81002.

Where to Buy

If you want to purchase a home that is already built or, more correctly, already *assembled*, shop at existing or brand-new communities, just as you would for a site-built house. Ask at the sales office about any developments that interest you and about whether a particular community features site-built or factory-built construction style.

If you own land and want to have a manufactured or modular home put on your lot, you can contact one of the more than one hundred companies nationwide that build these houses. They are represented by thousands of retailers around the country. The company you call will be able to put you in touch with the retailer nearest you. Some manufacturers have their own sales centers in certain parts of the country, too, where you can also buy a house.

Financing

If a manufactured or modular home is permanently set on a foundation and is sold with land or erected on land owned by the new homeowner, it usually can be financed with a real-estate mortgage. Mortgages can be secured from the same variety of lenders that offer financing for site-built homes, including FHA and VA sources. The key in this case is that the home and land are considered a single real-estate entity under state law.

FACT

Manufactured homes on rented land and houses that are considered personal property rather than real estate (such as the old-style mobile homes) are treated differently than other houses and are not financed as real estate, that is, with a mortgage.

Manufactured home retailers can arrange financing for these purchases, or you can shop around for better terms from banks and other lending institutions in your area.

Mobile Homes

True mobile homes—those erected before 1976 and usually situated in mobile home communities—are another housing option. We are not talking about "trailer camps" but about "parks" where newer—and larger—homes are almost never moved from their original site. Some of these parks are very attractive, and the larger homes in them may appreciate slightly in value rather than depreciating, the way the old, single-width mobile homes have in the past (although some parks may still have a single-width, old-style "trailer" in residence). They do not appreciate at the same pace as traditionally built houses, though, or high-end factory-built ones.

If you are interested in mobiles, you do want to see some return on your investment so that you can use that money toward your next real-estate purchase. Shop carefully, and take heed of the suggestions made earlier for buying on rented land. Remember, too, that pre-1976 homes were not subject to the same safety standards as HUD-regulated, post-1976 manufactured homes. You'll be better off with a newer mobile home.

One of the cardinal points made throughout this book, as you have probably noticed, has been keeping an eye on resale value when you buy any home. The same is true here. Location means virtually everything when you put up the "For Sale" sign, but a quality home that has been kept in good condition runs a close second. Whether you can afford a top-of-the-line manufactured or modular house or a very simple style, make sure that there is a resale market for it in the area you choose.

Chapter 10

Shopping the Neighborhood

Whether you are looking through homes with a real-estate agent or just driving around on your own, there are important factors for you to keep in mind besides just the house itself. The most important factor in smart homebuying is location. As you've heard before, in real estate, what matters most is location, location, location.

Choosing the Right Town

Location will make a difference in the size of your property-tax bill, the quality of schools, and probably how long you will stay in that house. It will certainly make a difference in whether you profit from its sale.

No other factor equals the importance of location, and nothing else should be considered as carefully when choosing your home—or, for that matter, in deciding to buy property of any kind. In real estate, location means more than the piece of the earth described in your deed or the area staked out by a surveyor's red-flagged stocks. That is just a lot. Location is that lot, the neighborhood around it, and the town in which the neighborhood lies. You may not be able to afford the top-of-the-line house and location, but understanding why one location is more valuable than another will help you get the most for the money you can afford to spend.

How's the Neighborhood?

First consider the community. We are certainly a transient society. How many of us today are still living in the towns where we were born? The automobile has allowed us to move beyond the few streets in a small town or the many streets in a large city to the next town and the one beyond that. Trains and planes take us even farther afield. There's evidence of this everywhere—for example, when you read obituary notices, you may find that even if the deceased has lived in the same town his whole life, his surviving children are scattered across the country.

Do you recognize your own family pattern in that picture? Are all of you in separate time zones? Or have you grown up and stayed pretty much in or around your hometown or at least in your home state? Whether you are looking for a home within a 20-mile radius of where you are now or one that's 2,700 miles away, there are some factors that apply in choosing any community.

Services

Learn about the services that are available in the community you are looking at. Here are some you should consider:

- **Refuse collection.** Some towns provide it; others do not. If yours is the latter, you will either have to make regular trips to the town dump or pay a private company for garbage collection. The cost can be anywhere from $10 to $40 a month.
- **Sewers.** Large cities use sewers, and rural areas use septic tanks. In the suburbs, you may find both in the same town. Is there a sewer use fee? If so, add it to your list of costs.
- **Water.** Is city water free (included in your property tax bill), or do you pay the city separately for the water you use? Do you pay a private water company? If your property uses well water, is the water pure and plentiful? Don't forget that the pump on a well draws electricity, so that water is not really "free."
- **Road service.** How well will your streets be plowed in winter? Sometimes you can get an indication by how well they are maintained during the fall "pick-up-leaves" season. How quickly do potholes get repaired?
- **Police protection.** What is the crime rate like? Can you go out safely at night? Are break-ins common? Does the town maintain rescue vehicles, or must you pay for private ambulance services? How large is the police force in relation to the population? How does this compare with other areas? You can learn all this from a phone call to the community-relations department of the local police force.
- **Fire department.** Is the fire department full-time or volunteer? Most cities have full-time personnel; most suburbs and rural areas use volunteers or a combination of full-time, part-time, and volunteer firefighters. How well are they equipped? Is equipment paid for by taxes or by contributions? If your real-estate agent cannot help you with answers to these questions, you should call the local fire department.
- **Library services.** A town's main library, and its branches, are a good clue to its character. How large is the library system in relation to the

town? Does it belong to an interlibrary exchange group so that books can be borrowed from other branches? Does it feature any special collections? Is there a solid children's department? Are there many library activities, or is the building limited to books and quiet reading? Call the library and ask, or better yet, stop in and pose your questions. That will give you an opportunity to look around. Is the place busy? Check bulletin boards. What is going on in the library and around town? A bulletin board chock full of notices indicates a lively community. Look on the library counters as well, for brochures about activities and programs.

- **Social services.** Does the town sponsor programs for senior citizens, teenagers, and children? Are family counseling services available? (They may be—on a countywide basis.)
- **Recreation.** This is a subjective area, which may be less important to you since recreational facilities might be available in a nearby town or even close by across the state line. If recreation and cultural facilities are high on your list of must-haves, you would be wise to look into what your town has to offer. Even if you don't expect to take advantage of them, keeping resale value in mind, your town should offer some amenities, such as parks, clubs, community groups, and similar activities to draw residents.
- **Accessibility to work.** Commuting time for you (and your spouse) is likely to be of major interest in your choice of a new town. How far are you willing to travel, twice a day, five days a week, in order to get to and from work? For most folks, a one-hour commute each way is about the limit they are willing to spend getting to work.

Overall, city residents expect to have public transportation available, and suburban dwellers are generally resigned to driving a car to work or to facing a train commute each day.

Access to workplaces is also a major factor in determining property value. Towns surrounding major corporate headquarters usually rank high in desirability. Second are towns along major interstate highways or on rail commuter lines that provide access to many workplaces. Transportation within the residential community has less effect on property value, even if that may be very important to you.

A Community's Character

Communities have personalities just like people do. Choosing a hometown is a little like choosing a mate or a friend. The personality you choose doesn't have to be exactly like yours, just as long as it's compatible with yours.

Look around carefully at the town you are considering. Do you want to live in an area with wide diversity, or are you more comfortable with people more similar to you? Do you want lots going on in your neighborhood, or a simple, quiet area? Would it bother you to know that 20 percent of your community's population changes each year because of company transfers?

ALERT!

In a community where a lot of people move in and out regularly, it may be hard on you (or your children) if your new friends are likely to leave soon.

How about your hobbies and interests? Is there a spot for fishing, if you would like to catch a prize? Is there an arts group or a little theater troupe, if those are your interests? If religion is important to you, how far will you have to travel to attend the services of your choice? Is there an active congregation of like faith in the community? Do you enjoy eating out? Are there enough good restaurants?

Look into hospitals, too. This is especially important if you have a chronic illness or small children and are more likely to go to the emergency room than most people.

It can be difficult to assess the character of a town that is more than, say, 40 miles from where you live currently. It is especially tough when you are planning a long-distance relocation. Get a short-term subscription to two of the local papers in the area you're moving to.

One might be the big daily and the other a smaller, weekly publication, perhaps what is known as the "alternative" paper. You could also look for the area's local news Web site—many papers are featured online. There you will see what residents are talking about—and what they're complaining about.

An excellent way to evaluate community character is to head for the planning or zoning board office, usually located in the town hall. Request the town's master plan, and spend a few minutes studying it. Although the information is free and readily available, few home-buyers actually look for it. On that map you will see all the current streets with their zoning indicated as well as proposed zoning and development. Future highways, open spaces, and the potential for high-density housing or commercial development will be apparent to you within a few minutes of study. Keep in mind, though, that zoning can be changed; do not assume that every line on the master plan is carved in stone.

Once you have narrowed down your choice of towns to just a few, visit the library of each one. Tell the reference librarian that you are considering buying a home in town and would like some information on the community. The library may have a community profile that has been prepared by the League of Women Voters, the town's chamber of commerce, or some other civic group. It will usually have material on local history and community activities, too.

Checking out the Towns

As you visit communities you are considering, use the questions in **WORKSHEET 10.1** to rate them between one and five on how well the following aspects of each town meet your personal needs and goals. You can then compare towns by comparing either totals or one factor across the board (for example, schools).

WORKSHEET 10.1   Town Comparison Worksheet

	Town 1	Town 2	Town 3
Name of town	_____	_____	_____
Accessibility to the workplace	____	____	____
Local transportation	____	____	____
Character of the community	____	____	____
Recreation (space)	____	____	____
Recreation (activities)	____	____	____
Schools	____	____	____
Municipal services	____	____	____
Taxes	____	____	____
Special considerations	____	____	____
Shopping	____	____	____
Medical facilities	____	____	____
Accessibility to places of worship	____	____	____
Child-care facilities	____	____	____
Opportunity for post–high-school education	____	____	____
TOTALS	____	____	____

Evaluating Real-Estate Taxes

Property tax is the primary source of revenue for the American municipality, whether it be a city of millions or a single-traffic-light hamlet. The character of the community's real estate is a major factor in determining the tax structure.

Everyone pays property taxes in some form. Tenants pay in their rent, and homeowners and condo owners pay taxes directly to the local government or through their mortgage lender. Co-op owners pay in their maintenance fees. Condo dwellers actually pay two property taxes: the tax on their own unit and a portion of the real-estate tax for the common areas of the complex (paid through their monthly maintenance fee).

There are two factors used in formulating the amount you will pay in property taxes: mill rate and assessed valuation. A mill is one-tenth of one cent. It is the actual dollar figure you pay on each $1,000 of the assessed value of your property. So, if your home is assessed at $100,000 and your town's mill rate is 23.7, then you must pay $23.70 for each $1,000 of assessed value. Multiply 100 by 23.7 to give you a tax bill of $2,370.

Seems simple, no? But it gets more complicated. Many, if not most, municipalities express their mill rates in terms of rate per $100 of assessed valuation. Using the above example, this would be expressed as $2.37 for every $100 of your assessment. To calculate your tax bill, you would figure out how many $100 units are in $100,000 (answer: 1,000). Then you would multiply 2.37 by 1,000 to come up with the same result we got above: $2,370.

But just searching for the town with the lowest mill rate will not bring you the lowest property taxes. Not every town bases its mill rate on an assessment of 100 percent of fair market value. Town A might have a mill rate of 23.7 on 60 percent of fair market value assessment, while Town B has the same mill rate on 100 percent of fair market value. Thus, you will pay considerably lower taxes for the same amount of house in Town A.

ALERT!

When you anticipate your mortgage payment, always include the real-estate taxes! Your lender will almost always insist that you add to the mortgage payment a "tax escrow," which means that you will pay one-twelfth of your real-estate taxes each month. Your escrow is not a fixed amount. As taxes rise you will be required to increase your payment. Be prepared for this rise.

In a country as varied as ours, there are any number of tax rates, and indeed there are still places where homeowners are paying 11.5 mills on a 40 percent assessed valuation established in 1975! It is best to call the town collector's office or ask your real-estate agent for tax structure information on the towns that interest you. If you should discover that the low taxes of a particular community are based upon an evaluation done

twelve in high school was the traditional grouping in public schools for many years. Today, many communities are using school buildings to group children more closely by age. Kindergarten to grade four, grades five to eight, and a four-year high school has become a popular pattern. Some parents, however, may prefer a different grouping.

- What is the average class size in elementary school?
- What special programs are offered in elementary school? What about extracurricular activities?
- What subjects do junior high or middle school students study? At what grade can foreign language study begin? Are there advanced math courses for bright students below the high school level?
- What about computers? Are they used in the high school? At what computer-to-student ratio? Are they in the junior high and elementary schools as well?
- How do local pupils rate on standardized tests against other area towns? Other parts of the state or the nation?
- What courses are offered at the high school level? What courses are required for graduation?
- What percentage of each high school class graduates?
- What do seniors do after graduation? What percentage goes on to college? Which colleges? Professional training schools?
- Is there an emphasis on learning to think or on learning "right" answers? Are the students treated as individuals? How much freedom is allowed in the classroom? What is on the schools' bulletin boards?

Another important consideration these days is crime in schools. Are there guards in the hallways of the high schools that interest you? What about other forms of protection to ensure that the school is as safe as possible?

If schools rank high on your list of considerations, by all means take the time to visit several schools in that town before you make a commitment to buy a home. Principals are usually happy to discuss their schools and programs with prospective parents, and you will surely get a tour of the school facilities. (It is not a good sign if a principal does not seem eager to talk with you.)

Is It the Right Neighborhood for You?

What is a neighborhood? It could be a city block, a builder's tract, a condominium community, a walled private association of houses, or a rural road. The homes that surround yours are your neighborhood. Let's look at some aspects of the house-neighborhood connection.

Size and Style

Most of us tend to feel most comfortable in neighborhoods of homes in pretty much the same ballpark price as ours. The neighborhood helps dictate the price.

For example, an extremely large house surrounded by smaller ones will not appreciate as much as it would if it were located in a neighborhood of houses the same size as it. Neighboring houses affect the value of your house. A house with a two-story, $50,000-addition may only bring $8,000 to $10,000 more when sold compared to its additionless twin down the street.

You may get a bargain by buying the biggest house in the neighborhood, and you will have plenty of space and amenities for the money, but remember that you will not sell it for a whopping big profit. (The sellers you bought it from didn't, did they?) Most buyers want their property values secured by having their house surrounded by houses of comparable value.

Broadly speaking, the smallest house in the neighborhood fetches a somewhat better price than it would bring in an area of houses its own size. This is the reverse of the large house. In the case of the smallest house, the house's value is pulled up by the price of neighboring properties. It might take a little longer to sell the smallest house, though. Some buyers could be intimidated by the pressure to "keep up with the Joneses." Others are unwilling to pay extra for a prestige neighborhood and smaller house. Eventually, however, the right buyer does come along.

Boundaries

Edges of a neighborhood are generally not a good housing choice if you are considering profitable resale. The most secure house, that is, secure in terms of price, is the one right in the center of a like grouping of homes. Even a huge condominium community is affected by a nearby office building or industrial plant. The condos on the outer edge will resell for less than those in the middle of the complex.

There is an exception to this rule. Houses on the edge of neighborhoods that are bounded by woods, parks, or golf courses will sell better than those in the middle of the neighborhood. Those natural boundaries and open spaces are very appealing to buyers.

Maintenance

Unfortunately, you cannot force your neighbors to paint their houses or generally clean up their property. So be wary of buying next door to a handyman special with a junk car parked on the lawn.

A safe investment lies in finding a neighborhood where each person is especially proud of his or her home. You may think that maintenance is not an issue in a condo community since it is done professionally. But condos have personalities and images, too, and shoddy, haphazard maintenance can ruin resale values. Be sure your condominium is run by a board of directors that oversees and insists upon careful maintenance and that has money in the coffers to pay for it.

Some single-family houses are located in private associations that might own a clubhouse, golf course, swimming pool, and sometimes even the roads. Those associations usually have rules about home maintenance, and there is intense pressure on the homeowner to comply.

Good maintenance can add thousands of dollars to the value of older homes. This is especially true if there is a movement toward refurbishing throughout the neighborhood. The properties that are least affected by the maintenance of neighboring houses are country homes in rural areas, where a considerable amount of land separates the dwellings.

A final point about maintenance. In some run-down inner-city communities, newcomers and existing residents have banded together to make their own particular enclave attractive once again. It can be a smart move to buy into such a neighborhood, getting a good price while it pulls itself back up. The trick is knowing whether it is on the way back or continuing to decline.

Lifestyle

Are children's toys left in front yards or on the sidewalks where you are looking? Are kids allowed to play in the street? Is there graffiti on the stop signs? Are rural mailboxes dented and rusted? Do pets run free, or are they carefully walked and seemingly well trained? Are property boundaries not particularly noticeable, or are the majority of yards fenced or landscaped for definition? Are car parts or broken-down washing machines rusting in backyards, or are there signs in the grass noting that some landscaping service has just been there to maintain the front and rear yards?

It is difficult to place economic value on neighborhood style. However, it is important that you be aware of what styles different neighborhoods have as you go about your house hunting.

Travel Patterns

When choosing your neighborhood, consider your travel routine. How will you get to work? To shops? It would be smart to ride those routes in rush hour to get a feel for the driving you will do. How about the route to schools, places of worship, and the activities your family enjoys?

ALERT!

Choosing the wrong neighborhood can commit you to far more driving each week than you bargained for.

Look for the closest convenience store. You will not want to have to travel 5 miles each way every time you run out of milk. On the other hand, if there are deer in your backyard at dusk and the sounds of birds are important to you, you might opt anyway for the house that is far from amenities.

Traffic Patterns

Beyond *your* traffic pattern, you'll need to consider everybody else's. Visit the neighborhood you are considering on different days and at different times of day, especially the common rush hours. What looks like a quiet street at 1:00 P.M. may be the shortcut home for half the town at 5:00 P.M. And houses on busy streets do not sell well. The cute little development off a main highway may, from 7:30 to 8:30 A.M. every weekday, have cars lined up waiting to get out of that enclave, through its one exit to the highway.

Sounds and Smells

You may hear highway sounds from what appeared at first to be a quiet development. Traffic sounds will lower your property's value, as will heavy air traffic overhead or the noise of a working rock quarry just over the hill. What about smells? Living near a chemical plant may make life in your house unbearable on a warm summer day.

Take nothing for granted. Spend some time driving around appealing neighborhoods without the real-estate agent. Agents have a habit of choosing the loveliest approaches to property that is for sale. You are looking for the gritty truth.

Talk with the Neighbors

The very best way to learn about a neighborhood is by talking to its residents. Walk the streets on a sunny day, and strike up a conversation with the man walking his dog or the woman watering her lawn.

Ask nonthreatening questions—you do not want to appear as if you are passing judgment on the neighborhood. Here are some examples:

- Instead of asking whether there are many children in the neighborhood, ask where kids play. If you are told they play in empty lots or parks or that they cut through to the bike trails in the fields, and so on, then you know there are lots of children around.
- If you ask if French or Spanish is offered in the elementary schools, you will hear more about those schools than if you asked, "How are the schools," which might elicit a brief, "Fine."

- If you ask if the tax assessors have been around yet and the answer is "What tax assessors?" you know reassessment has not taken place recently and might be due soon, a process that could raise your property taxes. If the assessor has been by, you will get an earful on those results.

- Also nonthreatening is asking if the town allows basement sump pumps to drain into the storm sewers. That will get you more helpful answers than asking if there are basement water problems in the area, a question that might make people defensive. Residents might answer, "Gee, I don't know; no one has a sump pump," or you could hear "No, they don't, but . . ." and then a full explanation of how various neighbors solve water problems.

- Instead of asking if prices are going up in that neighborhood, ask if there have been other houses sold there recently. You will learn what was sold, at what price, and how long it was on the market. You might even find out the original price of the house or houses; such information can give you an idea of how much negotiating room you are likely to have.

A Look at the Lot

It is best not to decide you want to buy a house without first giving careful attention to the lot on which it is situated. You may think that while the house is eye-catching, the lot is just ground. However, you should be aware of the importance of that piece of earth, too. Here are some points to weigh.

Shape

Generally, rectangular or square lots with good frontage on the road and good depth behind the house are best. Pie shapes, triangles, and multiangles are more unusual, and they usually hurt resale value.

Size

Lot size in relation to property value is a slippery thing, governed more by neighborhood and area than by any rule of proportions. A quarter of an acre is a large lot in a city; an acre is the norm for more expensive housing in the suburbs.

Large pieces of property that cannot be subdivided rarely add to the value of a house. For example, that handsome Tudor home on Summit Lane would sell for $265,000 on a half-acre, since all of its neighbors have half acres. So even if it has an additional seven acres of land fanning out behind it and its neighbors on both sides, if it is virtually undevelopable (swamp or rock land), the extra land will not increase the resale value of the Tudor by a penny. It may, in fact, hinder resale, since the owners are paying property taxes on all that land. Owners of some such lots have dedicated (given) their excess land to the towns in which they live, for "open spaces." They thus reap income tax benefits and reduce their local property taxes while being assured that the land will remain in its natural state.

Contour

When choosing your lot and/or home, be aware of the area's contour as well as your particular lot's contour. Floodplain maps made by the U.S. government are available in many town halls and will show you the contour of the land throughout the town. Some parts of town may be considered flood-prone; homeowners in these areas may be required to carry flood insurance. Know if the lot you like is vulnerable to flooding, and you can save yourself a lot of suffering later.

Level land is best. Houses built on steep slopes are often hard to sell. Buyers are especially wary of houses built below the level of the road, where driveways slope sharply downward.

What is beneath the grass? "Dirt" may seem to be the obvious answer. Not always. Could there once have been a garbage dump there? A forest?

A swamp? These become essential questions prior to purchase if you are considering a house that uses a septic tank for waste disposal, since the composition of the earth will determine how well that tank and its lines will drain. Especially poor drainage could mean a nonworking system, which taken to its farthest limit could mean an uninhabitable house.

In some developments built over the last twenty-five years or so, municipalities have required that the results of percolation tests be recorded in the town hall. In a "perc" test, the rate of ground absorption is measured by digging a hole on the property and pouring water in. Sometimes notes are made on the composition of the earth to the bottom of the hole (clay, shale, gravel, rock, and so on). If your town has perc-test information, it is worth knowing.

QUESTION?

Where can I find the results of a "perc" or percolation test for a property?
Try the building inspector's office or a tax assessor's office first. Ask at the city or town hall as well. You may have to do a little research, but be persistent.

What is underground will also affect the house settling process. Houses built on rock will settle little. Those built on landfill may settle unevenly, especially if the fill consists of tree trunks and other debris collected as a development was cleared and constructed. You should watch out for fill lots if you are considering a house at a low point in a development, usually the youngest houses in the neighborhood. As a general rule of thumb, choose high ground if you can.

Position

Corner lots, the most desirable location for business, are usually not particularly desirable in residential real estate. They are more exposed, and they require trees or fencing for privacy. Cul-de-sacs are popular with families with young children and are especially salable if the road widens to a circle for a turnaround.

Positives	TOWN	Negatives
Good schools (small classes, special programs, wide course selection in high school)		School problems (overcrowded classrooms, double sessions, sparse budget for extras, high dropout rate, incidence of crime)
Low taxes		High taxes
Good commuting with a wide employment choice nearby		Isolation, poor transportation facilities, depressed area with few job possibilities
Community pride		Dirty streets; high crime rate
Good recreation (parks, tennis courts, facilities for children, theaters, restaurants, etc.)		Poor recreation ("nothing to do")
Municipal services, many and well done (snow removal, road maintenance, refuse removal, city sewers, city water, police, fire, and rescue squad)		Poor municipal services (few services, the necessity of paying for private services)

Positives	NEIGHBORHOOD	Negatives
Socioeconomically homogeneous		Wide range in house value and style, with commercial properties mixed in with residential
"Neat as a pin"		Poor maintenance (unkempt lawns, peeling paint, trash and junk cars visible)
Trees, good landscaping, gentle hills, cul-de-sacs, curved streets		Flat land, all-alike houses, rectangular all-alike blocks; no shade trees
Proximity to parks and open spaces; between one and five miles from a shopping center		Close proximity to commercial or industrial development or to housing considerably lower in price

Positives	LOT	Negatives
Pleasant views		Unpleasant views
Trees, shrubs, flowers, carefully planned foundation planting		Bare grass, no foundation planting
High ground; level lot or gently sloping		On the lower side of the road with steeply sloped land; cliffs, gullies, or hills behind house; low point of the area
Mid-block, mid-neighborhood		Corner lot, edge of neighborhood
Rectangular or square-shaped lot		Irregular-shaped lot
Backyard line abuts park, woods, or open spaces		Backyard line abuts commercial property, schoolyard, high-density housing, or lower-priced neighborhood

ALERT!

Remember, no two house hunters are likely to make the same choices and have the same requirements in a home. Recreation, for example, can mean deer hunting to one and the opera to another. The lot you choose could come with two acres of fruit trees, or you might be content with a patch of asphalt just big enough for two lawn chairs. Select the factors that go along with the house you like that are important to *you*.

Be Prepared to Expand Your Search

Ask your agent to show you more than you considered prior to beginning your search for your new home. You will often find that by expanding a few blocks, a few miles, or to the next neighborhood or subdivision, you can get more for your money. It is a good idea to spend time exploring new territories on your own as well. Drive by at various times to observe traffic patterns, people going to and coming from school and work. Visit houses of worship and grocery stores. Get comfortable wherever you intend to live.

Chapter 11

 Negotiating the Best Price

You have secured a mortgage, explored the towns and neighborhoods you're interested in, and considered the pros and cons of a wide variety of housing choices. You have shopped until you nearly dropped, but your reward is at hand. You have found the home you want to buy. Now it's time to talk about price. You don't simply pay what the seller is asking. Using your negotiating skills, you'll be able to work out a better price for you that is also acceptable to the seller.

What Is Fair Market Value?

You will have to determine fair price of the home you want before you make an offer for it. This is defined as the highest price a ready, willing, and able buyer will pay and the lowest a ready, willing, and able seller will accept. To be completely accurate, fair market value cannot be established until a property is actually sold. But the trick of an estimate is to come as close as possible to the figure for which you could turn around after the closing and quickly sell the house again (within three months or so—that is about how long "quickly" is in real estate).

FACT

You can make your market evaluation by comparing the property you want to buy with similar properties that have been sold in the area during the past year. You will already have a feel for the price from all the house hunting you have been doing.

When you are ready to start negotiating, ask your realty agent to show you *comparables*. As mentioned previously, the term "comparables," in a real-estate setting, refers to the listing sheets that agents have describing properties that have recently been sold. Those sheets will contain all the pertinent information on the property, including the original asking price, all price reductions, the actual selling price, the date of the closing, and the date of the original listing contract. You can use the date of the original listing to determine how long the house was on the market before it sold.

Almost every real-estate office that belongs to a multiple listing organization will have a comparables file or a computerized comparables book. Even independent agencies that do not share listings will keep a file of properties sold by their own offices and agents. The single-office file works well in large cities where many brokers are independents and tend to work only in tightly defined neighborhoods rather than trying to cover the entire city. It also works well in condo or co-op sales, where one or two real-estate agencies usually handle all the sales within a particular building.

After you have seen comparables, make a list of selling prices and addresses of the properties that you consider similar to "yours." Take home photocopies of those listing sheets, if the agent is willing and allowed to give them to you. Compare and rate each property against the house you want to make an offer on.

When you finish that homework, you will know exactly what other people in the area have had to pay for a certain amount of house in the same or a similar neighborhood. From here, stepping along to an evaluation of what "your" house is worth is relatively easy.

Once you have determined what you think is a fair selling price for the property, compare it with what the sellers are asking. If your evaluation price is higher than the asking price (that rarely occurs), do not get out your pen to sign an offer. Look again at the property, the neighborhood, the location, the lot, the time on the market, local conditions—everything. You may have missed something very important. However, if everything checks out, then act quickly. The sellers may just have underpriced their property; so buy before word gets out and another buyer appears and starts a bidding war.

It is much more likely that the asking price will be more than your estimate of fair market value. That is what negotiating is all about. Put yourself in the sellers' shoes for a moment. Why do you think they set the price so high? To allow room for negotiating? Because they have installed new carpeting? They want to be repaid for their newly remodeled $14,000 kitchen? Take the position that the amenities or upgrades do not always add to the resale value of a home.

You would be smart to buy a small notebook for this process, and make it your negotiating journal. Record the addresses and prices of your comparables. Then record your ideal price for the home you want, your estimate of its fair market value, and the top price you're willing to pay. Keep the journal on hand as you go through the negotiating process to help determine how much you want to raise your offer.

You should figure out your ideal price for the home (likely to be a "steal" price), your estimate of fair market value, and your absolute "top-dollar" price. Gee, you ask, why would I want to pay a top-dollar price that is higher than the fair market value of the property? Because until the contract is signed, the fair market value is still an estimate, and even professional real-estate appraisers can differ in their fair market value estimates. Therefore, you must leave yourself a margin of error, a realistic dollar space that will keep you from becoming too rigid during the negotiations.

Most important of all during this negotiating stage is that you do not tell your real-estate agent your "top-dollar figure"—or your "steal" figure either. Remember, the agent represents the seller. If you tell the agent that you are willing to go up to as high as $123,000 for a house listed at $125,000, then $123,000 is probably what you will end up paying. You have to play your hand close to the vest during the negotiating process, even with your agent.

QUESTION?

What if I'm no good at negotiating?
Relax, it's not as scary as it may sound. If you are using a real-estate agent, he or she will be your go-between. You won't be talking directly to the seller in most cases.

The Market at the Moment

Besides checking comparables and working the numbers, it is important that you gauge the state of the market in your area at the time you want to buy. For example, if it is a hot sellers' market, where properties are moving quickly, and the home you want is a desirable one with potentially wide market appeal, start your negotiations fairly close to market value. You do not want to lose the property playing games over price.

In some situations, although this is uncommon, a house or a location is so "hot" that simultaneous offers are made. Sometimes the best of these is simply accepted, with no negotiating. More often the sellers negotiate with all prospective buyers simultaneously. They are "out for the kill." If you truly want that property in such a situation, the following are some tactics that will help.

- Offer your best price, but be willing to move up another $500 or $1,000. Do not, however, get caught up in auction fever and bid the house up far above its market value.
- Ask for as few extras in the sale as possible.
- Make the closing date as agreeable to the sellers as you can.
- Have loan approval from a mortgage lender.

On the other hand, if the market is soft where you are looking (sometimes called a buyers' market), if the seller is under need-to-sell stress, or if the house is not particularly appealing to most people—they cannot see the potential that you can, or their needs are different from yours—you can move more slowly and negotiate over a wider range. In these situations, it is possible to get a much better deal with a bit of patience and perseverance.

Your Initial Offer

You may hear people say that 10 percent below asking price is a good first offer. It isn't, really. There is no one "good" initial offer based on asking price. Why? Because there are so many variables in real estate and because sellers rarely set their asking prices with consideration to market value or other rational thought processes. They want to get the most they can for their properties, and many have emotional ties to their homes that turn simple Cape Cods into mental castles. Would you offer 10 percent less than the asking price of a home that is overpriced by $25,000 or more?

FACT

Earnest money is a sum of money that you provide along with your offer that demonstrates to the seller the seriousness of your intent to buy.

Each and every piece of real property is unique, and so is each selling situation. So, you can understand why generic rules of thumb in real estate are dangerous. But if you must have a guideline, a first offer that is 10 percent below your fair market value estimate—not the seller's asking price—will keep you from insulting the seller. It will also keep you from having your first offer snapped up because it was higher than the seller thought he would actually get for the property.

So now you have a figure in mind for your first offer. How do you go about making that offer?

Your offer cannot just be verbal. Most residential sales agents will refuse to present a verbal offer to the seller that is not accompanied by an earnest money check and specific information on financing, closing date, and other details of the sale. A buyer cannot call an agent and say, "Ask them if they'll take $139,500." That buyer could be asking the same question of four different agents about four different properties, a situation that can end up presenting serious problems. Your offer must be presented to the sellers in writing.

Most agents will want you to sign a contract before they present your offer to the seller. If you sign the contract, and if the sellers agree to your offer and also sign that form, you have bought the house.

When your real-estate agent hears the word *offer,* he or she might whip out a binder, a short form that includes your name and address, a few lines about the property being bid on, and the amount of your earnest money deposit (usually $500 or $1,000). If you are handed a binder, be certain it contains the clause "subject to review by the buyer's attorney within five business days." That will allow you to have your lawyer look over the form (and will also allow you an out if you change your mind about that property).

The Counteroffer

The counteroffer is the seller's response to your initial bid. Sometimes it names the actual amount they want for the property, but not usually.

Most sellers still have some room in their first-response prices, even when they say, "Not a penny less." You now must work toward a meeting of the minds.

In your negotiating journal, record your first offer, its terms, and its contingencies (or have your agent give you a copy of the offer form after it is completely filled out and signed). When you get the counteroffer, record not only its facts and figures but also what the agent says the sellers said. Do they want a quick closing? Is this their bottom price? Are they anxious to sell? Do not take a word of what you hear as gospel truth, though. In negotiating, you must always keep testing for what is "real" and what is just a negotiation tactic. The counteroffer is usually returned to you on your original offer form, with numbers crossed out and new numbers written in and initialed.

Your Second Offer

Your second offer should not be your top dollar, but it should be closer to your estimate of the market value. Have the agent write out a whole new offer form. Do not work with scratched-out figures and initials on the original sheet, since this will only confuse people.

Add to your negotiating journal the facts of this second offer and any asides that are mentioned by anyone. Keeping such a written account of who said what and when may prevent arguments, misunderstandings, and denials later. It will also give you a chance to review what happened throughout the process.

At each step of the bidding, it is worth mentioning to your real-estate agent the flaws of the house—something to the effect that of course you like and want the house, but it does need kitchen remodeling, or you really wanted a two-car, not a one-car, garage. You want your agent to know—and relay to the sellers—that you are not so committed to this house that you will pay anything to own it. There are other homes out there that could suit you, too. Even though you may feel this is the perfect house for you, if the sellers know that, they will have the upper hand in the negotiating, and you are likely to pay a higher price for it.

As You Move Toward Agreement

Most homes are sold upon or before the buyers' third offer. Sometimes, however, the negotiating goes on for many days. The procedure is always the same—offer, counteroffer. You and the sellers are making adjustments, circling about each other, and trying to find a place to meet. Here is where the advice of a good realty agent can be invaluable!

Keep Your Emotions in Check

Getting emotional—whether the emotion is on the buyer's or seller's side—can heat up the negotiating process to the point where the real-estate agent wants to run for cover! This is not good. Acting rationally is essential when you are negotiating to buy a home. Here are the most common emotions that carry away both buyers and sellers.

Love

For you, this means love of the house you are negotiating for, but you should try not to fall head over heels for it. If you start thinking that this is the only house for you and that you will never find another house as good anywhere, you might as well forget about negotiating effectively. Try to remember there are other houses that will suit you just as well—and maybe better—even if you haven't found them yet.

If you lose the house you love, and you have the luxury of time, it is a good idea to wait a while before going out house-hunting again. You do not want to buy on the rebound if you can avoid it. Purchasing the wrong house is a costly mistake.

Anger

This emotion makes an appearance in most real-estate negotiations at some point or another. The buyers may get angry at the sellers, the sellers may get angry at the buyers, they both can get angry at the real-estate agent(s), and the agent(s) can get angry at them. Buying a house can be stressful, and no one wants to be taken advantage of.

It might be hard to stay calm and rational, but that should be your mantra during the negotiating process. Here are some suggestions for doing just that:

- **Use time for cooling off.** If you feel yourself (or your spouse) about to scream, say, "I'd (we'd) like to take some time to think about this before saying anything more." Hang up the phone, leave the room, or leave town for the day if you have to.
- **Define the cause of your anger.** People sometimes find themselves furious without knowing why. Ask yourselves, "What got this started?" Once you answer that question, it is easier to say, "How can we settle this?"
- **Stick to the point.** If you are negotiating over a closing date, do not let who is going to fix the broken toilet get into the discussion.
- **Do not slam doors or burn bridges.** It is hard to come back from "Take your stupid house and stuff it."
- **Do not accuse.** "This is all your fault" gets you nowhere. Ask instead, "How did we get to this point, and where should we go from here?"
- **Do not lie.** Never lie—not at all, over anything. If you said something yesterday and changed your mind overnight, say so. Do not deny what you said. Do not fib about your financial situation—you will be found out anyway. Conveniently "forgetting" something counts as a lie here, too. Nothing sours a deal faster than contradictions about money.
- **Do not pound your fist on the table, and do not raise your voice.** Your point can be made without throwing a fit. Speak so softly that your listeners will have to listen harder.

Pride

Many a real-estate deal has been lost over a comment like, "No way! They're not going to have the last word! No way!" So, no sale. Negotiating is not a game of winning or losing. It is a coming together. You have to be able to give up a little to get a little.

Possessiveness and Greed

Sometimes it is difficult for sellers to part emotionally with their property. Some fight to keep every stick that is not nailed down, and they expect to be paid dearly for every one that is. That could be seen as possessiveness.

When people buy, however, they want the most for their money. "That should go with the house" is the usual attitude, since they are anticipating the out-of-pocket expenses for everything that does not go with the house. That could be seen as greed. There is no right answer here. If you get into an argument over bits and pieces, ask yourself if possessiveness or greed are not factors. Sometimes just recognizing those feelings helps to resolve the issue.

Negotiating with FSBOs

When you're dealing with homes that are "for sale by owner" (or FSBOs), no real-estate agent is involved in the negotiations. The same principles for negotiating apply, but there is, of course, no middle man.

How do you begin the negotiations? After your second visit to the home you like (the visit where you have explored the house more thoroughly than you did on your initial visit), wait a day or two before making an offer, to heighten the sellers' anticipation and to make your offer sound well thought out.

ALERT!

Get a lawyer to help with a "for sale by owner" deal. You should always have a lawyer in a case where there is no real-estate agent involved, but do *not* use the same legal counsel as the sellers use.

To determine fair market value, go through computer printout sheets you have secured from real-estate agents for similar properties in the neighborhood. The bargaining process is similar in this case to bargaining through a real-estate agent, but sitting down face-to-face with sellers is always difficult. Keep rational and friendly, and remember that your primary tool for acceptance is that fair market value. Your offer hands them a quick sale, no more disruption in having a house on the market, and no sales commission to pay.

Still, they probably will not accept your first price. So, back you come with a second bid. That should usually be the fair market value minus the usual real-estate commission in the area (probably 6 or 7 percent). Of course, the sellers aren't using an agent, so there is no commission to be paid here.

In the best possible scenario, the buyer and seller will split the amount of the real-estate commission and set the selling price between market value and the price the owner would have netted after paying an agent's commission (if they had used one). All of the extras, such as closing dates and financing, can be worked out then and there, or with the attorneys for both sides present. The attorneys will draw up the contract to buy.

That's how a neat, tidy sale works. But life does not always follow such a script. The sellers may be new to this business and hold out high hopes for a top-dollar price. When you come up against a stone wall, do not beat your head against it, no matter how much you like the house. Write down your best offer, with your name, address, and phone number, and leave it with the sellers. Tell them to call you if they change their mind, and then continue house-hunting. You might want to keep in touch with them from time to time to ask how they are doing.

Do not make another offer, but if they do come down a little, perhaps you will be willing to go up a little. This is how negotiating works.

Also, you should never give sellers an earnest money deposit. That check should be handed to your lawyer.

Secrets of Successful Negotiating

Here is how to cleverly navigate the back and forth over price between you and the seller:

- **Know a property's value.** There is nothing more important to successfully buying and selling real estate than knowing the market.

As you negotiate, showing and telling them what comparable houses have sold for will help you to bring the sellers' price down. Of course, the real-estate agent will probably be doing this for you, but do not ever count on anyone else to fight for your money as diligently as you will.

- **Be flexible.** Do not lose a property that you really want over a few dollars a month, which is what financing an extra $500 in sale price would cost you. Set limits, but do not be so rigid that you cannot respond or rethink a decision. "Never," "absolutely not," and "take it or leave it" are phrases that will slam the door on any deal.

FACT

The *closing* is the date when the title of the property is actually transferred from the seller to the buyer. This date can be a valuable tool in negotiating to buy a house.

- **Never show your hand.** Do not tell anyone, especially not your agent (who is, remember, ultimately working for the seller, no matter how helpful he or she is to you), what you will do next. Act as if the offer you are making will be accepted. If you don't, it won't be.
- **Ask for concessions as you increase your bid.** When you present your first offer, do not ask for extras. If it is accepted, you should have plenty of money to buy them, since your first offer was lower than the total amount you have to spend. But each time you increase your offering price, ask for something more. That can be almost anything you see: chandeliers, draperies, carpeting, appliances, lawn mowers and garden equipment, lawn furniture, and sometimes even living-room or dining-room furniture. Ask as you offer. The sellers may say no to your bid but yes to your request for extras at their higher price. But when you increase your price again, even if just a little, those extras are already part of the deal in both your minds.
- **Never ask for all the extras at once, however.** It is too overwhelming, especially with a low first offer that you are gradually increasing, as you should, in $500 or $1,000 increments. Once a seller says no, which is easy to do when the requests seem too

numerous for too little money, it is harder to get a reversal than it is to get something new added later. Remember, negotiating is a give-and-take process.

- **Use the closing date in your negotiations.** Time is money, so the saying goes. In negotiating for a home, time can be worth money if you use it as a tool. Try to find out early in the game what the sellers want out of the sale in terms of time as well as in terms of price. Do they need a quick closing because they are carrying two mortgages? Do they need time to find another house? Do they need flexibility in a closing date because they are having a house built and do not know exactly when it will be completed?

Negotiating the Closing Date

With your original low offer, you will be asked to name a closing date. If it works for you, name one that is not likely to be to the sellers' liking. If they need a quick closing, set your offer date for three or four months in the future. If they want a distant closing, ask for one in four to six weeks. Then, as you make responses to their counteroffers, you can increase the bid by very little cash but sweeten the deal by moving the proposed closing date into line with the sellers' needs. It is almost always worth money.

If the closing date is very important to you, work toward your ideal date in your negotiations. But be prepared to offer more money to get the date you want.

Other Negotiating Tactics

Use financing in your negotiations. If you plan to pay cash for your home, or if you have been preapproved by a mortgage lender, use your strong financial position as a negotiating tool. If you bid a little low, tell the agent to explain to the sellers that this is a no-risk offer. There is no mortgage contingency—the sellers don't have to wait to see if the buyers will qualify for a loan. This is a strong card!

Know when to stop negotiating. Some deals just cannot be made. If your sellers are not ready to sell at a reasonable price, start looking at other homes.

It is typical to think that you could have negotiated better. But learn from your experience. You have done well by buying the property. You will have the opportunity to profit from your purchase. Sometimes winning is not negotiating the lowest price, but making the seller feel he or she received the best price while at the same time knowing you got a good deal, too.

Chapter 12

Negotiating the Best Contract

What goes into a contract to buy a home? Virtually everything related to the sale of that home. There is really no such thing as a standard purchase contract, although your real-estate agent may claim that's what he or she is giving you. There is certain information that is required for a contract to be legally binding, but virtually anything can be included, even down to the most minute of details.

Finding a Good Lawyer

You are not required to have legal counsel in order to purchase a home, but it is wise for first-time buyers to engage a lawyer. It's smart for anyone buying a property "for sale by owner." And it is wise to have counsel if you are buying a condominium, cooperative, or any community-type home where you must belong to an owners' association. Going through the raft of printed documents—prospectus, rules and regulations, and so on—should be done by someone trained to look for red lights. That someone is ideally a real-estate lawyer. Do not engage anyone who has another specialty.

Sometimes getting the home you want is more important than negotiating the best price for your home. Value is perceived. If you want it, buy it. You'll never look back.

Call in a lawyer at the stage when you have bid on a house and need the lawyer to review the sales contract. Or call a lawyer when you are shopping for a condo, town home, and the like, when you have been presented with all of the documents about the home that interests you and need help with explanations.

How do you find a lawyer? Your real-estate agent can help you. Your mortgage lender is likely to have some names, too. You can also call your local bar association and ask for the names of lawyers specializing in real estate, particularly local residential real estate. Best of all is to ask friends or family members whom they have used in realty transactions. The best reference is a satisfied customer.

When you find a lawyer, ask about fees for reviewing contracts and giving advice. Is this set at an hourly rate? A flat fee? No charge if you go on to use that individual for the house closing? Ask the lawyer what the usual role of counsel is in house closings in your area. Will the lawyer be present at the closing? What is his or her closing fee?

Remember that lawyers' fees are not set according to any local or state formula. Shop around for the best terms the way you would for any consumer purchase, but also consider the reputation, knowledge, and experience of the lawyer you choose. What is a the typical cost? From $200 to $750 or more, depending on your area of the country and the complexity of your purchase.

Who Writes the Contract?

A contract is usually prepared by the buyer's agent, if the buyers have an agent, or the buyer, with help of course by their attorney or legal or financial consultant. Occasionally a seller will offer a contract to a purchaser, certainly in the case of properties featured for auction and at new developments. One party has responsibility for drafting the contract. More often than not it is prepared on the buyer's side. If appropriate, all parties can get together to sign a contract presented, but the proliferation of fax machines allows people to present, counter, and accept offers without all traveling to the same place. It allows processes to happen faster and more easily.

What a Contract Must Have

To be legally binding, the contract can be anything from a handwritten note on a dinner napkin from a local restaurant to the fanciest of printed forms. There is some information that must be included in every contract, but any contract *can* include almost everything. First, here are the essentials.

The following six items must be included in the contract:

1. **Date.** A contract must be dated to be a legal instrument.
2. **Names.** That means the full names of all of the buyers and all of the sellers—in other words, Mary and Thomas Jones of 142 Eaton Lane, Bayberry, Connecticut 06439, not, for example, John Jones et ox (which means "and wife"). If, for example, three former fraternity brothers are buying a house, then all three names and addresses must be listed on the contract.

3. **Price.** The full purchase price should be listed; that is what you are agreeing to in the contract.
4. **Address of the property being sold.** A street address is acceptable, unless there are no numbers on the houses—in which case you'll need at least a block and lot number from the local tax map. If you are buying a condo or a co-op, be sure the apartment number and the building number, if necessary, appear in the contract, along with the street address.
5. **Date and place of closing.** This is a date that is frequently changed, but naming a place and time to transfer the property is an essential part of an agreement to purchase.
6. **Signatures.** Each person who rightfully owns and is selling the property and each person buying that property must sign the contractual agreement. If any one signature is missing, the agreement can be invalidated.

ALERT!

Ask your real-estate agent for a blank contract to take home and look over at your convenience. You can make sure you understand all the details before it's time to draw up your own contract.

Other Considerations and Contingencies

Of course, beyond those required items, you can include a number of other things in the purchase contract. Some of the most common clauses are discussed here. You may want to add some of these to the bare-bones contract.

Mortgage Contingency Clause

If you are going to have to borrow money to buy the property in question, and you have not already been approved for a loan, your contract should be subject to your being able to secure a mortgage. Then, if you can't get the money, you are legally released from your contract to purchase, and you will get all of your earnest money back.

The phrase might be written as follows: *subject to a first mortgage in the amount of _____ for a term of _____ years at an interest rate no higher than _____.*

It is important that the length of the term of the mortgage and the maximum interest rate that you want (what you can afford) be spelled out in the contract. If your contract just states mortgage in the amount of $90,000 and the bank turns you down, the seller or someone else could offer to give you a mortgage loan of $90,000 for five years at 18 percent. You would be legally committed to accept it and buy the property (which, of course, you couldn't do) or lose your deposit money. True, this is not likely to happen when dealing with honest people, but not all people are reputable. It is safest to include in the contract that it's subject to your being granted a mortgage at the currently prevailing interest rate.

The mortgage contingency clause should also have a cutoff date. Allow yourself plenty of time to get a commitment from a lender.

A nice feature to offer buyers when you are selling a home is a home warranty. Home warranties can be purchased for less than $400 and will cover all mechanical systems and appliances in the home. For a buyer, this offers great security. For the seller, it eliminates worrisome inspections and more postcontract negotiations. The buyer will have to pay a small deductible for repairs if they arise, but for the small price of a deductible they will often find they are avoiding the cost of replacing a heating unit, hot water heater, stove, refrigerator, or other potentially expensive appliance.

Termite Inspection

You will probably want to have the house inspected for termites. In some parts of the country, and especially with attached housing, a "termite bond" must be shown at the closing, showing that the house is treated annually to prevent those pests. Sometimes this is the seller's responsibility, but if it is not required by law, you will want to pay for an inspection yourself.

A termite contingency in the contract can allow you to withdraw your offer to buy if there is significant termite damage. Or you can negotiate with the seller for those repairs.

Home Inspection Contingency

You also may want your contract subject to an assurance that the plumbing, heating/cooling, electrical systems, and appliances are in working order and that the house is structurally sound. You can negotiate over who pays for a professional inspection, but most buyers prefer to pay for this themselves and be sure the inspector is working for them. You can also negotiate over any repairs that the inspector finds necessary.

House Delivered Vacant

You probably want the house free for you to move into immediately after closing, if that is your choice. If sellers are delayed in leaving for some reason, they often pay a per diem rent to the new owners for the time they stay in that property. Your lawyer can work out those details for you.

Whether you can have an entire two- or three-family home delivered vacant depends on the rent laws in that community and on how they protect renters with a lease. It's possible that only the unit you will live in yourself will be delivered empty.

Sale of Existing Home

If you already have a home, and it is for sale, you might want a clause in the contract making the purchase subject to the sale of your current home. However, this is a point not all sellers will agree to, unless perhaps it is a very slow sellers' market or the sellers are in no particular hurry to move.

The Promise of Clear Title

You will want a clause in your contract stating that the seller provides a title that is free and clear of "clouds on the title." If real estate taxes have not been paid by the owner, then a tax lien may appear on the title. If work was completed to improve the property and the contractor was not paid, they have the right to lien the property. If the seller once entered into a contract to sell the property to another party and backed out of the sale, and the buyer sued the seller for specific performance, then this suit would appear on the title. All of these things are "clouds on the title" and you need to know about them if they exist.

You can negotiate over who pays for the search, and, of course, you can negotiate to accept some or all of the clouds on the title.

FACT

Personal Property

Your lawyer will tell you that everything that is not nailed down (attached to the building) is personal property, not real estate. This is true, but some sellers think nothing of pulling out built-in (and, therefore, attached) dishwashers and detaching and removing all the lighting fixtures the day before the closing.

The best contracts will have a personal property addendum attached. On this sheet of paper, everything that even vaguely resembles personal property or anything about which there might be a question is listed under one of two headings: "Included in the sale" and "Not included in the sale." Both the buyer and seller should sign that page. The list can include everything from appliances to light fixtures to blinds in the windows.

Subject to Buyer's Review of Community Covenants

You will want to be sure you can live with the homeowners' association regulations—if you are buying into a community with such an association—before you agree to purchase that home. Be sure to get those covenants from the seller or real-estate agent, if they have not already been offered to you.

Day of Closing Inspection

A good contract will provide that the buyer be allowed to inspect the property on the day of the closing, before the title transfer takes place.

Everything should be as it was promised, with no unpleasant surprises.

It is smart to include this clause even if you are not sure you can make it personally to this inspection. Maybe you can have a friend or relative look through the property for you. Just the possibility that there will be this walk-through is often enough to keep many sellers a little more honest.

Closing Costs

These are negotiable, too, as is so much in real estate. Who pays for what is up to both you and the seller, although some costs are traditionally the buyer's. Just remember that "common practice" is not law. Tradition can be broken. Everything is negotiable. After you've negotiated, specify in the contract who pays for what.

Liability and Maintenance

Adding a clause about liability and maintenance means the seller promises that you will receive the property in essentially the same condition that it was in when you signed the contract. If a storm later causes a tree to fall against the roof before the closing, repairs must be made by the seller. Your lawyer might also add a line to this clause that reads something like *Seller agrees to cut grass, maintain landscaping, and provide for snow removal until closing, and to deliver the premises in question in broom-clean condition.* That latter phrase can spare you from having to spend days hauling junk out of your new home before you can even move in.

Subject to Review by Buyer's Attorney

If you are using a lawyer to handle the sale for you, include a clause allowing your attorney to review the property, noting that that review will take place within three to five business days of the date of the contract.

ALERT!

Remember two points about the contract: First, as you have read often in these pages, everything is negotiable, and second, if it is not in writing, it is not enforceable—for either side.

Writing the First Check

Most real-estate agents ask that your check be made out to the broker of record in their firm or to the firm name. When you do this, add the words *trustee* or *fiduciary agent* after the broker's or firm's name in order to protect your money. Your check can then only be deposited as money held in trust.

Real-estate law in every state provides that this earnest money will be returned to you if the offer is not accepted and a contract-to-purchase is not entered into. Yes, the return may take some time if the check has been deposited in the broker's account. In practice, though, most realty agents clip the earnest money check to the contract and carry it around until a deal is struck. Then they deposit the check.

An earnest money check is standard procedure when working through a realty agent. Do not, however, give an earnest money check directly to a seller, ever. If you are dealing with "for sale by owner" sellers who insist upon earnest money before a contract can be executed, write that check to their lawyer or yours, and write *fiduciary agent* after the lawyer's name. The money will then be held in a trust account until the negotiations are complete, the contract signed, and its contingencies met. If the deal falls apart, you will get it back. But if you give earnest money directly to the sellers, you may never see it again, or you may have to go to court for its return.

An Additional Deposit

After a contract is signed, you will be expected to hand over a check to your real-estate agent that when added to your earnest money deposit will come to 10 percent of the purchase price. That figure is very negotiable. The down payment may and often does exceed the earnest money, but the earnest money is always applied to the down payment. The lender for the purchaser will require verification of the earnest money deposit to assure that in fact the buyer did pay the deposit. If you have only $10,000 instead of the $20,000 that is 10 percent of a $200,000 house, the sellers may be amenable to accepting that amount. That check is the down payment and is held in escrow until the closing.

Can You Change Your Mind?

What happens if you do indeed change your mind about the house and want to scrap your purchase plans *after* you have signed a contract? You may still have an out. If you included a *subject to a lawyer's review contingency clause* in the contract, the lawyer may be able to let you off the hook. He or she is likely to find *something* that does not set well with you. Or you might not meet one of the contingencies of the contract. For example, you may find the inspection report too negative and determine that you do not want the problems that come with that particular house.

Once everyone finally agrees on price, closing date, some contract contingencies, and what goes with the house, you might consider the house sold, go out, and buy a bottle of champagne. Wait! Don't uncork it yet. Save it for after the house inspection and the closing.

However, after all contingencies have been met, the contract is legal and binding. If you've changed your mind, your only recourse is the mercy of the sellers, and they may have none. Or they might choose to let you out of the contract, but they might want to keep your $500 or $1,000 earnest money. (To try to get that sum returned would cost you more in legal fees than the money at issue.) A sympathetic seller may also give you back your earnest money if he or she is able to sell the house quickly to another buyer.

But if indecision is your forte or you have some doubts about the particular house you have signed a contract to buy, it is wise to try to cancel the deal as soon as possible. Certainly you do not want to back out after you have paid the deposit on that property!

 The House Inspection

One of the contingencies of a sale should be a house inspection by someone you designate, with the results of that evaluation satisfactory to you. You want to ensure that there are no unpleasant surprises after you move in—things that may cost you substantial sums to repair that may not have been obvious to an observer just walking through a home. Having a professional inspector look at a house before the buyer plunks down an enormous amount of money—or takes out a mortgage for, perhaps, the rest of his or her life—is one of the best ideas to come along.

Why Have an Inspection?

An inspector's job is to bring to light any important problems with the house—disasters already there or those about to happen. You might still choose to buy the house, but you will have room to negotiate the price if you can say to the owner, "Well, the house inspector says the roof's in very bad shape. He estimates it's well over ten years old, so it's about due for replacement." Your comments can open negotiating for a lower price and/or repairs or replacements.

No house is perfect. It is pointless to search for a home in mint condition, with the idea that you can save money in repairs. Mint-condition homes are not very common.

On the other hand, just because a house needs work is no reason not to buy it—as long as you are aware of its defects and what they are likely to cost you, either immediately or a few years down the road.

The Cost

House inspections can cost anywhere from $150 to over $500, with the average running about $250. The price you will pay for a professional will depend on the part of the country where you are house-hunting and the individual inspector's, or inspection company's, rates. This is a small expense compared with an investment of $100,000 or more.

Call a professional only after you have made an offer to buy, that offer has been accepted, and you have signed a sales contract. It is rare for buyers to have more than one house inspection performed during the entire house-hunting process.

Sometimes mortgage lenders will require a professional inspection before approving a mortgage loan. This is not to be confused with an *appraisal,* which is always called for by lending institutions. An appraiser, chosen by the lender, does not usually go inside the house and is concerned with the neighborhood, the overall appearance of the property, and whether it represents a safe investment for the lender.

The Report

A house inspector also will help you become acquainted with the property that is about to become yours. If you have never seen a home heating plant close up and have no idea how one works, this is your chance to ask questions and learn.

More and more sellers, especially in a slow market, are offering prospective buyers home-inspection reports that they have ordered and paid for. If you are interested in a home that has such a report, good for you. You will save the expense of getting your own inspector, and you can take that report around the house with you, checking points made by the inspector. There are two points you should check carefully:

1. Make sure that the report is dated recently, and that it is not many months old.
2. Make sure that the inspector is a reputable individual and not the seller's brother, Freddie, with a report handwritten or typed with no letterhead.

When You Inspect a House

Before calling in the pros, do your own inspection. In so doing, you may be able to avoid the aggravation of making a bid on a house, hiring an inspector, and then learning that the house is not worth your investment or that it will cost a fortune in repair bills to bring it up to par.

You will likely go through many homes in your search for the right one for you. Some you will be in and out of in five minutes, maybe less. A very few you will walk through, pause here and there, perhaps ask some questions of the agent, and take the agency's computer printout on the place so that you can remember the details—the number of rooms, property taxes, and the like. "Hmmm," you think, "this one is a possibility."

On your second, or even third, visit to that house that you think has real potential, you should get down to the nitty-gritty and really look at it. On this visit, wear old clothes and bring a flashlight with a bright beam, a yardstick or tape measure, a marble or small ball, a pocketknife or ice pick, and a pad and pencil.

Before you head for the house, jot down some questions you still need answered by the sellers. Perhaps they will be out at the time of your visit, but the real-estate agent can relay those queries for you.

You might also note any special problems or concerns you are likely to have with any house you buy. Do you need room for a piano? Will your rather sizable sofa fit against the only solid wall in the living room? Will the girls' room be large enough for their twin beds?

The Condo or Co-Op Inspection

As with the single-family home, first do your own inspection. Then call an inspection service to recheck the unit and the applicable common areas, such as the heating/cooling system, the laundry area, and so on. You can get permission for entry into locked areas from the board of directors or from the building superintendent or managing agent. Do not fail to make this extra effort, and remember to go along with the inspector. Though you may never see those areas again, what you learn on your tour can help you understand how the entire condo/co-op community works.

What to Look For

The things you are checking will be gone over more thoroughly by a house inspector, so when you come face-to-face with a system or house feature you do not understand, just move on. Leave it for the pros. The following sections will give you an idea of what you should be looking for.

The Foundation

The foundation is any construction that is below or partly below the ground level and upon which the house is built. It could be a concrete slab, walls, and a crawl space or a full basement. The most common materials in today's construction are concrete, concrete block, and cinder block. In very old houses, stone is most common. To prevent termite infestation and dry rot, all wood parts of the house should be at least 6 inches off the ground. Hairline cracks in the slab that are visible as you walk around outside are not usually a cause for alarm. All houses settle somewhat. Major separations or extensive crumbling, though, should make you nervous. If a footing sinks, leaving the support of the structure uneven, the soundness of the house and every working system in it can be endangered.

Look for large cracks in the foundation walls that can be seen from both inside and outside the basement. A house with a serious settling problem will have doors and windows that bind and diagonal cracks in the wallboard or plaster, especially above doors and windows. Repairing the problem is very expensive.

The Crawl Space

A foundation that lifts the house 18 to 36 inches off the ground is called a crawl space. It is most often built of concrete block or cinder block. The floor of this area is often the ground itself; if this is the case, serious moisture problems can occur, especially if ventilation is inadequate. At least one foundation wall ventilator should be built in at each corner, with all four ventilators being kept open year round.

A wet crawl space can cause joists to rot and can send harmful ground vapors up into the house, causing mildew and dampness. Adequate ventilation often can correct the problem. If the space is floored and heated, venting is unnecessary.

Crawl spaces are difficult to inspect, and many homebuyers just do not bother. If you do not want to check the crawl space, make sure that an inspector does it for you. (Some of them want to skip this, too.) The inspector should look for standing water on the ground, especially near the walls and in the corners. When he or she pokes at beams, an ice pick should not sink into the wood. That could be a sign of termites or dry rot. The inspector should also look for rodents' nests. Rodents love the darkness of crawl spaces.

The Basement

Here is where you will see more of the working systems of the house than anywhere else. One thing to look for is dryness. Basement dampness (as opposed to standing water) is often due to condensation. That can be corrected with a dehumidifier.

Seepage from outside groundwater is a much more serious problem and can undermine the structural soundness of a house. First, check for water in the corners. If you see some, it may be due to the faulty positioning of a downspout. Your water problem could be solved by moving, extending, or repairing the downspout. However, such puddles could also be the result of a collection of groundwater around the footings, a serious problem that can cause uneven settling. If you see water, suspicious stains, or a newly repainted floor and cracks in the foundation walls, you might want to cross that house off your list. Or, if you really want the house, get the advice of a professional inspector quickly.

ALERT!

Beware of stains on the basement walls. If you see yellowish-brown markings at the same level all around the basement, it is probably dried moisture and is likely to be the high-water mark. That basement does flood or has flooded!

Overall, be wary of newly painted walls in a basement area. Of course, many sellers do paint long-overdue areas when they are getting ready to put a house on the market, but it pays to be particularly cautious when you see fresh paint in basement areas to ensure that it isn't covering something up that you should know about.

If there is a sump pump, ask the owners how it works. Ask where the pump drains. A dry well at some distance from the house is good. Even better, if allowed by your town, is a storm sewer system in which the water is permanently taken away from the foundation. A pump that takes the water up and out through the basement window does not accomplish much. This is a little like bailing a leaking boat—the water is still on the other side of the wall.

"Gee, there's an awful lot about basements," you may be thinking. That is because water in a basement is one of a homeowner's principal fears, and it should be one of yours at this stage of the buying process.

Termites

Look for traces of these critters around the exterior of the house and while you are in the basement. Look for evidence of wood decay and dry rot. That evidence can take the form of a tunnel-like line running in the problem area. The house does not have to be constructed of wood, either, to suffer from a termite problem. Termites can hit wood trim around stone houses as well as wood foundations and subflooring.

Termites can be such a serious concern that you may want to hire an exterminator to look for them or for signs of other itsy-bitsy things eating away at the house. A house inspector sometimes checks for these pests—but not always.

Use an ice pick in areas where you think you see some evidence of termites. Those contact points between wood and concrete are the most vulnerable to all wood deterioration problems. Problems exist if your blade slips into the wood or if you encounter a spongy rather than a solid resistance. Termites can hit wood fences around a property, too, as well as freestanding garages and sheds.

Are certain regions more susceptible to termites than others?
Yes. While they can be found in various parts of the United States, they thrive in southern California and in the Southeast, where the damp climate fosters termites.

Unfortunately, termites are not the only little devils that could be gnawing away at the home you want. You could have, for example, powder post beetles. They eat wood the same way termites do. Beware, in any event, of floors that feel soft in one or two spots when you walk on them. Something is probably feasting on them.

A careful eye can save you hundreds, even thousands, of dollars. At this stage, the price of the house can be lowered, the seller can take on repairs, or you can split the cost. If you overlook a trouble spot and buy the house before finding the problem, there is no question about who will write the check for the repair.

The Working Systems

The working systems—electrical, heating, and plumbing—are best handled by professionals. Still, there are some points even a novice can check.

ALERT!

Be sure there are enough outlets. Too many appliances and gadgets plugged into extension cords is a sign that the outlet supply is inadequate.

You can find out whether or not the wiring is adequate by looking around the house. If there are a dishwasher, clothes washer and dryer, a few television sets, an electrical stove and oven, central air conditioning, and a computer or two in the bedrooms, you can be reasonably certain that wiring is not a problem. Try the light switches. Check to be sure the doorbell rings. If it is broken, that is one repair you can have the seller make before closing. You will need that chime during the busy days of moving in.

Having an electrical system upgraded in an older home—maybe just a plain old home—is certainly possible. Inadequate wiring is not something that should cause you to change your mind about the house, unless you cannot afford to upgrade it.

Does the heating system provide enough heat? How much does it cost to run? Determining its safety is a job for the experts, but determining if the heating is adequate is something you can do. Ask the owner of the house for the heating bills for the previous winter and the name of the fuel supplier. Then call the oil or utility company and ask what a typical bill for a house of your square footage would have been for the previous winter. Do the same with central air conditioning.

What about the plumbing? You can examine the condition of exposed pipes, but an inspector will likely know more than you about their condition. Old iron pipes or lead fittings could need replacement. Also, be sure to run water from faucets and to flush toilets. Is the water clear or rusty? Look for leaks, low water pressure, and drains that empty too slowly.

Radon and Lead Paint

You've probably read about these problems over the last decade. They can still be serious concerns for some house hunters.

Radon is a colorless, odorless gas that came to public attention in the mid-1980s and has been determined to have serious health risks, including cancer. It is found in the ground, as well as in some building materials. Most homes built since 1990 have radon-resistant features. Radon testing is still a routine part of most home purchases. High radon levels can usually be corrected, and remediation can be arranged before the closing.

Most house inspection firms will do radon checks. If yours does not, ask your real-estate agent where to get this done.

Lead-based paint is present in most houses built before 1950. If ingested, it can be very harmful to children, causing brain damage and even death. The federal government has explanations and guidelines for covering this problem. Call your local housing authority and/or health department.

Other Things to Note

There are many other parts of a house you should investigate, although the aforementioned are the most important and potentially most costly. For your own purposes, note room sizes, traffic flow patterns, size and state of the kitchen, and number of bathrooms. Ask the owner about storm or screen windows. If there aren't any, determine their cost and decide whether you will want to buy them.

Are floors level? Test them with a ball or marble. Do they need refinishing? Any creaky boards? What about the stairs? Any problems there? Are all of the appliances that will stay with the house in working order?

The Seller's Disclosure

Most states require that the seller provide to the purchaser a written residential home disclosure.

This disclosure is required in order to inform you, the purchaser, of any material defects in the real estate. It is against the law to not disclose information to a buyer, and you should know to request this information when looking at a property. You will have to sign a receipt as well, usually on a copy of the form, showing that you received the disclosure.

Read the disclosure. Usually you will find one of three things with disclosures. First, you may find that the seller knows of no material defects with the property. Second, you may find that at one time there was a problem, like a leaky roof, and that it was repaired.

Or third, there is a problem that requires attention. If you find a defect after closing that was not revealed to you on the seller's disclosure, you have the ability to recover damages as prescribed by statute in many states. Penalties are quite large in some cases. The seller in most cases will have the right to remedy the problem for you.

Disclosures are generally not required when you buy a new home, as it has not been lived in and there should be nothing to disclose. New homes should be inspected by you and your licensed inspector prior to closing, looking for material items and punch-list items (items that the builder is contractually obligated to fix before closing).

Disclosures really apply to resales only. Items may include the following:

- Indications of whether there has been flooding in the basement of the property through sewer back-up or from foundation leakage.
- Roof or skylight leakage.
- Knowledge of environmental problems, that is, asbestos pipe wrap, underground storage tanks, or radon.
- Structural problems.
- Termites or bug infestation.
- Problems with heating ventilating and air conditioning.

You can obtain a disclosure from your state or local real-estate board office or from your real-estate agent. These disclosures will vary from state to state but are there for your review to inform you of potential problems with the property. Some states do not require disclosure when a property is sold as part of an estate or when it is sold by a trustee in cases where the administrative seller has not lived in the property and has no knowledge of any history.

Always ask your agent for a seller's disclosure if you are seriously interested in a property.

If you read a disclosure that indicates an existing problem, it may be that the seller does not have the funds to remedy or fix the problem. Read the disclosure carefully, as it may provide a negotiating tool for you if you are capable of attending to an item, and you can reduce the purchase price accordingly.

Calling in the Pros

Once you have some idea of the workings of the house that interests you, you are ready to call in a professional. Perhaps you know a home remodeler in your town or an engineer who does house inspections. Those folks can be fine to use, if you are very sure they are qualified to look at every area of a house. There are home inspection companies, too; some of them are local franchises of nationwide concerns.

Be certain your inspector can be objective and that he or she owes no allegiance to a real-estate agency or company that you might later choose to do repair work on that property. In the latter case, for instance, hiring a person who does home repairs would clearly be a conflict of interest, which you want to avoid. Your best bet is to hire someone who has a contractor's license or experience in residential construction. An engineer might be able to give you advice on repairs and new installations that a house inspection service cannot and is not required to, but you are likely to pay more for the engineer's services.

How do you find a good inspector? It is best not to ask the seller to recommend one. And, of course, do not use the real-estate agent's recommendation either. In the latter case, even the most honest of inspectors, might avoid making too many waves for fear that the sale will fall through and the realty agent will decide not to recommend him or her again.

Some real-estate agents supply buyers with three or four names and addresses of inspectors/inspection services that other customers of theirs have used. That is different from making just one recommendation, so feel free to check any, or preferably all, of those suggestions. Even in this case, do not mention to the inspector that he or she was recommended by the realty agency. Make your call sound as if it came from out of the blue or perhaps from an advertisement in the Yellow Pages.

After the inspection, you should be given a typed report, and quickly. Most companies will have this document in the mail to you in a few days.

You can also ask friends and business associates for referrals. In large corporations, personnel offices that handle transfers often supply the names of inspection firms. You might also call your mortgage lender or your lawyer for recommendations.

Finally, in a pinch, check out the Yellow Pages. You will find large, nationwide inspection services and small local firms there. Neither type of firm is necessarily better than the other. You can also look for those who are members of the American Society of Home Inspectors (ASHI), which sets professional standards for its members. Those who are not members— usually small, independent local services—may still be fine.

When you make your initial phone call to an inspector, ask if he or she actually goes on the roof and, gets into the crawl space under the house. Some check these areas as a matter of course, others charge extra, and still others will not go closer to a roof than standing in the driveway, looking up, and jotting down notes from there. Which do you want?

Also, testing for radon and asbestos, well-water contamination, or termites usually costs more than a basic inspection. The home inspector/inspection service might, in fact, direct you to someone else for those reports, perhaps to an individual or company that specializes in certain problem areas of a house, particularly environmental hazards.

FACT

For the name of a home inspector in your area, contact the American Society of Home Inspectors, Inc., (ASHI) 932 Lee Street, Suite 101, Des Plaines, IL 60016, ✎ (847) 759-2820, ✎ (800) 743-ASHI, or visit ✎ *www.ashi.com* for more information.

Ask the inspector what type of written report you can expect. If possible, look at a sample report from their firm. Does it give the ages of specific systems in the house or just a notation of their current state? Does it offer projections of when parts or systems might need repairs in the future? Does it estimate the cost of those repairs and of remedies to existing problems? (You can get answers to some of these questions by accompanying the inspector on his or her tour of the house, a trip that will definitely be worth your while. While the inspector talks, you take notes.) Ask whether the inspection company carries any type of liability insurance to cover any damage to the house created by the inspector during his or her tour or major defects the house inspector misses. How long will the inspection take? A general inspection can run about an hour and a half; a more detailed look that runs two hours or more is likely to cost more. The house inspector, incidentally, should not comment about the wisdom of your buying a particular house, even if you ask—and don't bother asking.

Checking out Complaints

It is a good idea to call your local Better Business Bureau and consumer affairs agency to see if any complaints have been lodged against the service you are thinking of using. However, this is not a fail-safe way to protect yourself, since a lack of complaints is no guarantee that a company does a good job. It could simply mean that disgruntled consumers failed to contact that agency. Still, a few consumers are likely to have written about really bad outfits, and those reports will be in the files.

ALERT!

The Council of Better Business Bureaus, the national organization of local offices, offers a booklet of tips on home inspection for $2. Write the council c/o Publications Department, 4200 Wilson Boulevard, Arlington, VA 22203, or call them at ✆ (703) 276-0100.

Evaluating the Problems

Should you buy a home with problems? What is most important here is to put the problems you have found into perspective. With some faults, you may choose to walk away from the best bargain you have ever seen because of the risks (or higher costs down the road) involved; with others, you may have the time, money, and motivation for the repairs needed. Following are some aids in helping you with the decision to buy or not, now that you know a home's faults.

Red Lights

Any item on this list should be enough to turn you away from your prospective purchase:

- Unsafe or inadequate drinking water.
- A nonfunctioning or malfunctioning private sewer system (septic tank or cesspool).
- Location in a floodplain. (The U.S. Geological Survey has mapped most floodplain areas in this country. If your property is on low land near a river or stream, investigate. Federal flood insurance is available to residents of floodplain areas. Most lenders will not write a mortgage without it.)
- Uneven settling or a buckling foundation.
- Uncontrollable basement water problems.

Yellow Lights

These items indicate caution, and potential trouble or costly repair ahead:

- Peeling, cracking, or bubbling exterior paint.
- A roof almost in need of repairs.
- Deteriorating gutters and downspouts.
- Leaks in the roof at the flashings.
- Excessive moisture in the attic due to poor ventilation or inadequate insulation.
- Pests (termites, bats, mice, squirrels, or roaches).
- Inadequate electrical service. (This can be brought up to date at a cost.)
- Inadequate insulation.
- Plumbing pipes or fixtures in need of repair or replacement.
- Leaks around the bathtub or from under a shower stall.
- Windows in need of repair or replacement.

Green Lights

The following findings on a home inspection report should do nothing to disrupt your confidence in the soundness of your potential purchase:

- An aged or inadequate water heater.
- Nonworking appliances (built-in ranges, ovens, dishwashers, and so on).
- Hairline settling cracks in the foundation.
- Leaky faucets.
- Dirt, grime, and eyesore decorating.

Be Reasonable

Recognize what is serious and what is not. Don't let an aggressive home inspector kill a deal for you. Be reasonable while protecting your interests. Figure deferred maintenance into your purchase price. Realize that a property that is not new is not new. Don't expect perfection. Get the home you want, and let the little stuff slide. Ⓔ

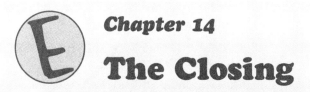

Chapter 14

The Closing

The closing is the event that makes it all official. The title of the house is turned over to you from the sellers, and the property is finally yours. There's a lot that happens at this solemn event, and it's exciting as well as a little nerve-racking. But you'll be prepared for it after reading this chapter!

Closing Ceremonies

After your mortgage has been approved, your signed contract accepted, and its contingencies met, you will be notified of the date of settlement—that is, when the transfer of title to your new home takes place. Procedures vary. In some regions of the country, notably the Northeast, the closing might be a lawyer's office, where the room is crowded with people—the sellers, the sellers' attorney, the buyers, the buyers' attorney, the lender's attorney, and the selling real-estate agent. In contrast, the scene of a settlement on the West Coast might be a small office with one person working alone—an escrow agent. No one else need come, and no one does.

QUESTION?

What actually happens at the closing?
Ask your real-estate agent or your lawyer. Both are excellent sources of information about local closing procedures and customs. Ask them to describe exactly who does what, where the closing takes place, who must be present, and how long it will take.

Between those poles are many possible closing scenarios. Depending on local custom, settlement may be conducted by an escrow agent, a lending institution, a title insurance company, a real-estate broker, or attorneys for the buyers or sellers. Even the wording of the settlement/closing procedures will differ from one area of the country to another, since terminology, like procedure, is a matter of local custom.

ESSENTIAL

Your real-estate agent may offer you a copy of the RESPA (Real Estate Settlement Procedures Act) booklet after your offer for a home has been accepted, or it may come from the lender with your loan package. If you do not see one, ask for a copy. Visit ✐ *www.hud.gov* to find out more about RESPA.

There is one stabilizer, however. In response to buyer and seller confusion over the diversity of closing procedures across the country, and in response to the prevalence of some unethical practices and paybacks, the federal government stepped into this area of real estate in 1974 by enacting the Real Estate Settlement Procedures Act (RESPA). That law governs most of the steps in the transfer of property and protects the homebuyer with its disclosure requirements. Thus, you can anticipate no unpleasant surprises!

RESPA assures that you will know fairly accurately what services you will be charged for, although you may not know the amount of the fees. Essentially, though, at a closing, a sizable number of papers are shifted from one party to another for signature. And you pay a fairly sizable number of costs.

Keep in mind that unless everything is paid at the closing, the property does not change hands. You cannot earnestly plead, "I'll get that check to you as soon as I get paid Thursday." No payments, no house.

Following is a common closing protocol, assuming you will take part in the closing "ceremony." As soon as it is possible to do so, your lawyer's secretary calls and tells you what your closing expenses will be. If that does not happen, by all means call that office and ask.

QUESTION?

What if I don't have a lawyer?
Your mortgage lender will apprise you of settlement costs.

The secretary will give you a specific figure and ask you to bring in a cashier's check for that amount, made out to the lawyer. You pay the lawyer for all the expected charges, and using your money, he or she makes disbursements. That is practical, because the money will be paid out in so many different directions. Also, bills for various services needed for the closing will be sent to your lawyer for payment by you at the closing. It would be wise to keep several hundred dollars in your checking account, though, to bring along in the unlikely event something else pops up.

Closing Costs

Closing costs can run as high as 6 percent of the sale price of the home, which is certainly a considerable expense. If you're buying a $100,000 home, you could pay $6,000. In reality, these costs vary so widely that it is impossible to give you a specific figure. Costs depend on what the lender charges, the customs in your community and your part of the country, what you have already paid before the settlement, and the fees you have negotiated for the seller to pay.

If you have bought a home with an assumable loan, you will pay only a few hundred dollars at settlement; that is one of the advantages of that type of financing.

The following sections discuss what fees you might expect to pay before you truly own your home. Note that there are no exact figures listed for most of these charges, which again is because they vary so. The individual fees can range from twenty-five to several hundred dollars. Not all of the charges may be applicable where you live, either, so do not assume that you will be billed for each service listed. You might count on paying somewhere around 2 to 3 percent of your loan amount. A high estimate of closing costs can approach 6 percent.

Mortgage-Related Charges

The following are mortgage-related charges:

- **Loan origination fee.** This fee covers processing your mortgage. It might be stated as a percentage of the loan or as a flat fee.
- **Loan discount or points.** This is a one-time charge to "adjust the yield" on the loan; it translates into making the loan more profitable for the lender. One point is 1 percent of the loan. The buyer usually pays the points, but sometimes the seller does. (And sometimes there are no points charged.) Buyers using VA-backed loans do not pay discount points, but FHA buyers might.
- **Appraisal fee.** Mortgage lenders require an appraisal of the property that you want to buy, for their own protection. The fee is usually paid

by the buyer, but it can sometimes be paid by the seller, if both agree. The appraisal charge is sometimes included in the mortgage insurance application fee.

- **Credit report fee.** This fee may also be paid when making a written loan application rather than at the closing. Whether you get the mortgage or not, the charge is nonrefundable.
- **Lender's inspection fee.** Here is a charge that is applicable to buyers of new homes. Representatives of the lender must make several inspections at various stages of the building process.
- **Mortgage insurance application fee.** This fee covers the processing costs for applying for private mortgage insurance (PMI), if you plan to purchase such coverage. Sometimes it is paid in advance of the closing.
- **Assumption fee.** Those assuming a loan pay this charge; it covers the processing work involved in the assumption.

Special Items

These items are required by the lender to be paid in advance of taking on your new mortgage:

- **Interest.** Usually buyers must pay this charge at the closing. You pay interest on your loan for the period of time between the closing date and the date on which the first scheduled loan payment is due.
- **Mortgage insurance premium.** The initial premium is often paid in advance, at the request of the lender. It may cover several months or be a full year's premium.
- **Homeowner's insurance premium.** Your lender could require a first check for this policy. After that, you are likely to cover homeowner's insurance in your monthly mortgage payment. (Chapter 19 explains homeowner's insurance in detail.)
- **Hazard insurance premium.** If it has been determined that your home is in an area calling for some type of hazard insurance (flood or earthquake protection, for example), the lender will require proof of payment of the first year's insurance premium at the closing.

Reserve Funds

These funds (also called escrow funds) are to be deposited with the lender:

- **Hazard insurance.** Some lenders require that a certain amount of money toward the next year's premium on hazard insurance be deposited and put on reserve. Try to negotiate payment of interest on your reserve fund.
- **Private mortgage insurance (PMI).** A part of this premium may be placed in a reserve account rather than be paid in advance at the closing. Again, try to negotiate for interest paid on it and, for that matter, on any deposit.
- **Real-estate taxes.** This can be a hefty charge of several hundred dollars. Most lenders require a regular monthly payment to the reserve account in your name for city and/or county property taxes. They may also call for an amount of up to six months' taxes to be paid at the closing and held in an escrow account. If you cannot avoid this, at least try to knock down the interest paid on this sum.
- **Special assessments.** Like the tax escrow account, these monies are held in escrow to make payments due either annually or at intervals throughout the year. The funds can be spent for local improvement assessments such as sewers, traffic lights, and sidewalks, or they can represent neighborhood or homeowners' association dues. If you have a clean credit record, ask the lender if you can pay those fees yourself, directly. He or she might say yes!

Charges for Title Services

This is an important, but little known, area of home owning. Title services ensure that you truly do become the owner of the property you are buying and have written proof of that ownership. There are several fees, as you might have guessed, in connection with the process of gaining title, as follows:

- **Title search, title examination, and title insurance binder.** The latter is sometimes called a "commitment to insure." These are charges made for title search and guarantee services. Who pays for what, whether it's you or the seller, may be dictated by local custom or by an agreement negotiated before the signing of the contract.

- **Title insurance.** This policy protects against any defects in the title that may be discovered after the transfer of ownership has been conveyed. For example, a contractor who has not been paid for his work could place a lien on the house.

A lender's title insurance policy, which protects only that institution, might be required. A policy for a new homeowner is an option but one you might want to pursue. The premium for each is a one-time charge. Sellers sometimes pay for an owner's policy as part of the sellers' assurance of clear title. Buyers usually must pay the fee for the lender's title policy, but often only the amount of the mortgage, rather than the purchase price of the house, need be insured. All of this is negotiable.

Other Settlement Charges

Finally, you are approaching the end of this lengthy list of (possible) fees. What follows is an assortment of remaining charges, not all of which might apply to you in your particular situation:

- **Settlement or closing fee.** This amount goes to the closing agent. Whether it is paid by the buyers or the sellers can be negotiated before the contract is signed.
- **Document preparation.** An amorphous-sounding service, this is a final preparation of legal papers, for which you may also be charged. Be sure, however, that you are not paying twice for the same service. It might be included in the preparation of the mortgage.
- **Notary fee.** This fee is paid to a licensed notary public to authenticate the execution of certain documents, where applicable.
- **Attorney's fee.** If a lawyer is required by the lender, the fee will appear on the Uniform Settlement Statement. If you have engaged an attorney to represent you for this purchase, his or her charge will be a separate bill to you. Ask your attorney how it is being handled in

your situation. This, too, is money due at the closing, no later.

- **Government recording and transfer fees.** Charges for legally recording the new deed and mortgage are usually paid by the buyer. They are set by state and/or local governments. Local government tax stamps may also be required, and they, too, carry a fee.
- **Survey.** This is often required by the lender and paid by the buyer. You might be able to save a little money by updating the previous survey made when the seller bought the property. The size of the lot rarely changes, after all.
- **Termite inspection.** Sometimes required by the lender, local custom, or law, this bill is usually paid to those rendering that service in advance of the closing, but you must show proof that the service has been provided.
- **Broker's commission.** If you have made an agreement with a buyer's broker, his or her fee will be due at the closing. One expense you do not have to worry about is any other realty commission. Sellers pay the agent who sells their home.

And that's it. About time, you might say. By all means ask for an explanation of any charge you do not understand.

Closing Day Tasks

Here are a few other details that will need your attention on or just prior to closing day:

- **Utilities.** Arrange to have the electric and water meters read the morning of the closing, and then have an account for those utilities set up in your name. Do not wait until the last minute to make these arrangements.
- **Fuel.** If the house is heated by oil, have the oil company measure what is left in the house the day before closing, if that is agreeable to the seller. Sellers usually charge buyers for any sizable amount of remaining oil when title changes hands. Otherwise, make some other arrangements, calling on your lawyer for advice if need be. If gas is

the fuel, have the meter read on the day of the closing so that the bill for that usage can be sent to the seller, and have a new account opened in your name.

- **Before-closing inspection.** If possible, inspect the property on the morning of the closing.

In your closing-day inspection of the property, make a list of any problems or questions that can be raised at the closing. Your bargaining time is dwindling, and the seller wants to sell that day. But if there has been water damage, for instance, from a pipe that burst after you last saw the property, you are entitled to have something knocked off the sale price or to have the seller write you a check for the estimated cost of repair.

What should you bring with you to the closing? There are some things you will need to have with you.

- **Money.** During those busy preclosing days, be sure to purchase a certified check and have some money in a checking account for unexpected expenses.
- **Personal identification.** No doubt you carry this with you anyway, but you may need to show some proof that you are indeed who you say you are. Your identification is likely to be a driver's license, but a passport or birth certificate will also work. A state identification card might suffice.
- **Your "home" file containing important documents.** In this folder, which you have very likely been keeping since your offer was accepted, perhaps even since you started house-hunting, you should have a copy of your loan commitment letter and the contract to purchase. You should also have a copy of your homeowner's insurance policy, (see Chapter 19), as well as any hazard insurance, showing you have made at least a first quarter's premium payment. In addition, you should have in your folder the lender's statement of settlement charges and correspondence from your attorney. Any notes

you jotted to yourself should be kept in the file, too.

- **Your wits.** Do not assume that you are now in the hands of the professionals and can just sit back at the closing and watch the papers fly. Mistakes certainly do happen at a closing, and just as often they are made by the pros as by those who are a bit out of their element in that setting. Ask questions if there is anything you do not understand. After all, this is your $100,000 or $200,000 (or more!) on the line, no one else's. You might indeed be charged for the same service twice, and you could be the only one who catches the error.

Is Anything Tax Deductible Here?

Unfortunately, not much. Your portion of any real-estate taxes and interest paid in advance is tax deductible. Points are deductible. Your insurance premium is not. Save an itemized list of expenses paid at the closing to show your tax adviser. While most other closing costs are not deductible, they might be added to your home's purchase price to arrive at its adjusted cost basis; so they do serve some tax purpose later.

Buyers always question whether moving expenses are tax deductible. Some are, but the majority are not. Here, too, your accountant can advise you.

Finally, "In Closing . . ."

Plan to celebrate! You have earned it. If you are buying as a couple or as friends, bring champagne to the closing so that you can toast each other later in your new home, where you will no doubt head immediately after taking title. You might want to make plans to go out for a celebratory dinner. If you have been particularly friendly with your real-estate agent, invite him or her to come along. If you are buying alone, have a special lunch or dinner with friends. If this is your first home purchase, it calls for some special commemoration of this rite of passage. If it is more your style to drive right over to the home center, purchase a mailbox, and have your name pasted or painted on it, then go with that. Do something you will remember—you're a homeowner now!

It is up to you to make sure that your "home" file is complete. But then, as a successful homebuyer, you already know how much depends on *you*.

Your house-buying homework is almost over—but not quite. Do follow up with phone calls in a week or two to your lawyer and/or real-estate agent for material that you did not receive at the closing but that was promised you. It will take four to six weeks for the lawyer to send you a copy of the recorded deed, but other information you requested should be forthcoming more quickly.

Chapter 15

Building Your Own House

Perhaps you consider building a home to be a money-saving venture. Or maybe you just like the idea of creating your own home from scratch and having a say in each aspect of its design. Building a home brings with it some concerns that are different from buying an existing home.

Simple Ways to Acquire a Lot

The first thing you need if you're going to build a house is land. Owning a piece of land immediately lowers your home-building cost. You may already own a small plot of land. Or perhaps someone in your family has half an acre that no one is using. That may sound funny, but it is surprising how many folks inherit or buy a parcel of land and have no clear intention for its use. Some people just like the idea of owning land, even if it sits there year after year, doing nothing but growing weeds.

If you have a relative in this situation, you might be able to purchase his or her parcel inexpensively. A relative may be thrilled to see the land put to good use, or perhaps he or she is just tired of paying taxes on a quarter-acre and cannot seem to sell it on the open market. You can offer to take it off their hands for an attractive (to you) price.

Or maybe your folks, or an investor outside of your family, will join you in purchasing a lot that can be subdivided. You can build on yours; the investor can either hold his or hers or sell it to another would-be home builder.

Does anyone in your family own a lot that could be split into two parcels so that you could build on one and he or she could continue to hold the other? Be sure to check the zoning restrictions. Can the land be legally subdivided? Or will you all have to apply for a zoning variance (an exception to the zoning laws)? Naturally, it is assumed that the land in question is in a viable location and can, according to local laws, have a home erected on it.

Building a home is not likely to work for you if you are on a tight budget *and* have to spend a lot of money for land. But if you live in a part of the country where land prices are still relatively inexpensive, then buying a lot and erecting a manufactured or modular home can quite cleverly ease you into home ownership at not too high a cost.

Does the Government Offer "Free" Land?

The government *does* have some land suitable for private citizens—land it no longer needs or thinks would be better in private ownership. This land is undeveloped, with no improvements, and is usually part of the original public domain established during the western expansion of the United States. Most of this land is in the eleven western states and Alaska, although there are a few scattered parcels in the East.

The land varies in size and description—some of it is desert, and some is rural. Prices vary, too, but the land must be sold at market value, with no bargains (and no preference given veterans either). Large urban cities offer land as well! Areas that are prime for redevelopment and had previously been overlooked can be purchased for as little as $1 when a city wants development. Often you will find that the low sales price coincides with a firm commitment on behalf of the purchaser to hold the property for a long time and to build on the property.

For more information, contact your state or regional office of the U.S. Department of the Interior, the Bureau of Land Management at *www.blm. gov,* or your local city department of planning and development.

Shopping for a Site

If you go land shopping, keep in mind that costs for vacant acreage have been rising steadily, and do not be so eager to buy and build that you make a serious error with the lot you select. Not all land is valuable. You may be able to pay as little as $2,000 for a one-acre lot somewhere, but it might be impossible to build a home on that site. It may not be accessible to utilities. It may be so far off the beaten track that it is difficult to reach. It could have poor drainage. Maybe it is not zoned for a home.

More than a few buyers have been dismayed (frantic might be a more accurate word for it) to learn that the lot they purchased is too small, according to local government restrictions, for the house they want to build—or for any house. Make sure the lot you buy is large enough for the home you have in mind.

You may not be able to afford land in an established residential neighborhood—if, that is, there is any open land left—or in farm country, where land is being sold to developers in parcels of thousands of acres apiece, if it is being sold at all.

Not discouraged? Good. Following are some important points to note when shopping for a home site:

- Be sure to look at environmental concerns. It will pay to check into what your state environmental agency has, or has in mind, for land trust purposes and where it could be putting a total moratorium on development.
- Don't buy too close to a major highway. You might find that the state highway department is planning to widen a road right into your parlor. Check as many master plans and environmental agency reports as you can for the area you are considering.
- Find out if the land can be used as a home site. What type of permit must be obtained? Are there water and sewer hookups? Is your lot large enough, according to local zoning laws, for the construction of a home? All of this can be checked at your city or town hall.

FACT

A land trust may be established to protect and conserve open space, leaving it untouched by development forever. This may make it harder to find land to buy.

- Check also that the lot is not too steep for building, another unpleasant surprise for some buyers.
- Find out if there are government restrictions. With the rapid growth in housing development over the past ten years, cities have imposed height restrictions.
- Also check the soil. You might have to add topsoil to your lot or take some topsoil away from it. Rock that is too close to the soil can add to the expense of the foundation or make digging one totally impractical.
- A high water table or a ground not stable enough to support a house could mean you run into still more expense. Be especially wary of acreage over a landfill, where flooding can occur as the water table

rises. Ask about all of this at your town engineer's office.

- Find out if you can erect a manufactured home—your most affordable choice—on the lot. Some municipalities have regulations against such houses.
- Utilities are another point to check. Is the lot you are looking at serviced by public sewer and water? If not, you will need a septic system and a well.
- Be sure that you get clear title to the land. You can do the title search yourself at the town hall, you can pay a title search company to do it, or you can buy title insurance, which will insure you against potential lawsuits. For the latter two options, see "title" in the Yellow Pages.
- Will you be landlocked? The selling of landlocked lots is illegal in many states. Small plots in the middle of nowhere that can be reached only by helicopter cannot be marketed anymore. There must be an access road.
- What will be going up around you? Again, look at local master plans to see what kind of growth is forecast. Ask around, too, to see what is in the talking stages for the acreage around the lot you have selected.
- What about the shape of that lot? The more road frontage on an already completed thoroughfare, the more valuable the piece of land will be. The more expense required to develop the land, the cheaper your purchase price should be.

Do not forget to consider resale value. Being plunked in the woods far from even the nearest hamlet might suit you fine. But when it comes time to sell, buyers who feel the same way might be fewer than you would like.

You will also need to consider how you will you pay for your lot. Financing is important. Many sales of land are cash only. Sometimes the seller holds a short-term mortgage. Check with mortgage brokers. Some can put you in touch with a conventional lender who will finance your lot if you intend to build on it within two years.

You cannot forget the local political entity where you buy. Learn to whom you report building plans, requests, problems, and the like. Be sure you know jurisdictions, town borders, and county lines. If you have to appear before a zoning board or a city council meeting to petition for a zoning variance, try to get a reading on those people. How do they feel about development, even on the small scale you are planning? Are you likely to win your variance?

There's Building, and There's *Building*

A little clarification might be in order here. When you hear someone say, "We're building a house," that could mean one of three things:

1. It could mean they are having a manufactured or modular home delivered to their lot and erected on that site.
2. It could mean they have a home going up in a new development, where they are buying from that developer. They have a choice of a few designs and work closely with the builder and his or her staff on features, product choices, and the like.
3. It could mean they are having a home designed especially for them, either in or out of a new development.

Buying a House Before It Is Built

Buying a home before it is built carries its own potential price savings. In the real-estate section of your local paper, you will often see advertisements with headlines like "Preconstruction Prices Through September 15," "Preconstruction Prices for Phase II of Pheasant Run," or "Special Preview Offer." What does all of that mean? Is it good for you, or is it just another sales come-on?

As the name suggests, a preconstruction price is the first price at which a home in a new development is offered. At that stage, the lot that is being developed is probably still no more than a sea of mud and a sales trailer. Developers concede they underprice a little at the beginning to get the ball rolling. Nothing brings in customers more than seeing other people buy.

How much can you save at this stage? Houses sold when the development is complete can cost 20 to 30 percent more than the price of preconstruction homes! Thus, assuming you can wait for your home to be built and that the builder is reputable, buying early can be a very good deal indeed. You are locking in a lower price that is likely to be unavailable later when the homes have been built. Additionally, you will have a say in choosing the tiles, flooring, and paint colors for the home as it is being built. Buying early also gives you a choice of location; you do not have to take what is left.

ALERT!

One drawback is accepting that there will be some uncertainty about when you will actually have the house. Sometimes there are construction delays and delivery snags. If you need to get into your new home right away, you may not have the luxury of being able to wait.

It is important that you know your builder. It is best to go with someone who has done similar construction and has completed such jobs satisfactorily. Look for a builder with a record of other single-family home projects, not someone who has built shopping centers, for instance, and who is just now dipping into the residential area.

Drive around your potential builder's other projects, even if you have to head 30 miles out of town. Talk to those homeowners if you can, too, and ask them if they are satisfied with their houses. If this is the builder's first job, you cannot know if he or she will finish. What if the builder disappears with your deposit and leaves the community awash in unpaved roads, half-built homes, and unlandscaped yards? Alas, that has been known to happen—and more often than one would like to think.

If you are one of the early residents in a development, will you feel comfortable living virtually alone until more people move in? Maybe you will be the first buyer or perhaps the fifth. In any event, you are likely to be living in a fairly unfinished neighborhood for some time. What about the safety factor? Can children play in the area without the danger of their running into construction materials or, worse, machinery? Will you mind the noise of construction?

Once a contract is signed, the sales figure—preconstruction or not—is usually protected, no matter how many times a developer later raises the cost of other homes in the development. If you are concerned about a delivery delay, ask for a clause in the contract requiring the builder to notify you two months in advance of the completion date; thus, you will establish a time frame for changing residence.

If you are buying a small home and are already considering expanding it in the future, be sure that you can do so following local regulations. Also, check the covenants of the new-home community.

Saving on a New Development Home

Here are some ways to save money when you are buying a home that is not yet built:

- **Buy at preconstruction prices.** If you won't mind not having a house for a while, and it won't matter that you will be one of the pioneering families in the development—having few neighbors or development niceties—you can save substantially.
- **Select a model home.** You may have to wait until a development is almost sold out, but you will probably have a home with all the bells and whistles—put in to entice buyers—at a discounted price. Of course, you'll have to take the model as it comes, and you won't have any choice about options, upgrades, or design features.
- **Speaking of options and upgrades—skip some of them.** Select standard features and fixtures, and save the upgrades for later. You don't really need top-of-the-line kitchen cabinets—at least not right away—do you?
- **Leave a portion of the house unfinished for now.** If you can wait a while for that third bath or fourth bedroom, you can save money by just having it framed out, then finished later.
- **Don't automatically take the developer's mortgage package.** It might be good, but maybe you can do better by shopping around. Check at least three other lenders in your area, and compare interest rates and

other terms. For a first-time buyer, often the bank you have your accounts with, that is, the bank that knows you best, is the easiest lender for you to use.

Financing Help from the Developer

In some new home communities, the developer will do all he or she can to help you buy, including shaving down-payment requirements, sometimes to 5 percent (or even requiring nothing down), and offering financing at attractive rates. Developers are able to do this through their relationships with the banks or other lenders who are handling the financing for their projects.

By all means, jot down all of the information the developer provides about mortgages and interest rates. But then do some comparison shopping. His or her rate might not be the best. And it is likely to be short term.

Discount financing programs are apt to be in force for no longer than probably three years. After that, they convert to current market rates. So bring out the calculator again to determine how much you can save with what is offered.

QUESTION?

What exactly should you check when walking through a newly built house?
Check both the things on the punch list and anything that it does not cover. Inspect everything from the attic for ventilation, to the stairs for creaks, to the walls to be sure they are straight.

Checking out the Place Before You Move In

You might be allowed one inspection of your home after it is framed up (so that you can see what is going up behind the walls) and then another inspection after the drywall is installed (to avert any problems during the final inspection). Last comes your final walk-through, which will be followed by one by your lender. At the last look at the house before closing, you have the opportunity to assure yourself that the builder has completed the job to your satisfaction. Anything that has not been completed or is not up to standard should be jotted down on what is known as a punch list, a sheet prepared for buyers for just that reason.

Do not be so taken with how marvelous the house looks that you do not check every detail. This is your chance to have things set right. Ask the builder to fix any points you ticked off on your punch list before the closing. Then make a final inspection to see that those problems have indeed been corrected.

Sometimes a builder will contest your complaint. If a problem remains unsolved as closing nears, you can delay the closing until all of the questionable points have been cleared up. If the builder offers you cash instead of repairs, decline and ask for the repairs. They could cost more than the builder's cash allowance.

If you have any concerns about the house after it is built, hire a home inspector to take a look at your new home. Inspectors are not only for resale homes!

Be sure that you take walk-throughs. This is not something you want to rush. Remember that you will have to live with any unreported faults or pay to have them corrected. Remember that you hold all the cards before the closing. If ever there is a time to get the corrections you want, this is it. Your leverage drops significantly after you take title to the house.

The Custom-Built Home

If you know exactly the type of house you want but can't seem to find the development home that fits, then you are probably considering a custom-built home. Building your own home can be a creative, exhilarating experience. It can be a frustrating, time- and money-consuming one, too.

Working with Professionals

How can you make a custom-built home project run as smoothly—and economically—as possible? First, know where you are going to place that special home. You read earlier about buying a lot. If you have good land, with access to water and sewer facilities and on a level lot in a community where you can, in terms of zoning, build just what you want, then, literally and figuratively, you have a good foundation for your construction project. And second, choose the right architect or custom builder for you.

An Architect

An architect's fee will increase the cost of your new home by about 10 percent, but you might make that up in resale value, not to mention your enjoyment of a well-planned house during your years living there. By overseeing your project carefully, an architect might be able to get discounts for you on materials. That alone could save you his 10 percent fee.

You will want an architect who shares your vision of a home, whether it's a Victorian, a sleek stone and glass contemporary, or a charming, compact Cape Cod. An architect whose portfolio consists of homes you cannot identify with is obviously not on your wavelength. Keep looking.

Talk with some architects in the area where you are looking. They know the land, the weather, and any eccentricities of that area better than one who lives far away.

If you do not know where to begin looking for an architect, contact the American Institute of Architects, 1735 New York Ave. NW, Washington, D.C., 20006, at ✆ (800) AIA-3837, or you can visit them at ✑ *www.aia.org* for more information. They can refer you to a few members in your area. Ask those you interview for references, of course, and drive around to those homes not only to see them but also to talk with their owners. Are they satisfied with the finished product?

Once you choose an architect, have agreed on an overall design for your house, and have the drawings and specifications, you need to solicit bids from the person who will build that house—the builder (sometimes known as the contractor).

The National Association of Home Builders can provide you with names of local builders. It is best to get price estimates from three builders, or even more, and do be sure they have at least five years' experience building homes (erecting shopping malls or condo complexes does not count here). Should you go with the lowest bid? Not automatically. The builder could have written in inferior materials or building practices that will give the profit he or she needs—at the expense of your house.

ALERT!

Check your local consumer affairs agency to be certain that the builder you are considering does not have any complaints lodged against him or her.

Just as you did with the architect, ask the builder for references and contact those people. Did their home come in on time? Was it on budget or close to it? Have any problems surfaced since they moved in? Did the builder fix them promptly?

Once your building project has begun, you can hire the architect to oversee the work, if you don't have the time to do it yourself, or if you are not familiar with construction yourself. He or she is likely to charge $100 an hour or so.

The architect's strength is conceptual—the look of the house, traffic flow, and so on. The custom builder's strength is technical. He or she knows which screw works better in which type of wood, for example. You can get an excellent custom-built home using either route.

The Custom Builder

This is an alternative to going the architect route. A custom builder, who does not have to be an architect—and indeed almost never is one—can "design" your home, to your specifications, on a computer and then construct it. When you are ready to go scouting for someone to construct your custom home, follow all the recommendations already listed for finding a builder.

Naturally, if you engage a custom builder, he or she will oversee the project as part of the job. Since your builder is also designing your home, the cost for those plans will be included in the overall fee.

Paying for Your New Home

A custom home follows a different financing path than that of a resale home or even a new development house. Typically, you need a lender to give you a construction loan that automatically becomes a mortgage when the home is completed.

In the past, the money you borrowed was released in stages to pay those working on your home. When the building was complete and everyone, including subcontractors and any others expecting a check, had been paid, the lender and local building inspector inspected the house and then gave you a certificate of occupancy (known informally as a "c of o"). Then you could move into your home. You repaid the money you borrowed to have the house built by taking on a traditional mortgage.

Now the process is simpler. Many lenders now offer what are called "combo" mortgages, where both construction financing and the permanent mortgage are rolled together into one loan package. In addition, the net value of the lot can often count toward the down payment.

Here are a few more points to consider:

- Do not make your home so unique that it will please only you. Every area of the country has tales of those homes—usually designed by their architect owners. They are startlingly unique and sit on the market waiting for a buyer, sometimes for years. Examples of such houses include a home built underground, a one-bedroom house, or anything else that strays very much from the more usual realty offerings in your area. (Generally, homes built in vacation areas—second homes—can be "one-of-a-kinders" more easily than those built in the more traditional year-round communities.)

- No matter how carefully you plan, your home is likely to take longer to build than you plan and cost more than you budget. That is a given.
- It's smart to have a real-estate attorney when building a custom-designed home.

New-Home Warranties

You will most likely receive a builder's warranty—usually a one-year protection plan—against problems with your new house. Like most warranties, these plans cover the house against structural defects and malfunctions of the working systems. However, if your builder goes out of business or is no longer on the scene for some other reason, you will be out of luck; your chances of being reimbursed for repairs will be practically nonexistent.

However, if you have an insured, independent warranty, you will still be covered. Such plans are usually ten-year policies written by an independent warrantor, for example, Home Owners Warranty (HOW). If anything goes awry with your builder, your claim—if considered a legitimate one—will be honored by those warrantors.

Try to secure both a builder's and an independent warranty. Chances are the builder will provide a one-year protection plan. But in the event he or she refuses to offer a warranty, you should purchase a policy on your own. A few hundred dollars is a small amount to pay to insure the proper functioning of a much larger investment.

You Can Do It!

Although from the onset building your own house may seem like a tremendous responsibility, and it certainly is, you *can* do it and enjoy the finished product with pride. It is not as difficult as you might think. Take your time to feel comfortable with the process. Building new is not any more difficult, and sometimes can be easier, than rehabbing a home. By building you can do your own space planning. You can choose your own finishes, like flooring, windows, colors, lighting, and fixtures. Take the step with care, and you will be amazed at what you will end up with. Ⓔ

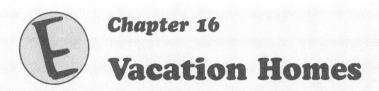

Chapter 16

Vacation Homes

A cabin in the mountains? A cottage by the sea? Do you dream of having your own place to spend summers or holidays each year? Buying a vacation home may be the way to go. Vacation homes are typically second homes, so you are probably already familiar with the steps involved in obtaining financing, site selection, and the many other issues that go into homebuying. Buying a vacation home will present some new issues to consider.

Is Owning a Vacation Home for You?

A vacation home is right for you in several cases: when you decide you can afford a second home, if you plan to spend quite a bit of time there, if you can obtain income from it when you aren't using it, and if you treat it as an investment that will appreciate with time.

FIGURE 16.1 Household Income of Second Home Buyers (1999)	
Annual income	**Percent of buyers**
Under $25,000	2%
$25,000–29,999	5%
$30,000–39,999	13%
$40,000–49,999	7%
$50,000–69,999	24%
$70,000–99,999	17%
$100,000–149,999	20%
$150,000 or more	12%

Source: *The 2000 National Association of Realtors Profile of Home Buyers and Sellers*

Let's start with the first point—affording a vacation home. If you put money away and know where you would like to spend your weekends, summers, winters, free time, retirement, then answering the question, "Can I afford this vacation home?" is an easy one.

FACT

According to the National Association of Realtors, the median income for second homebuyers in 1999 was $68,800.

Sometimes when traveling, people get caught up in the moment, and that's often the seduction of a second home or a timeshare. They may not put all the numbers together while they are vacationing and relaxing. But if you look realistically at your finances and you have the money, then a vacation home might be the ideal place for you to get away from it all and have peace of mind.

Check with your lender ahead of time in order to determine what they'll require in financing so that you're as prepared as you can be. You certainly want to consider the same factors that you did in buying a primary residence. You want to choose the place that is right for you and suits your needs. And this is a home that you should enjoy traveling to and being in— you don't want it to be a hassle or to create more work for you than it's worth. It's often been said that the two best days of owning a boat are the day that you buy it and the day that you sell it. Without proper planning, that could be the situation that you are in for a vacation home.

ALERT!

Lenders often require larger down payments for vacation homes than they do for a primary residence.

A wonderful time to buy your vacation home is in a down economic period. That's because the market for vacation homes drops in price in times when the economy is tight and other people aren't buying vacation homes.

"Why are you buying your vacation home?" is a great question to ask yourself. Will you have the time to enjoy it often, or is it something that you'll visit only twice a year? If you're acquiring your vacation home for occasional use, consider whether there's a way it can become a source of income during the times you are not using the property.

If the home you're interested in is near a ski resort, and you're planning to go there a couple of times a year, is there a real-estate agent who could rent it out and get you some income? Does it pay for you to acquire a multiunit property so that your units are always well preserved and you are receiving income from the tenant-occupied units? In choosing a vacation home an important question to ask yourself is whether this will limit your travel to other destinations. By having a vacation home, you may then feel obligated to use it year after year, instead of going to different vacation destinations. If you're the kind of person who likes to get up and go to different places each time you travel, then a vacation home may still make sense as an investment that will appreciate or as an income-generating property. These are all things worth considering as you decide whether owning a vacation home is right for you.

Benefits of Owning a Vacation Home

The benefits of owning a vacation home are obvious—it's a place to relax, it contains your own furnishings, you can keep everything you need there and avoid having to pack your bags each time you travel there (unlike going to a hotel or resort area). You know the area well (or will after visiting your vacation home a few times!) and, with careful planning when you buy, you'll see the value of your home go up over time.

Easy Travel

Many people like to have a vacation home within an hour or two of driving time from their primary homes. This allows them in any type of weather to get out of the city that they dwell in and find their haven close by. Others choose to have a vacation home in a warm-weather or tropical climate. Something that's easy to get to by plane, train, or automobile from where you live will allow a change of scenery during harsh winter months fairly easily.

ALERT!

Don't buy a vacation home solely for the appreciation you expect from the investment. Though it likely will appreciate, think of it first as a home where you will want to spend vacations.

Familiarity

Familiarity is extremely important to many people who own a vacation home. Many simply get in a car or board a plane for a long weekend without even packing a bag. Everything that they have and need—that extra set of golf clubs, tennis racket, and wardrobe—is already at their vacation home. Instead of having to get to a hotel, check in, and pay for meals at restaurants, you have in a vacation home a warm and friendly setting for yourself as the owner, your family, and your friends.

Estate-Planning Tools

As an estate-planning tool, vacation homes are a great way to gift property out of your estate by gifting percentages of ownership of property to your heirs. By gifting a percentage of ownership each year, you're gradually getting the home out of your estate, which will help decrease the taxes that will have to be paid on your estate upon your death. The appreciation of the home takes place within the estate of your children, grandchildren, or whomever you choose to have as heirs.

Obligations of Owning a Vacation Home

The obligations of owning a vacation home are the same as owning a primary home. Maintenance, repairs, and other expenditures are going to be *your* responsibility and no one else's. If you are renting out your vacation home, and you don't live fairly close by, make sure that you have a maintenance company available to handle any necessary maintenance and repairs for your tenants.

Never skimp on insurance. It won't save you money in the long run. Be sure to figure in the cost of insurance as you decide if a vacation home is affordable. You'll also need to budget in some money in reserve for maintenance and repairs that will crop up occasionally.

You'll need homeowner's insurance on your vacation home, just as you have for your primary residence. (See Chapter 19 for a discussion of homeowner's insurance.) You need to be protected against damages and destruction of property that may happen unexpectedly. Accidents can occur, and if you (or your renters) aren't at the property on a regular basis, you could be in for a nasty surprise on your next trip. Imagine that a pipe bursts while no one is using the home, that water floods the house, and that by the time you next visit the property, hundreds or thousands of dollars of damage has been done to the floors and furniture that have been sitting waterlogged for weeks. You must have insurance, not only for your dwelling, but for your personal property as well. And it's not a bad idea to have someone—you, your family, your friends, or your renters—visit the property on a fairly regular basis.

Types of Vacation Homes

There are many types of vacation home to consider. When you first hear the term "vacation home," it may be a single-family house that comes to mind. While this is certainly one option, there are other choices that you may find even more suited to your lifestyle.

Land and Farms

Land can be used in a number of ways to provide your vacation home. It is quite popular these days for urban dwellers to acquire farms within range of the city where they live so that they have a different environment from city life that they can get away to easily. But farms require the same kind of maintenance as any other property—with acres of grass that you have an obligation to mow and keep up. If you buy land on which you are capable of growing crops, you may offer a neighbor the chance to farm your land. Some people keep horses on their land as well.

Condos

Condominiums make nice vacation homes. That's because the condominium association or the town home association will provide maintenance for the common areas of the building or complex—leaving you one less thing to worry about while you're back at your primary residence. You won't have to deal with finding someone to shovel snow (if your vacation home is in a snowy area like a ski resort) or to mow the grass. They may often be capable of managing and leasing your property for you for a small fee so that you're retaining income during the months that you are not physically at the property.

If you buy a vacation home in a tropical area, make sure that you have a way to safely protect your home from damage from tropical storms and hurricanes when you are away.

Timeshares

Timeshares, or "vacation clubs" as they are now often called, are a very popular form of vacation home that offer the advantage of paying one fixed fee for the membership in the club, with the benefit of dwellings available to you the world over. A timeshare, or vacation club, works like this. You buy membership in the club, which guarantees availability of a certain type of property for a particular week every year. You can buy a week in California, for example, and return each winter to a sunny beach there. With a timeshare, you also have the option of trading your week with other members—you might trade your week in California for a week in Tahoe one year, if you like to ski. Some vacation clubs even offer time on a cruise ship as an option. Thus you have practically unlimited choices of destinations, all for the fixed price of membership in the club.

The many vacation clubs/timeshares that are available range from Hyatt, Marriott, and Hilton programs to the programs offered through the Walt Disney Company. When choosing a timeshare, read all of the materials carefully and be sure you fully understand what your obligations will be before signing on the dotted line. There are also agencies that sell resales of timeshare and vacation club memberships. You may want to do some research on the Internet for site locations, as well as visit local offices in prime vacation spots. You may find that you can get a better deal in a timeshare buying a resale than you can buying directly from the primary source of the vacation club.

Of course, with a timeshare you don't have the luxury of leaving your own things in the home year-round, but you do get access to great vacation homes without the obligations of owning a single-family house or a condo that you have to maintain from hundreds of miles away.

With a timeshare, you benefit by having the opportunity to go to different places or to return to your favorite place again and again.

Renting out Your Vacation Property

If you won't be using your vacation home for much of the year, you may be able to rent it out by the week or even by the month, especially if it is located in a popular vacation spot. Rental income is a good way to help pay your mortgage when the property would otherwise sit empty.

If you are buying a home with the idea of renting in mind, look for homes with features that will make the property more attractive to other vacationers. Multiple bedrooms and bathrooms will be a plus. The location will also play a large part in determining how much money you can command for it—something close to the town center or near the local tourist sites will have a lot of appeal to out-of-towners.

Check out Chapter 18 on landlording before deciding to rent out your vacation home. Many of the same issues apply here.

You will probably choose to use a local real-estate or property management company to handle the details of finding renters, collecting payment, housecleaning, and the like. This will make the process easier and more hassle-free for you. Typically, a property manager is paid some percentage—8 or 10 percent—of the rental price of the unit.

Your Future Residence?

You may be buying a vacation home with an eye to someday moving there permanently. Perhaps you plan to live there after you retire. This can be a wonderful option. If you expect to live in this house in retirement, there are a few things you might also want to consider as you search for a vacation home. These include the following:

- **Accessibility.** Are there stairs to climb, either to get into the bedroom or even to get into the front door? Is there a way someone using a walker or wheelchair can get in and move around easily within the home?
- **Neighbors.** Who will your neighbors be? Are they mostly local residents? Or will you be the only permanent residents, surrounded by tourists on vacation? What age groups do you see out and about?
- **Property taxes.** Of course it's hard to predict how much your taxes may go up, but keep in mind that you'll need to be able to cover these taxes even after you've paid off the mortgage completely. Will your retirement income be sufficient?

Buying a vacation home to enjoy as a retreat now and a primary residence later can be a smart idea. You'll have that much more to look forward to, when you can dream about living in your favorite vacation spot every day!

Chapter 17

E Other Real-Estate Opportunities

There are instances in which homes are for sale with no agent involved. You may buy a home through the seller directly ("for sale by owner," also known as FSBO), buy a distressed property, or buy a house sold at auction. Read on.

Dealing with the FSBO

As mentioned earlier, the "for sale by owner" (FSBO, pronounced "fizzbo") is a case in which the seller would like to maximize what he or she can get for the real estate. These sellers will not have access to a multiple listing service, they will not want to consult with a real-estate broker, and they're attempting to sell on their own. Statistically, between 80 and 90 percent of FSBOs convert to listings with realty agents. FSBO sellers often find that they need professional assistance in hitting a marketplace. The commission that they had wanted to save ends up being a fee well spent.

If you're dealing with a FSBO and you're unprepared, without the proper contracts, disclosures, or due diligence materials, and the FSBO is inexperienced, you may need to consult an attorney or another experienced professional to help you get the property under contract and take it all the way through the closing.

There are many advantages to working with an experienced real-estate broker. If you are working with one, and you are interested in a property that is a for sale by owner, have your broker contact the seller, and if the FSBO is not willing to pay your broker a commission, then you should do it. Pay your broker the 3 percent fee or whatever fee he or she would have earned during the period if they had been working for a seller as usual.

Distressed Properties

Distressed properties are houses and condominiums in which the owners have defaulted in paying their mortgage, property taxes, or water bills. Foreclosure procedures vary from one community to the next, between federal and local agencies, and between government-backed and private mortgage holders.

In the case of nonpayment of local property taxes and water bills, you can contact your tax collector or other public official who conducts the tax sales and ask about the next auction of those properties.

There are a few points you should consider when pursuing properties that are up for auction. For one, the owners of the properties sometimes manage to come up with delinquent payments and so save their homes before auction, even after their property has been publicly listed. Thus, some of the addresses you see on the tax collector's list will never actually go to auction. Also, most houses have mortgages, and mortgage lenders do not allow their properties to go on the auction block for unpaid taxes. They pay the taxes and foreclose on the property. Finally, this is a complicated arena for the neophyte. Ask your lawyer to explain city tax sales. You might indeed decide to forgo this type of house hunt for one that is less complicated.

After you see the list of distressed properties and investigate the addresses, contact your lawyer to see if you may be able to purchase the property directly from the owner, who is about to lose it.

The U.S. Department of Housing and Urban Development (HUD) also sells its foreclosures. These are the homes taken by HUD for the nonpayment of FHA-backed loans. Those homes and condos are usually sold through sealed bids. Would-be buyers send in their best offer to the office handling the sale, and the highest bid wins the house or condo. Financing is arranged through a conventional mortgage lender and insured by the FHA. Down-payment requirements can be as low as a few hundred dollars with some incentive programs. Buyers can finance up to 100 percent of the closing costs, including the initial mortgage insurance premium required by the FHA. Sometimes HUD helps with repair costs, too.

Many of these distressed homes will need work, to put it mildly. They may be damaged far beyond the definition of a "handyman's special," so get as much information as you can. However, you're likely going to be able to get a distressed home for a much lower cost than you could otherwise find. As one HUD spokesperson put it, "When you buy a house well below market price, you have to expect to put in some sweat equity." Look for words in ads indicating repairs that are required or for the term "handyman's special." These may indicate distressed properties that you can get for a bargain.

In the private sector, houses are also sold by banks that have taken them back for mortgage default. Contact the real-estate-owned (REO) department of any bank, and ask whether they have a list of their foreclosed properties. Some banks deal directly with prospective buyers for those houses; others turn them over to a local real-estate agency to sell for them. Start with the bank first.

If a lender is really eager to get rid of an REO property, it could make the mortgage financing very attractive, with a low (10 percent or sometimes even 5 percent) down-payment requirement and good interest rates. That's what make REO properties worth pursuing—not their sale price, which is usually no great bargain.

To find foreclosed properties, call the number listed on the advertisement in your area newspaper offering HUD homes for sale. Or phone your regional or field HUD office. (See Appendix C for those numbers.) In addition, you might get in touch with the Department of Veterans Affairs for their list of VA foreclosures. The Federal National Mortgage Corporation (Fannie Mae) has homes for sale acquired through foreclosure. You can call Fannie Mae at ✆ (800) 732-6643 during business hours, or visit ✎ *www.fanniemae.com* for more information.

Distressed properties come in two forms. The first is when they're physically distressed, that is, when they require repairs and maintenance to put them in order. The second situation is when the seller is distressed, oftentimes from illness or an excessive financial obligation, or a management headache, turning a very good and reasonable piece of property into a good buying opportunity for you. Remember, "One man's ceiling may be another man's floor." In other words, the limit of what someone else can handle financially may be perfectly acceptable to you.

Look at elbow grease or a handyman special as being something that will benefit you by allowing you to put what's called sweat equity—or labor you invest that results in improvements that increase its value—into the property.

ALERT!

Don't assume every distressed property is in bad physical condition. That is certainly the case in some situations, but it is not always true.

When you're dealing with banks, savings and loans, credit unions, or other institutional sellers, you may find that what you perceive as a distress sale is not always available to you. Why, you might ask, if a bank has foreclosed on a piece of property, did they not view the property as a distress sale? Oftentimes a lending institution will be able to afford to carry the real estate without having the property be a negative obligation. If that's the case, then the institution naturally wants to get a reasonable payback on their books after having made a bad loan.

Buying Houses at Auction

Some houses, not necessarily distressed properties, are sold through auctions. Real-estate auctions grew in popularity in the 1980s and today are fairly commonplace. Sometimes just one home is being sold, perhaps to close an estate. In other instances, the auction will include, for example, a number of condominium units in a complex in which the developer has run into financial problems.

Auctions have an allure; auctions are exciting; auctions let you buy at your price, and they may just be your opportunity to get into home ownership. Before attending an auction with the serious intent of buying a house or condominium, you should do some homework. Try to acquire all of the printed material on the sale that you can (known as the bidder's kit), and visit the homes that interest you. Auctions are conducted as each auction company sees fit. Some are very splashy indeed, with local high-school girls dressed as auction company cheerleaders, complete with pom-poms, going through several rounds of spirited cheers at each intermission.

When real estate is in an auction, that means that the seller needs instant liquidity, or, in other words, that the seller needs to sell the house and get the money right away. What that means for you as a buyer is that you should be prepared with your financing in place and ready to go on auction day. That may be difficult, since most mortgage lenders require an appraisal and a thirty- to sixty-day turnaround time for preparing their appraisal, but maintaining a credit line or a home equity line that will be available to you whenever you need it will make you successful with auctions. Certainly, having the cash available to buy your property outright is possible as well.

If possible, it may be helpful for you to attend a couple of auctions before the one you are interested in. This will give you a chance to see how real-estate auctions are conducted and for you to become familiar with auction procedures before bidding yourself. You will find fewer auctions in good economic times, and it only makes sense that you will see more auctions during tough economic times.

Sheriff's Sales

There are a variety of auctions and auction scenarios for you to explore. An auction takes place every business day in every city throughout the country. These sales, called sheriff's sales or judicial sales, are foreclosure sales of real estate whose owners have become delinquent.

How It Works

After a property owner has been delinquent on the mortgage, the lender and circuit court of the county notify the owner of his or her right to redeem himself or herself by making the mortgage payments to the lender with any penalties of interest. If the owner does not pay, then he or she is considered to be in default of the loan, and the property will go to a sheriff's or judicial sale. These sales, which are conducted in municipal buildings or title company's offices, are conducted by order of the circuit court. In cases of a sheriff's sale, a buyer is obligated in most cases to bring a cashier's check or a certified check to the auction sale for 10 percent of the price of the property that he or she will be acquiring. So if a property will be offered at $80,000, but you know that you'll bid to $100,000, you're going to need to have a cashier's or certified check for $10,000 with you.

Full payment will need to be made to the sheriff within twenty-four hours after the sale. Usually the sale also needs to be confirmed in front of a judge within the next two to four weeks, thus giving the defendant (that is, the owner who defaulted on the loan) in the case one last chance for self-redemption.

ALERT!

Do not bid at a sheriff's sale without having an attorney or another qualified individual give you all of the information that you need regarding the potential liability that you will assume by being the successful bidder at the sale.

You won't own the property or get a deed to the real estate until after the date of the sheriff's sale and the judge's confirmation of the sale.

What You Get

At a sheriff's sale, you are buying real estate "as is," oftentimes without seeing it and certainly not subject to liens on the title of the real estate. You need to know how to adequately inspect the title as well as the property and make sure that, by winning a property in a sheriff's sale, you're not assuming obligations to pay many years of back real-estate taxes, mechanic liens, or any other obligations that might go with the real estate.

Conventional Auction

A conventional real-estate auction is usually conducted with multiple properties. If you're dealing with an auction house—and there are many throughout the United States—you will more often than not have access in order to inspect the real estate prior to the sale, and you will also receive a bidder's package. A bidder's package will include a physical description of the property, a copy of the title report, survey, leases, and other financial information that will accompany the property contract you will be required to execute if your bid is accepted. This material allows you to become familiar with all of the financial and legal obligations associated with the real estate you're interested in. Then, all you need to concentrate on at the auction is how you want to bid.

People tend to think that bidding at a real-estate auction drives prices up. That certainly can be the case, but you may find that the bidding starts even lower than what they ask for an opening bid, depending on the marketplace. You never know how it will go.

What You Get

In a public real-estate auction, you will be required to buy the property "as is," with no obligations by the seller. Most times you will also be required to make this a cash sale, not contingent on a mortgage. Also, in a public real-estate auction, you oftentimes have more than a day to deposit the money required to close the real-estate transaction.

There are two golden rules at auctions. One is *caveat emptor,* or "let the buyer beware." The second is "as is, where it is." That expression means what it says. There are no refunds, exchanges, or adjustments to what you buy at the auction. (However, depending on the laws of the state in which you are buying, you might have the right to cancel your purchase within an allotted number of days following the sale.)

Review the information in the bidder's package carefully with an attorney. Know what you are bidding on!

Watch for the announcement of dates when prospective bidders can go through the properties that are being auctioned. Naturally, you should take a detailed look at any home that interests you. You can bring a house inspector or engineer with you, too, to give you an idea of any serious problems and the price for fixing them. Here are some things to keep in mind:

- Remember to keep the renovation expenses in mind when deciding what to bid.

- Be certain the house you want will be delivered vacant. Government-sold properties usually are, but other sales might not be.
- Ask about the title, too. Will you own the house free and clear? Check with the people at the administration desk at the auction, or ask in advance at the auction company or real-estate agency handling the sale.
- Ask in advance how the auction handles the actual buying of the homes. Some are strictly cash sales. You will almost certainly be required to pay some small amount of money in order to bid.
- Be sure you understand whether, if you are a winning bidder, you will be given an allotted time after the auction to secure financing or whether you must be preapproved before the sale.

ALERT!

Remember, you cannot blame a seller for not telling you the basement floods regularly. Keep this point in mind as you raise your hand or card to bid.

The Bidding Process

There are many attendants in the auction room to help bidders. They usually wear blazers imprinted with the name of the auction company or some other distinguishable outfit. Ask them any questions you have.

Pay very close attention. It will help if the property you want is not one of the opening two or three properties up for auction. That way, you can become familiar with the speed of the process before your prospective home comes on the block. Be very sure you are bidding on the property you want. With the speed of the proceedings, mix-ups can occur.

Once the auction starts, things move rapidly. There might be a few minutes of rest between house number nine and house number ten, but once the bidding starts on ten, it can be over in less than a minute. If you want number ten, you have to react speedily. There is no time to agonize over whether to increase your bid. The auctioneer's chant is also likely to be unfamiliar and distracting to the novice auction attendee.

You don't have to be the first bidder at the auction. Oftentimes, getting a sense of where the bidding is going before you raise your hand is an important feature to watch. Remember the winner at the auction is the last bidder—the last bidder becomes the owner of the real estate.

In some auctions, a hand signal shows your intention to bid; in others, you are handed a card with a number on it when you enter the auction room. You raise the card when you want to make an offer on a property.

Don't be shy. Speak up for the home you want, perhaps loudly if it's over an excited crowd. If you are concerned that you will not be able to speak up or that your reflexes are too slow for this speedy show, bring a friend who can do the bidding for you. Be careful that you do not get so carried away by the adrenaline-pumping proceedings that you overbid. Set a firm limit before the auction that represents your top offer for any property. You can arrive at that figure by comparison-shopping at similar homes for sale in the nonauction arena.

With some auctions that involve a few dozen properties, an on-site lender can offer good financing terms because that institution expects to finance a good number of homes sold during that sale. Ask about their terms, of course, but you should also shop around to see if you can do better.

The Best Time to Buy

The best time to buy property is really the time that you determine is a good time for you. That makes sense, right? There are always opportunities to purchase property. In the United States, there is always a distress sale somewhere. There's that real-estate auction and your neighbor having to move because of a job. All of these features create opportunities that you can't predict by looking in your crystal ball. You'll know when the best time is to buy; it might not even be a time when you're expecting to buy something. But if you sense that it is right, no one knows better than you.

Chapter 18

Is Landlording for You?

One of the best ways to ease yourself into a home of your own and into the beginning of what could be a profitable investment career is by purchasing a house that has rental space. Mortgage lenders will often take that rent into account when calculating your worthiness for a mortgage. The rent from your tenants could also pay a good deal of your housing expenses—perhaps your entire mortgage payment or maybe even mortgage and real-estate taxes.

Could You Become a Landlord?

If you're interested in buying a house with more room than you need—a two- or three-family home, perhaps?—you can rent out the extra space to help cover the cost of your mortgage. A landlord's success will depend on several things, of course, and there is a lot to know about the responsibility you'll be taking on.

Benefits of Being a Landlord

Having an apartment to rent can be a particular relief for those in less stable professions—those who are self-employed, for instance, those whose industry goes through major swings, or those whose job is otherwise subject to the vagaries of the marketplace. No matter what happens at your workplace, the rent check will be slipped under your door each month; there will be *some* money coming in.

There are other benefits besides the steady income. The repairs and new installations you make to that rental apartment are deductible from your federal tax return. The apartment's share of your repairs to the house as a whole—a new roof, for example—is also deductible. So if you live on two floors of the house, and the tenants live on one, one-third of the price of a new roof can be deducted.

Check with your accountant for the latest on tax deductions and on depreciation allowances. They are always changing.

Most real-estate investors start with small rental properties. From there, you could find yourself launched on a very profitable sideline or a full-time career as a landlord of several houses, maybe even small apartment buildings.

The Flip Side

On the other hand, here are some points to give you pause with this type of purchase. There will be people—strangers—walking around above or below you. If you have lived in an apartment building or a house converted to two or more apartment units, you are probably used to this and it may not bother you. Others may find it disquieting, for a while at least. But you'll adjust to it soon as it becomes an everyday part of your life.

Private homes that have been converted to two or three separate living units—the type of purchase that you will probably be seeking—do not usually appreciate as quickly in market value as single-family houses. They can also take somewhat longer to sell when you are ready to move.

What Being a Landlord Entails

Can you—should you—become a landlord? You will have to be just as responsible owning a two-family house as those landlords who run large apartment complexes would be. If something is broken, you must fix it—and promptly. *You* may be able to put up with a roof that leaks, because money is too tight for a roofer right now. But if the *tenants* are on the top floor, you will have to come up with the cash for repairs immediately. This is not just an ethical point. Tenants are entitled by law to premises that are habitable; any serious lack of repairs that leaves those renters without heat, light, or water, or with rain leaking in through a damaged roof, can result in a call to the local landlord/tenant enforcement agency and/or withholding rent.

Generally, those who own and live in buildings with three residential units or less (almost always houses that have been divided) are exempt from many local regulations that govern landlords of larger properties.

Smaller repairs are a different story. You do not have to drop everything to fix things that are not basic to the apartment and that do not contribute to making it fit for habitation. You can add minor repairs—an outlet that does not work anymore, for example—to your list and get around to them within a reasonable length of time.

If rent control is in force where you live, you will have to adhere to those regulations. Rent-control regulations are set by law, and they restrict how often you can raise the rent and by how much.

In a community with rent control, you may find yourself carrying Mr. Second Floor, who pays $200 a month for an apartment that could go for substantially more. In that event, be sure you count only on that $200 a month as added income and not on the higher amount you could charge if a new tenant were to move in. Mr. Second Floor could be there quite a while.

Some local laws protect the elderly from having to move when a new owner takes over a building. Be sure you are aware of what the laws are in your area.

If you buy a two- or three-family house with landlording in mind, you are entitled to ask for at least one unit (that is likely to be where the owner is living) delivered to you vacant. Have that point included in the sales contract.

Your local housing agency may say that a tenant living in the home with a lease is entitled to stay until his or her lease runs out. If there are no leases, you can ask that the whole house be delivered to you vacant, if you like, and you can start with new tenants. All of this is subject to local regulations, naturally. You may find you do not have carte blanche to do what you like just because you own the house.

Your state department of community affairs, your local property owners' association, or even your tenants' association can fill you in on your rights and responsibilities. Make the acquaintance of these folks before you start house-hunting for a rental property so that you do not sign on a dotted line and then learn about your restrictions.

Finding the Right Property

Finding the right house is extremely important. Your ability to rent the apartment in your house will depend on several factors. Is the house convenient to the downtown or perhaps to a suburban office park? Or to a college or university? Where will the tenants—and you for that matter—park cars? Does the house need so much work that paying for repairs through a home-improvement loan will cancel out a few years of rent coming in? (That is all right if you can do without profits for that time.)

FACT

An ad you take out in the paper to advertise for renters is tax deductible.

Several areas of the country are facing or are already in the midst of a rental housing shortage. Over the last several years, many developers have steered clear of new rental construction, preferring condominiums. Also, more renters are staying in apartments these days because they cannot afford to buy. Still, while this shortage is pronounced nationwide, it might not be true where you live.

It is best if the house you buy has a separate entrance for tenants so that they do not have to walk through any part of your apartment to reach their own. The only way you can discard that generally applicable standard is if you are buying in a college town (where houses are apt to be too expensive for the first-timer buying on a shoestring) or in a downtown, "hot" back-to-the-city market, where many people, especially the young single ones, are interested in living.

Are apartments in houses a rarity where you are because there are dozens of new rental complexes in your town? If so, you will be competing with features like waste disposals, bathroom exhaust fans, built-in microwaves, and the latest refrigerator models, features not found in most older homes. That's not to mention the pool, tennis courts, and clubhouse you almost certainly do not have! You will have a hard time finding tenants unless you are offering rents substantially lower than those of the glossier complexes or you have something special to offer. That could be a house in a historic district, with architectural features in your rental apartment not found in new construction, a home within walking distance of downtown, or some other special attraction that will make your place a particularly appealing place to live.

Ask yourself who your tenants are likely to be. Nose around a little during this stage. Read real-estate articles in your local papers, not just the advertisements. What is the rental situation like?

WORKSHEET 18.1 Should You Be a Landlord?		
	Can Do	**Not Me**
You can become knowledgeable about local rent laws and landlord/tenant relations.	☐	☐
You can be called at all hours of the day—and night— by a tenant with complaints.	☐	☐
You can (or can learn to) screen new tenants carefully.	☐	☐
You can afford to make emergency repairs to a tenant's apartment as they arise.	☐	☐
You can keep up with nonemergency repairs and general maintenance of the building.	☐	☐
You can complain to the tenants if they are being too loud or violating some other part of the rental agreement.	☐	☐
You can keep after a tenant who is late with the rent, perhaps seeing that problem through to an eviction.	☐	☐

Making Improvements

The tenant's unit does not have to be as nice as yours, but be sure it is nice enough to bring in the best rent you can command. Will it need much in the way of repairs? Can you make them, or will you have to farm out the work at high labor costs?

It is interesting what a few low-cost improvements can do to a rather boring apartment in an ordinary-looking house. Many a professional renovator has made a bundle by adding touches that resulted in higher rents than the average (and a nice, higher sales price when it was time to move on).

For example, when looking at the tenant's kitchen, consider new doors (and doors only) for bedraggled cabinets. You might add a mantelpiece to the living room, even if there is no fireplace (and even if there's no possibility of putting one in). The opening can be filled with a basket of flowers or greens. The mantel provides a focal point for the living room and is a very desirable decorative feature.

Keep wallpaper neutral and paint even more so. White is preferred throughout.

You might have the floors sanded if they are hardwood. That is often the flooring of choice these days. If the house is an old one, a medallion around the ceiling lighting fixture in at least one room can be added at low cost. Ceiling fans add an interesting touch, besides being practical and energy saving. All of these expenses should be included in your doodling as you walk through houses and estimate your fix-up costs.

Open for Business

Once you have closed on your two-family property, you probably will waste no time in fixing up the apartment and looking for a tenant. In fact, most homebuyers in your situation work on the tenant's unit before their own, to get that rental money coming in as quickly as possible.

QUESTION?

How do you calculate the amount of rent to charge?
You can check the classified advertisements in your local papers for an idea of what other owners are charging for similar apartments.

When you're deciding how much to ask in rent, remember that there are all sorts of variables to consider. For example, the apartment down the street may not be as fancy as yours, but it is only two blocks away from the grammar school, while yours is eight blocks away. That could make it worth more than yours, even though your unit may be larger or nicer.

You can talk to some local real-estate agents about rents. Some offices have in their windows index cards showing listings of apartments for rent, with pictures and prices. You are under no obligation to any real-estate agency. Most help as a service because they hope to secure your rental unit as their listing and, in the future, your house when you decide to sell. It pays them to be nice. Renting is often a sideline to their more profitable business of selling. If you do give a real-estate agent your listing, he or she will find you a tenant, usually at no fee to you. The tenant often pays the realty office.

ALERT!

If you're using a real-estate agency to rent your property, be sure that the agent checks references of prospective tenants. Some are in a hurry to conclude a deal and do not bother.

Would you rather run an advertisement yourself to find a tenant? List only your telephone number, not your name and not the address of the property, just its general area. Do put in the rent you are asking, along with a brief description of the apartment and the neighborhood. It is a pain in the neck for would-be tenants not to know the rent, and you will just be bothered by phone calls from the curious if you leave it out.

When calculating rent, remember to take into account what it will cover. Will the tenants pay their own utilities? That generally means water and gas or electric. What about the heat? Is the house metered for two units, or are you all on a master system? If you will have to pay some or all of these costs yourself, the rent should reflect that cost.

Dealing with Tenants

The first thing you'll need to do after placing an ad is prepare to screen the prospective renters who respond.

The Tenant Search

Screening tenants is not an aspect of landlording you will enjoy. Work up a form for each interested person to fill out with their name, address, phone number, number of years at their current address, previous landlord, employer, and number of years on the job (the self-employed should supply tax returns for the previous two years).

You are looking for a tenant who can afford your rent and whose current landlord has no gripes. Still, you cannot, in truth, count on a landlord's reference. He or she might be delighted to see a troublesome tenant move and so will tell you what a prince that tenant has been. References can be rather dicey these days, in any event, with employers, landlords, and so on being too worried about legal reprisals to say anything negative. General references are not going to be much help either. Who is going to list anyone they think will say anything bad about him or her?

Verify employment, at the very least, to be certain your tenant can afford your rent. Checking your prospect's credit report, while it may seem intrusive, can also tell you whether you are getting someone in a position to pay you each month or someone deep in debt. Look up "Credit Reporting Services" in the Yellow Pages.

Not allowing pets could be a hasty decision you will regret. Because some apartment complexes ban them and because many landlords will not allow them in their rental units, you stand to have a larger pool of applicants if pets are allowed. Try, if you can in your community, to secure a pet deposit of an extra $200 over your security deposit, or ask for a deposit that covers rent for, say, a month and a half. You will probably have to spend some money cleaning up after the tenants and pet leave, and you cannot count on using their security deposit because tenants often do not pay the last month's rent, saying, "Let my security deposit cover it." At least you will have the extra half month—or more if you can manage to get it.

A written lease is far better for you than a handshake. You can pick up a standard apartment lease from a stationery store or office supply center.

Fill in all of the blanks, even if it is with "NA" (for "not applicable").

You can add your own special clauses to a lease. For example, you might type or write, "Landlord permits this tenant to bring in his two cats, Tinsel and Doodad." That sounds better than just "pets allowed," which would allow your tenant to gradually acquire three dogs and four cats.

It is important to meet every potential tenant that is going to live in your building. Even if you depend on a rental service to find tenants, you should still take the time to meet your tenants.

Keep a Professional Attitude

Property ownership comes with its own pride. Certainly you as the owner think that your piece of real estate is a great place to live, and you feel strongly about its upkeep. How will you react if you end up with an irresponsible tenant whose carelessness causes damage to your property?

Even though you may be upset or angry, be careful to maintain a professional attitude and act in a strictly businesslike manner. Try to avoid foolish things like leaving threatening messages on voice mail; they will only come back to haunt you.

Be aware that when you are refunding security deposits, in every area of the country interest is usually required to be paid to the tenant, as well as on their pet and key deposits. Failing to pay this interest will put you in jeopardy with a local tenant bill of rights and sometimes require that an automatic penalty be thrust upon you at a multiple of their security deposit. Oftentimes a receipt must be enclosed if something has been deducted from their security deposit when your tenants leave the apartment and damage has occurred.

Handling Basic Maintenance Repairs

You will undoubtedly have maintenance-related issues to resolve. You have to tend to them in a timely fashion to hold up your end of the rental bargain and to keep your tenants happy. One big reason that people sell rental property is because they find the maintenance challenge too frustrating.

Preventing Problems

Doing preventive maintenance can help you avoid major problems, as well as giving you the luxury of doing it on your schedule, rather than having to drop everything to deal with a problem that occurs later. For example, consider having the sewer line cleaned up after you buy the home. One common problem is drains backing up and causing flooding in basements after a big rain. There is no way to know when or how often the previous owner rotted out the sewage line. Items like replacing the air filter in furnaces, oiling and maintaining furnaces, replacing batteries in smoke detectors, or even simply turning on stoves and water faucets in your building are things you can do to make sure they operate properly.

FACT

Many landlords use the Daylight Savings Time change each spring and fall as a standard reminder to do minor repairs, such as replacing air filters on heating units or refreshing the batteries in smoke alarms.

Working with the Tenant

Even if you have written into your lease that the tenant is responsible for taking care of certain maintenance items, don't count on its happening without some attention from you. Tenants don't care or have the experience to maintain your property. Some tenants will try to negotiate a lower rent in exchange for maintaining the premises. This has its pluses and minuses. According to many tenants' rights ordinances throughout this country, the burden of maintenance and repairs falls on the landlord. Oftentimes, a tenant will have the right, after written notification of a material defect, to repair an item and bill you or to deduct a portion of rent for their discomfort and dissatisfaction. One way to make small repairs less of a hassle is to have the tenant call in a repairman to fix the issue, then deduct the cost from their rent. That way, you don't have to be there, and the tenant (who *will* have to be there) will be able to explain the problem, which he or she is more familiar with than you are, to the repairman.

Be sure you can trust your tenants before leaving them responsible for making a repair. Otherwise, you are opening yourself up to being taken advantage of by tenants who abuse the situation. A tenant may claim she had trouble getting a repairman out to fix her electric stove and was unable to cook for two weeks, and therefore might claim that she should be reimbursed by you for two weeks' worth of restaurant bills from eating out! If something does go wrong, and you don't feel you should have to cover the costs that they want you to cover, you may still choose to work out some sort of compensation with them, if they are good tenants. You don't want to drive out tenants who pay their rent on time, and generally take good care of their unit, over something minor.

When negotiating with a tenant for some type of compensation for defects in the dwelling, remember that they will usually ask for less than you volunteer to give them. This is like any other type of negotiation, in which you should always have the other person speak first. Everything is negotiable.

Rental Property Is Like a Second Job

Buying your first property as a multiunit, living in one and renting the others, can be a great way to live inexpensively while saving up and earning equity. That will allow you to step up the ladder, either to other investment properties or to a single-family home, perhaps, that you could not have afforded without this type of investment. But remember that owning rental property is a business, and like every business it must be taken seriously. You must be prepared to screen tenants, do repairs, comply with municipal regulations, and assume other responsibilities. If you don't mind the second job, or if you see ownership and management as your future, landlording might be right for you! Ⓔ

Chapter 19

Protecting Your Investment

So, you say, *now* are we finished? Almost. Insuring your home is one crucial part of homebuying that will stay with you for the duration of time you live in your new home. You're making what is probably the largest purchase you've ever made—you don't want to take chances with losing that investment. So what do you need to know about homeowner's insurance?

The Importance of Homeowner's Insurance

Homeowner's insurance will protect you against both known and unknown perils that could wipe you out financially. Choosing homeowner's insurance is nowhere near as nerve-racking as negotiating to buy a home, signing up for a mortgage, or sitting through a closing. Lenders will not even consider offering you a mortgage if you do not have homeowner's insurance from day one. They aren't willing to take the chance on their investment. You will be required to make payments for as long as your home is in their portfolio. With many lenders, your mortgage payment will include homeowner's insurance and sometimes property taxes. If you buy the insurance on your own and let your policy lapse, the insurance company will send a copy of the cancellation to both you and your lender. Your lender could start foreclosure proceedings if the coverage is not reinstated quickly.

What Is a Homeowner's Policy?

As may remember from Chapter 14, which covered the subject of closing, shortly after your offer for a home has been accepted and the wheels start rolling toward the closing, you will need to start shopping for homeowner's insurance. You will be required to show your mortgage holder proof at the closing that you have purchased a homeowner's policy and have paid at least the first premium.

ALERT!

Insurance companies are given ratings by various research groups based on customer approval. Deal only with companies that have an "A" rating.

Do shop around for an insurance policy the same way you have for a home and a mortgage. Make some phone calls. Your real-estate agent may have a suggestion. Indeed, many realty agencies have an insurance branch within their office. By all means, speak to that person about coverage. You don't have to be concerned about conflict of interest here.

Get a couple of additional estimates, too. Rates and coverage vary, so shop around to see what your options are.

Varieties of Policies

The most basic homeowner's policy protects your home, shrubbery, trees, and outside structures from nearly a dozen perils, including fire, theft, vandalism, lightning, and windstorms. A broader policy adds another seven or so items, including protection against damage from frozen pipes, falling objects, and sprinkler systems—virtually everything but war, nuclear accident, floods, and earthquakes.

Standard homeowner's policies in any category also offer peripheral coverage for calamities befalling your home. For example, if you have to evacuate the house in the event of a fire or some other disaster, a typical policy usually covers living expenses.

Your Choice

Generally there are three packages, with HO-1 being the most basic and HO-3 the most comprehensive. Note that you are covered only for the misfortunes listed on your policy, so read the document carefully. Think, too, about the age of the home you are buying, its location— waterfront, for example—its siting, landscaping, and so on.

You may want to consider insuring your home for more than it is worth, since it would probably cost you more to rebuild it in the future. If you have a $100,000 home, consider insuring it for $150,000.

The standard homeowner's policy consists of coverage for 100 percent of the replacement value of your home (80 percent replacement value is the least you should consider). It is important that you secure replacement coverage, which is what it would cost to rebuild the home at today's prices. If you do not know what that cost would be, ask your insurance agent or call in an appraiser.

You should also have coverage for your personal belongings, as well as liability coverage to protect you if someone is injured in your home or on your property. The policy should not cover the land. After all, you can, in all likelihood, build on it again. Similarly, the foundation is likely to be there following almost any calamity, so do not insure that either.

There are many variations on the homeowner's package and limits to certain categories of coverage. Investigate them all. Given the variables of how much the carrier you select charges, the amount you are insuring your home for, and the extent of extra protection you want, you may pay anywhere from a few hundred dollars to over a thousand dollars annually in premiums. The average cost of a policy for a $100,000 house at an 80-percent replacement value is $350–$450 a year.

QUESTION?

Will your premiums increase if you file a claim?
Yes. And not only are they likely to increase, but also, depending on the amount and frequency of your claims, a company can choose not to renew your coverage, or to ask for the maximum rise in premium payments allowed by law.

On the Personal Side

Your personal possessions are also insured with a standard homeowner's policy when you insure the structure itself. That coverage also extends to those items when you are away from home and have them with you, in the event of theft or even loss.

The usual coverage for the contents of a home is 75 percent of the home's insured value. So a house carrying $150,000 worth of insurance will be covered by $112,500 for personal property, including furniture and clothing. That is for the standard actual cash value coverage, which deducts for depreciation. You will almost always have to pay extra—perhaps another 10 percent—if you want that property insured at full replacement value.

Then there is liability coverage to cover you in case someone is hurt on your property and sues you over it. Court awards for even relatively minor injuries that used to be $100,000 a few years ago now are as high as $300,000. And what if a guest incurs a serious injury while on your property? That could cost you even more. Thus, the $100,000 liability limit, which was common for years, has been increased over the last several years. You will probably find that for as little as an additional $20 to $30 a year in premium costs, you can raise your liability protection to $300,000 per incident.

The Umbrella Policy

You might also give some thought to an umbrella policy. This liability protection is a separate policy that picks up where both your homeowner's and automobile policies leave off. Umbrellas can cost about $200 annually for $1 million of coverage, going up to $250 or $300 for as much as $10 million. By all means look into this coverage, even if you do not have a home or lifestyle you think would warrant such protection. Guests tripping on stairs, the cleaning woman slipping on unshoveled snow that has turned to ice, or the postal carrier getting seriously bitten by your cute little doggy can all result in lawsuits. Umbrella coverage includes some libel protection, too, and it provides some coverage if an incident occurs while you are engaged in volunteer work. In this increasingly litigious society we live in, you might well want to consider an umbrella policy.

The cost of an umbrella policy will increase with the number of people covered under it as well as with the number of cars you own.

Special Valuables

Do you have a few pieces of important jewelry you want insured? Do you have some silver you value? Most policies will cover up to, say, $1,000 for loss of jewelry, furs, and watches and up to $2,500 for silverware. (Figures vary from one carrier to another and according to coverage purchased.) But there is often no provision for such special items as antiques, art, or valuable collectibles. They can be covered with the purchase of a personal articles floater, at an additional cost to you. Coverage applies whether or not the articles are in your home at the time of loss. It also includes damage or breakage, which is not covered by the standard homeowner's policy. Most standard policies provide coverage for original cash value minus depreciation. You can upgrade your coverage to include replacement cost, a far better protection for you. Before you decide just how big a floater you want, have those valuables professionally appraised.

What about the house itself? Do you feel it is worth more than the amount an insurer is willing to cover? Few starter homes are that lavish. Still, you might be buying a charming, detail-laden, old fixer-upper. Possibly there are certain features, built into the house when it was constructed perhaps more than a century ago, that are unique and cannot be duplicated today. The house might even be a designated regional, state, or national landmark. Replacement cost, using modern materials, could not bring that house back to its original state.

If you have a house with some historic or architectural distinction, you should first have the house appraised professionally before you approach an insurance agent or broker. You may have to shop around a bit for a policy that takes all of this into account. Insurers are wary of coverage above replacement value because of the fear of arson for profit. Still, finding the right policy is not impossible.

You can call the National Trust for Historic Preservation in the United States for guidance on insuring valuable historic homes. They are at 1785 Massachusetts Ave., N.W., Washington, D.C., 20036, ✎ (202) 588-6000, or visit them at ✎ *www.nationaltrust. org* for more information.

Still More Coverage

There are special insurance packages for still other calamities. The three most common are flood, hurricane, and earthquake coverage.

Flood Insurance

Flood protection does not come with a standard homeowner's policy. That fact can come as quite a surprise to a homeowner who hasn't read his policy carefully, until the day he finds 3 inches of standing water in his living room. Your homeowner's policy *is* likely to protect you against flooding that occurs, say, from a burst pipe in your home or from some other similar type of accident; but flooding from a storm or from storm drains around your property is *not* covered. For that you need a special policy. If you live in a particularly flood-prone area, your lender will require you to purchase this special protection. It runs about $150 to $200 for $85,000 worth of coverage each year.

Flood insurance is offered by the federal government, through the National Flood Insurance Program, administered by the Federal Emergency Management Agency (FEMA), 500 C Street S.W., Washington, D.C., 20472. If you have any questions, call that office at ✆ (202) 566-1600, or visit them on the Web at ✍ *www.fema.gov*. You can also purchase a flood insurance policy through most insurance offices.

ALERT!

If you want flood coverage, whether it is required by your lender or not, it is best to sign up when you buy your home. There is a waiting period after an application is taken, so you cannot buy a policy when you hear a big storm is heading your way and expect to be covered.

Hurricane Coverage

A standard homeowner's policy provides coverage for windstorm damage, and under that heading comes damage from hurricanes, tornadoes, cyclones, and hailstorms. If you live in a particularly dangerous locale for those storms, you can purchase a special windstorm insurance policy through an independent company or a statewide insurance pool. Florida, to take one example, has such a pool, offering windstorm policies to homeowners in some two dozen coastal counties in that state.

Earthquake Coverage

Earthquake insurance can be secured for a high fee and a high deductible. This is of particular interest to homebuyers in California, where news from seismologists is aired more frequently than folks there find comfortable. You can secure an earthquake policy from your homeowner's insurance agent, who must offer earthquake protection to Californians.

Insurance for a Condo or Co-op

These housing styles are each covered by two insurance policies. One policy is purchased by the owners' association or cooperative board for the entire building or complex, for which you pay a prorated share of premiums as part of your monthly maintenance fee. You purchase the other to cover your own apartment and its furnishings. There is a special insurance policy designed for condo owners and renters' insurance coverage for co-op residents.

Those individual policies are as important for you as insurance is for the master association to carry for common areas. If there is a problem in your unit, such as damaged carpeting from that ubiquitous burst pipe, you will need your own insurance coverage. The condo or co-op's policy will not help you.

How to Lower Your Insurance Costs

By keeping up with your policy and making changes when needed, you might be able to take advantage of special discounts. If you answer yes to any of the following questions, check with your agent or your insurance company to find out whether you qualify for lower rates:

- **Can you raise your deductible?** That is the amount of money you must pay before your insurance policy kicks in. Since insurance is meant to avoid terrible financial loss, why not absorb small losses yourself, saving anywhere from 12 to nearly 40 percent on some policies.

- **Have you purchased a home security system?** Again, you could be in for lower premiums, depending on the type of system you installed.

- **Are the residents in your home nonsmokers?** Some insurers offer to reduce premiums if a household does not smoke.

- **Have you stayed with one insurer for several years (the exact number is theirs to call)?** If so, you may receive special consideration. Some insurance companies reduce their premiums by 5 percent if you are with them for three to five years, and they might give a 10 percent discount if you remain a customer for six years or more.

- **Are you about to retire?** If so, you could get a break on premiums. Retirees are often charged less for homeowner's insurance because, it is assumed, they are home more often and apt to catch problems around the house before they blow up into full-scale catastrophes.

- **Do you qualify for a group rate?** Some employers, alumni associations, and business groups have worked out a plan with an insurance company that brings employees or members competitive rates. Ask your company's personnel director or the director of your alumni or business association.

- **Do you buy your homeowner's insurance and car insurance from the same carrier?** Some companies will offer you a 5 to 15 percent reduction in premiums on that two-policy package.

Shop around for the best terms and coverage. All companies are not alike. Making some phone calls to compare policies and rates can save you money. However, be sure you are comparing coverage, service, and price, not just price alone.

Keeping Track of Your Policy

You cannot afford to just pay the premiums each year and otherwise forget about your homeowner's insurance. Check your coverage annually, and update it periodically if housing prices rise and the replacement cost of your home goes up. If you have bought a fixer-upper and have done extensive—and expensive—remodeling, or if you have purchased new furnishings, check your insurance package. An inflation guard policy that automatically adjusts your plan each year to cover rises in building costs covers only inflation, so do not rely on that for total security. (E)

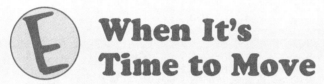

Chapter 20

When It's Time to Move

So you've done it! You've managed to get through the homebuying process successfully. Of course you are excited at the thought of moving into your new home. But you probably do not look forward to the logistics of getting from one place to another. Who does? Moving is always at least a little upsetting, sometimes downright traumatic. There seems to be so little time, so much to plan, so much to do—and so much money to spend.

Moving into Your New Home

This is an event that, like a wedding, depends on organization for success. Moving can be a mammoth production, with some folks badly needing a "cruise director" to take them in hand.

You might be concerned about how you will get along in your new home. Will the neighbors be congenial? Will you miss the friends or relatives you are leaving behind? Will you worry about those relatives? It is no wonder that on life-stress tests, moving is right up there with divorce, losing a job, and other major heart thumpers. Some 20 percent of us move every year. That's a lot of nerve-racked Americans.

Still, it does not have to be that difficult. The process can be broken down into three major steps: looking into the new community, taking inventory, and selecting a mover.

Looking into the New Community

You have obviously explored your new town, since you have purchased a home there. But even if your new town is near your present one, it is different, so do some armchair homework to become as well acquainted with it as possible before you arrive there.

The Newspaper

Subscribe to the Sunday edition of the newspaper in that community, if it is different from the one you read now. (Or check it out on the Web.) Reading the paper is one of the best homework steps you can take. It will give you an idea of jobs that are available and their salaries. You will see what nationwide store chains are operating in that community, and, in the social pages, you will become familiar with the names of schools and social and religious groups you may later want to join.

Perhaps more important, though, you will find in the news pages of that paper a sense of how the community functions, so you can hit the ground running when you arrive. You can get up-to-the-minute news on zoning or school battles, job downsizing, or an infusion of federal aid coming to perk up the place.

You can find the name, address, and circulation figures of any newspaper in the country by consulting the Gale Directory of Publications and Broadcast Media. It is in the reference department at most public libraries.

The Chamber of Commerce

Write to that office in the new town, too, or check out the local community on the Web. More and more communities and chambers of commerce have Web sites. Request information. They can send you reams of printed material that will round out your picture of the community. Ask for the "newcomer's package." You can also query them about any other matter of special interest to you, such as jobs in your field of interest, schools for those with disabilities, nearby golf courses, and the like. These folks are naturally going to be great boosters of the town, so keep their enthusiasm in mind when you are evaluating the package.

The State Department of Tourism

If you are moving to a new state, write to this office at the state capital, or check them out on the Web. You might do that even if you are just moving to another corner of the same state. Ask for material on your favorite sport or outdoor activity—for example, boating, camping, cycling, or visiting historic sites and state parks. It might be nice to know what fun activities are waiting out there for you, after the stress and fatigue of moving.

Taking Inventory

Now is a good time to take stock of all your belongings, from what is in the hall closet to what has been stashed in the corner of the basement for the past ten years. Decide what will go with you and what to either give away or sell. There is likely to be an initial reflex action to say to yourself or someone in your household, "Now is our chance to finally get rid of all this stuff."

"Stuff" can be pitched out in any number of ways these days. It will take a fair amount of organization on your part, however, to determine just what goes where. Make lists if that will help, or set aside certain parts of the house or apartment to hold items designated for sale or charity. Following are some of your choices for getting rid of things.

Charities

You can give unwanted items to Goodwill Industries, the Salvation Army, veterans' groups, or any number of other charities. Many will pick up at your door, saving you drop-off time. It is important to contact those organizations in plenty of time; do not wait until moving week. They may schedule furniture pickups only on certain days of the week, or they may not want what you have to offer.

Classified Ads

Sell unwanted items through classified advertisements in your local paper or through notices tacked up at supermarkets, social centers, the library, and so forth. Again, place the ad with enough time to sell the items before moving day.

Garage Sales, Yard Sales, and Tag Sales

Whatever you call it, you can hold one of these, too. They certainly prove the maxim that one man's trash is another's treasure. The success of any sale depends in large measure on where you live, when you hold the sale, and how well it is publicized. If you can band together with others on your block or in your building, the sale becomes that much more attractive to would-be buyers. Naturally, you should choose a season when the weather is good and hold the sale on a weekend. Interestingly, it has been found that some holidays attract garage sale buyers (Memorial Day, Independence Day, and Labor Day), while others do not (Mother's Day, Father's Day). Many moving companies publish booklets on conducting sales; the booklets provide information about arranging stock, pricing, publicizing the event, security precautions, and so forth. Ask your mover.

You could also hire an individual or company to run a tag sale for you. This takes the work out of your hands entirely and can be useful if you do not have the time to become involved, if you are not sure of the value of your things, or if you feel so attached to some items that you break down at the thought of seeing them carted down the driveway by someone else. (Tag sale operators prefer owners to be away from the house on the day of the sale, to avoid just that emotion.) Not every community or region has an individual who conducts tag sales; but if such a person exists in your community, his or her fame is usually spread by word of mouth.

A tag sale operator will inventory your furnishings, price them (calling in an appraiser if necessary), arrange them in the most attractive setting, publicize the sale, and run the operation on sale day, bringing in assistants if necessary. The fee can range from a flat daily fee to a percentage—usually 25 percent—of the sale's income.

Auction

You can call in an auctioneer. You might, in fact, want to reread Chapter 17 to get a feel for the auction milieu.

The work is taken out of your hands. The auctioneer can be particularly helpful if you have objects that need appraising or if you have expensive collections. The fee can be a flat rate or a percentage of the day's sales. You might want an auctioneer if you have valuable art, china, or collectibles and want his or her services just for that collection.

FACT

More and more people are using Web sites like ✍ *www.ebay.com* and ✍ *www.yahoo.com* to sell goods over the Internet. You will need either a digital camera to photograph your stuff or a scanner so you can scan prints of the items you're selling. You will have to pay for the service and pay a fee when you sell and pack and ship the item, but it can be amazingly profitable (and easy!) to sell things over the Internet. Each Web site will give you a tutorial on how to use the site.

Storing

Then there is self-storage. You have probably seen these one-story complexes along major highways; such facilities have grown in number over the last couple of decades. They appear to have replaced, in number and in popularity, the old, several-stories-high warehouse.

It works like this. You lease space on a month-to-month basis in buildings like those one-story complexes or, in a city, in multistory buildings. Rental space is broken into a few dozen or a few hundred storage cubicles. You can expect to find a wide range of charges across the country. But broadly speaking, you can rent a small 5' x 5' cubicle for around $40 a month, while a 10' x 10' storage space rents for around $75 a month. Some units are quite sizable—24' x 26', for example—and rent for several hundred dollars a month. Check to see what kind of insurance the facilities offer, and look to see if your items are covered in your existing homeowner's or renter's policy.

In some buildings, you are given twenty-four-hour access to your belongings; other facilities have set hours. Just about everything but hazardous and combustible materials can be stored, and most facilities understandably frown on food kept in cubicles.

So if you are moving from a large to a small space and cannot bear to part with items that won't fit into the new place, consider self-storage. Besides furnishings, you can stash out-of-season clothing and sports equipment, holiday decorations, luggage, and porch and patio furniture. Newer units are climate controlled, so there is no need to worry about dampness or mold.

One of the most popular aspects of self-storage in suburban locales is that in those one-story buildings, you can drive right up to the door of your unit any time of the day or night. Your belongings are easily accessible, probably more so than in a full-fledged warehouse.

Finally, you can store items you will not need in a warehouse, if there is one around your area. In some locales you can still find great big barns in cities or along major highways that are used for storage. They are used, for example, by people storing estate furnishings or by those going abroad for a period of time and needing to store a whole household's worth of furnishings.

Before You Go

Here are some things that you will need to do before your move:

- Contact your local utility companies to disconnect any services as well as to arrange for services in your new home.
- Transfer checking and savings accounts if necessary.
- Provide change of address notices as appropriate to your local post office; magazines; credit card bills; children's school records; financial, medical, and dental records; as well as to your family and friends.

Selecting a Mover

If you are twenty-three years old and are moving the contents of your studio apartment to a condominium across town, you may decide to hire a truck or van for a few hours and do it yourself or with a couple of brawny friends. If the truck costs $25 to $50 or so an hour and you take the guys out for beer and pizza afterward, your moving expenses could come in under $100.

Or you can hire the van and a couple of brawny fellows who come with it. Their charge might be $40 to $75 an hour, depending on where in the country you are. This, too, is quite a bargain if you are not moving an eight-room house across three states. The fellows are not likely to supply you with boxes and other packing materials, though.

FACT

You could also box up your items and ship them by mail to your new home. You take more risks with this method, but it may be significantly cheaper than more conventional moving methods.

If you want to rent a van from one of the national companies and drive it yourself to your new location, you can expect to pay—again, depending on a number of factors—a few hundred dollars. These trucks come in a variety of sizes.

If you are moving an eight-room house or if you are perhaps a tad older than twenty-three, you should probably hire a moving company. You should know a couple of things before you pick up the phone: first, that moving can be very expensive, and second, that the field has its share of charlatans. You do not want to wind up with an overinflated estimate, or a no-show mover, or one who seems to drop every carton marked "Fragile."

Expect to pay anywhere from $500 to over $1,000 for a local move with a moving company. An interstate move can run from around $3,000 to $10,000 or more. (The price is significantly bumped up if you have them move a car or two.)

Which Company?

That's a good question. You have a choice of local movers in your area or the large nationwide companies. Naturally, you should check any mover you select with your local consumer protection agency.

It is smart to get estimates from three movers. When you call, a representative from that carrier will come to your home to look over what you plan to move and give you an estimate.

To keep kids upbeat about a move, give them materials from the chamber of commerce of the new town and let them plan the first sightseeing tour once you get to the new place.

For short, intrastate (within the state) moves of fewer than 40 miles or so, the estimate can be an hourly rate or based on cubic footage of the goods. The charges for interstate (from one state to another) moves are based on the weight of the goods and the distance the movers will travel. Be certain you give each mover the same information about what is going and what you are leaving behind so that you can accurately compare the figures you are given. Too much changing your mind only confuses everyone, including you—and adds more expense to the move. To be really on top of things, have all your goods inventoried before the estimators pull up.

Some companies will offer you a binding estimate, which means that estimate is the cost you will be charged. With others, the estimate is just that, and the final charge can—and probably will—be higher. If you are given three binding estimates, the choice is then a personal one, unless one mover offers more auxiliary services than another—some free cartons, for example, or packing paper.

ALERT!

Pack boxes and a suitcase of essential items that you will need for your first few days, including clothes and necessary kitchen and cleaning supplies, and keep these with you. It may take a few days for the movers to get your stuff to your new place if you are moving very far.

What if you get two binding estimates and one nonbinding one? Sometimes the binding estimates are higher, just because they are binding. The nonbinding one may be a better deal for you if it is lower and if you are sure you have told the mover everything that will be going along. If on moving day you add a few more items, especially heavy ones, your cost will increase. Adding items on moving day to a *binding* estimate may throw the movers for a loop, causing delays, more paperwork, and additional charges.

Timing

Moving companies are busiest in April through October, with business peaking between June and September. That is because so many families move after the kids have finished the school year and before they start again or enroll in a new school.

On moving day, make sure that someone is there to meet the movers, indicate which items are to be loaded on the truck, and check that everything is done correctly.

Movers overbook during their peak season to make up for the slack from the remainder of the year. This practice can, of course, leave you cooling your heels and waiting for a van on one end or the other some fine August day. When looking over and signing the company's documents, remember that oral promises on pickup and delivery dates mean nothing. Get everything in writing. A growing number of carriers, especially the larger ones, offer payments for each day that their trucks are late. If you must move during the peak season, try to give the carrier as much notice as possible—sixty days is not too much notice.

Liability

Moving companies are required to assume liability for the value of the goods they transport. However, there are different levels of liability. Make sure you know how much protection you are purchasing from the carrier you choose. To ensure the most hassle-free as well as the least costly move possible, follow these eight rules:

1. **Watch what you purchase from the mover.** For example, you can easily skip paying for their boxes. Pick up ordinary cardboard cartons for free at the supermarket (you may have to tape them back together with strong mailing tape, as most of those boxes have been folded after their contents have been emptied). Other good bets for sturdy boxes include liquor stores and office supply centers. For packing dried or silk flowers, haunt florists for those long, slender boxes in which fresh flowers are delivered.

2. **Keep an eye on the movers' packing, if you're having them do it.** A common practice is "short" or "balloon" packing—putting too few objects in large boxes and stuffing the boxes with paper. All of that extra weight adds to your bill.

3. **Be sure to observe the weighing of the goods, since that will determine your final cost in long-distance moves.** "Weight-bumping"— weighing goods in a truck that is already full with dollies, pads, and even a couple of men—is not rare.

4. **Call if your mover is one day late showing up.** Believe it or not, some folks wait weeks for the carrier. Sure, most moving companies will reimburse you for hotel/motel costs and a percentage of food bills if late delivery is their fault, but who needs the aggravation? And they will not pay if you have to rent furniture while you are waiting.

5. **Stay with the movers all the way, if you can.** If not, at least have someone at either end looking out for your interests.

6. **Even if the movers offer some form of liability protection for your goods, look into extra coverage.** Check your own homeowner's insurance policy.

7. **Do not sign any receipt when the movers arrive at your new home until you have examined at least the most important of your furnishings.** On the receipt, you can note any damage and add something like "approved subject to unpacking boxes." Remember, if anything goes terribly wrong, your words on that receipt may be all you have to document your case. Get a copy of that receipt from the mover.

8. **If you are moving either to or from a cooperative or condominium building, check for rules that restrict moving to certain days of the week or within certain hours.**

ALERT!

If you are planning to move valuables such as art and antiques, you should call the valuables to the attention of the mover to be sure of adequate coverage. Check your homeowner's insurance policy, too, to see if it, or any special endorsements to it, mentions coverage during a move.

With most companies, any dispute that arises that cannot be settled between you and the mover will be settled through binding arbitration. That means both you and the mover must go along with whatever decision the arbitrator reaches about your problem. The mover will provide you with a booklet describing the arbitration procedure. The arbitrator's word is final.

The Corporate Move

If your company is relocating you, they are likely to help you every "state" of the way, monetarily and service-wise, or at least pay for the move. In addition, depending on the state of the national economy, corporations are likely to compensate employees for the difference in mortgage interest rates between their old and new homes for at least three years and to buy employees' homes or reimburse employees for the cost of selling those houses. Company benefits depend not only on the condition of the economy but also on whether the employee is transferred from a relatively low-cost community to a higher-priced one and, to some extent, on intangibles such as the value of the employee and the desirability or undesirability of the new locale.

FACT

There were some 300,000 corporate moves nationally in 1996, according to the Employee Relocation Council (an umbrella group of corporations that move their employees).

Many corporations offer career-counseling services for spouses in the new locale, for which they pick up the tab. They also sometimes have relocation agencies help the employee's parents or in-laws find housing there so that they can come along as easily as possible. More than one relocation agent these days is asked to find a house for the transferee as well as an apartment for his mother and one for his mother-in-law in the new locale.

All of this is mentioned so that you can see what some businesses are doing, how much you can ask from your own, and what you can reasonably expect to receive. The bottom line here is to ask. Relocating is expensive and is likely to cost you something, no matter how much of the tab the corporation picks up. But you may find the company that's transferring you willing to pick up the bulk of your expenses and contribute in any other way to an easy transition.

Relocation Companies

Relocation agencies come in all sizes and descriptions and can handle a variety of chores connected with a corporate move. Most large realty firms have a relocation arm, although the size of that unit varies. When it comes to private relocation companies, some specialists may be a one-person shop, operating in a small community that sees a lot of turnover of transferees. Such individuals work on a freelance basis for one or two large companies in the area.

The relocation company first talks to the transferee, at the request of the transferee's corporation, to learn his or her needs in the new community—for example, neighborhood, size and style of housing, nearness to schools, housing budget—so that it can put him or her in touch with real-estate agents in the new town. The relocation person spells out company benefits and policies regarding moves and explains the tax picture, too. He or she introduces the employee to the community—its cultural attractions, educational facilities, shops, and the like—and in general helps make the whole experience for the transferee run as smoothly as possible. The employee's corporation pays for all of this hand-holding.

Some companies immediately turn over the transferred employee to one of these agencies. Others provide those services in-house and so have no need of an outside company.

If your employer leaves you pretty much to fend for yourself in a move (perhaps just reimbursing you for your expenses), you should know that the larger relocation companies work only through corporations. They don't take on individual clients. That may not apply to the very smallest, one-person outfits, however.

To inquire about individual representation or if you have any other questions, you can call the Employee Relocation Council, 1717 Pennsylvania Ave., N.W., Suite 800, Washington, DC 20006, (202) 857-0857 or visit *www.erc.org* for more information.

To find an agency willing to take you on individually, check the Yellow Pages under "Relocation Services." You should investigate, at least minimally, any company you are thinking of engaging on your own by checking with your local consumer protection agency and Better Business Bureau. Ask the company or individual for references, and then call those people.

If you are paying, costs for a relocation service will vary. A specialist may charge you a flat fee for one day's or two days' work, or it may be an hourly fee or a package charge for however long it takes the expert to see you settled in. Most spend ten to fourteen hours with a client.

What You'll Need the First Days

Here are the basics you will need for the first couple of days in your new home. Pack the items in a carton and take them with you in your car. If it's more than two boxes, label each clearly for contents so that you can get to items easily, such as the following:

- Facial tissues
- Bed linens
- Towels
- Work clothes/loungewear/nightclothes
- Personal items (toothbrush, razor, and so on)
- Tool kit
- Extension cords
- Shelf liner
- A lamp or two
- Light bulbs
- Plastic trash bags
- Disposable plates, cups, utensils
- Aluminum or plastic wrap
- Can opener
- Soap, sponges
- Pots and pans
- Paper towels

If you have a pet, don't forget food and water bowls, pet food, cat litter, a litter pan, and a few favorite toys. Also, you might want to bring, for example, floppy disks for a computer project, or other items you would feel better about having with you rather than with the movers.

Settling In

Here are a few things you may want to do when you get to your new home:

- Arrange for automobile license and registration, if that is necessary, in your new town or state.
- Check to see if there is a professional organization in your career field or a branch of your alumni association. You might also look into religious, social, charitable, or sports groups that interest you. There is very likely a newcomer's club, too (check for meeting announcements in the local paper). And how about school—either working toward a degree or taking adult education courses? Join something. It's the only solution to feeling lonely in a new town.
- Some moving companies offer settle-in services to make the newcomer feel more at home. Sometimes that service consists of a flyer with the names and phone numbers of doctors, hospitals, child-care services, and the like.
- Entertainment books are published for many cities and towns around the country. They are filled with coupons for discounted restaurant meals and local attractions. The coupons will get you out and sampling the local scene. The books cost between $25 and $45, depending on the locale. To see if there is one for your new town, call Entertainment Publications at ✆ (800) 445-4137.
- If you are moving to a development or complex that has an owners' association meeting or social events, by all means go as soon as it is possible. These people are not just your new neighbors; they are potential good friends. Ⓔ

Appendices

Appendix A
Glossary

Appendix B
Mortgage Tables

Appendix C
Resources

Appendix A

Glossary

a

abstract of title. A synopsis of the history of a title, indicating changes in ownership and including liens, mortgages, charges, encumbrances, encroachments, or any other matter that might affect the title.

acceleration clause. A stipulation in a mortgage agreement that allows the lender to demand full payment of the loan immediately if any scheduled payment is not made by a given date.

access. The means of approaching a property.

acre. A measure of land. One acre equals 43,560 square feet or 208.71 feet on each side. A builder's acre is generally 200 by 200 feet.

addendum. Something added. In real-estate contracts, a page added to the sales contract. It should be initialed by all parties concerned.

adjustable-rate mortgage. A home loan whose interest rate changes periodically over the course of the loan.

agreement of sale. A written agreement by which a buyer agrees to buy and a seller agrees to sell a certain piece of property under the terms and conditions stated therein.

amenities. Features of a property—pool, clubhouse, tennis courts, and the like—that make it more attractive to a buyer (or renter).

amortization. Prorated repayment of a debt. Most mortgages are being amortized every month that you make a payment to the lender.

appraisal. Procedure employed by a disinterested professional to estimate the value of a piece of property.

appurtenances. Whatever is annexed to land or used with it that will pass to the buyer with conveyance of title, for example, a garage.

as is. A term used in a contract to mean that the buyer is buying what he or she sees as he or she sees it. There is no representation as to quality and no promise to make any repairs.

assessed valuation. An evaluation of property by an agency of the government for taxation purposes.

assessment. Tax or charge levied on property by a taxing authority to pay for improvements such as sidewalks, streets, and sewers.

assumption (of mortgage). Buyer taking over seller's old mortgage at the interest rate and terms of that original mortgage.

b

balloon mortgage. A home loan that requires a lump sum payment of principal at some specified date in the future (perhaps five or seven years).

bleedout. A term indicating that effluent from a septic system is rising to the surface rather than draining into the earth.

bona fide. In good faith, without deception.

bridging. Usually, crisscrossed pieces of wood wedged between supporting beams. They reinforce the beams and distribute the stress.

builder's warranty. A written statement by a builder assuring that a dwelling was completed in conformity with a stipulated set of standards. The purpose is to protect the purchaser from latent defects.

building codes. State or locally adopted regulations, enforceable by police powers, that control the design, construction, repair, quality of building materials, and use and occupancy of structures, all falling under a specified government agency for enforcement.

c

capital appreciation. The increase in market value for a property beyond the price you paid for it.

capital gain. The portion of your taxable profit realized on the sale of real estate that is not taxed at your ordinary income tax rate.

cash flow. The dollar income generated by a rental property after all expenses are met. Negative cash flow occurs when expenses generated by a property exceed its income.

caveat emptor. A Latin phrase meaning "let the buyer beware." Legally, however, in virtually no state is the law of caveat emptor still in effect.

certified check. Payment that is guaranteed by the bank upon which it is drawn. A certified check is usually brought by a buyer to a closing to pay those costs.

chattel. Items of personal property, such as furniture, appliances, and lighting fixtures, which are not permanently affixed to the property being sold.

circular pump. The pump on a hot-water furnace boiler that moves the water through the heating pipes and radiators.

closing. The meeting of all concerned parties in order to transfer title of a property.

closing costs. Expenses over and above the price of the property that must be paid before title is transferred. Also known as settlement costs.

cloud on the title. A defect in the title that may affect the owner's ability to market his or her property. That could be a lien, a claim, or a judgment.

commission. Payment given by the seller of a property to a real-estate agent for his or her services. Usually paid at the closing.

common facilities. Areas in a condominium, cooperative, mobile home park, apartment building, or private home association shared by all residents. Examples of common facilities include hallways, grounds, laundry room, parking facilities, swimming pool, and golf course.

condominium. Housing style where the buyers own their apartment units outright, plus an undivided share in the common areas of the community.

consideration. Anything of value but usually a sum of money. A contract to buy property must have a consideration in order to be binding.

contingency. A provision in a contract that keeps it from becoming binding until certain activities are accomplished. The buyer's securing a satisfactory mortgage is often a contingency to a sale.

contract. An agreement between two parties. To be valid, a real-estate contract must be dated, must be in writing, and must include a consideration, a description of the property, the place and date of delivery of the deed, and all terms and conditions that were mutually agreed upon. It must also be executed (signed) by all concerned parties.

convey. To transfer property from one person to another.

conveyance. The document by which title is transferred. A deed is a conveyance.

cooperative. A housing style where buyers purchase shares in the corporation that owns the building. The number of shares varies according to the size of the apartment unit being bought or sometimes its purchase price. Tenant-shareholders have a proprietary lease that gives them the right to their units.

d

deed. A written instrument that conveys title to real property.

default. A breach of contract or failure to meet an obligation. Nonpayment of a mortgage beyond a certain number of payments is considered a default.

depreciation. Gradual loss on paper in market value of real estate, especially because of age, obsolescence, wear and tear, or economic conditions.

discount. See *point.*

down payment. Your initial cash investment in purchasing real estate, usually a small percentage of the sale price.

duplex. A two-family house or an apartment unit that takes up two floors.

e

earnest money. Sum of money, as evidence of good faith, that accompanies a signed offer to purchase. Rather than cash, it is almost always a personal check, certified check, or money order.

easement. A right of way or access. The right of one party to cross or use for some specified purpose the property of another. Water, sewage, and utility suppliers frequently hold an easement across private property.

eave. The extension of a roof beyond the walls of a house.

efflorescence. White, fuzz-like powder that forms on basement walls when moisture is present behind the walls.

effluent. Treated sewage from a septic tank, usually 99 percent water.

eminent domain. The right by which a government may acquire private property for public use without the consent of the owner but upon payment of reasonable compensation.

encroachment. A building or part of a building that extends beyond its boundary and therefore intrudes upon the property of another party.

encumbrance. A right or restriction on a property that reduces its value. That might be a claim, lien, liability, or zoning restriction. The report of the title search usually shows all encumbrances.

estate planning. Orderly arrangement of assets (including a home) and a plan for conveying them to heirs and others in a way calculated to minimize taxes and delays.

estate tax. Federal and state tax on the transfer of wealth upon death.

equity. The value an owner has in a piece of property exclusive of its mortgage and other liens.

escrow. Money or documents held by a third party until specific conditions of agreements or contracts are fulfilled.

escrow account. A trust into which escrow moneys are deposited and from which they are disbursed. Both lawyers and real-estate brokers can maintain escrow accounts.

exclusive agent. A real-estate salesperson with the sole right to sell a property within a specified period of time. The property becomes an exclusive listing.

exurbia. Semirural area just beyond the suburbs.

f

fascia. A flat horizontal board enclosing the area under the eave.

FHA. Federal Housing Administration, an agency within HUD (see listing) that insures mortgages on residential property, with down-payment requirements usually lower than the prevailing ones on the open market.

fixed-rate mortgage. A home loan whose interest rate is set at the time the loan is taken out. The rate remains the same throughout the entire life of the loan.

fixtures. Items of personal property that have been permanently attached to the real property and are therefore included in the transfer of real estate. For example, the kitchen sink is a fixture.

flashing. Material used at roof angle changes or joints to prevent leaking.

flue. The passageway in the chimney through which smoke rises to the outside air.

FmHA. Federal Farmers Home Administration, an agency of the U.S. Department of Agriculture that insures home loans in rural communities.

foreclosure. Legal proceedings instigated by a lender to deprive a person of ownership rights when mortgage payments have not been made.

FSBO. Stands for "for sale by owner" (pronounced "fizzbo").

g

gentrification. Process whereby private or government-sponsored development in certain neighborhoods, usually inner-city ones, results in the displacement of low- or moderate-income families by those in higher income categories.

GI loan. See *VA loan*.

girder. A main supporting beam of the house.

grace period. An allowed reasonable length of time to meet a commitment after the specified date of that commitment. For example, most lending institutions allow a two-week grace period after the due date of the mortgage payment before a late fee is imposed.

grade (or grade level). The line of the surface of the ground.

h

housing code. Local regulations setting forth minimum conditions under which dwellings are considered fit for human habitation. A code guards against unsanitary or unsafe conditions and overcrowding.

HUD. U.S. Department of Housing and Urban Development, from which almost all of the federal government's housing programs flow.

i

index. The base figure used to determine the interest rate charged on an adjustable-rate mortgage.

installment payment. The periodic payment (usually every month) of interest and principal on a mortgage or other loan.

installment sales contract. A sales contract for property in which the buyer receives possession of the property but does not take title to it until he or she makes regular installment payments to the seller and fulfills other specified obligations. Also called a land contract.

interest. A fee paid for the use of money.

intestate. Dying without a valid will. The state then designates beneficiaries to receive the deceased's income and assets.

j

joint tenancy (with right of survivorship). Property ownership by two or more persons with an undivided interest. If one owner dies, the property automatically passes to the other(s).

joists. Beams that rest on the outer foundation or walls to support the boards of a floor or ceiling.

l

lally. Column. A steel column filled with concrete that supports a girder or sometimes other floor beams.

land (raw). Land available for building but lacking utilities or improvements such as electricity, roads, and water.

leader. A downspout or vertical pipe that drains water from a roof.

lease/purchase option. Opportunity to purchase a piece of property by renting it for a specified period, usually one year, with the provision that you may choose to buy after or during the leasing period at a predetermined sale price.

leverage. The effective use of money to buy property by using the smallest amount of one's own capital that is permitted and borrowing as much as possible in order to obtain the maximum percentage of return on the original investment.

liquidity. The speed at which an investment can be converted to cash. For example, there is little liquidity in a house, but shares of stock can ordinarily be sold quickly for cash.

living trust. Written agreement into which a person transfers assets and property along with instructions to the trustee for the management and future distribution of those assets. However, anyone with a trust still needs a will for assets not covered by the trust.

lock-in. An agreement that calls for a lender to make a loan at a specified rate of interest, even if rates change before the loan is funded.

loft building. Structure that was built for storage, manufacturing, or some other commercial use but is now used for housing.

lowballing. The practice employed by some builders of underestimating maintenance and carrying charges in a new condominium or cooperative project to make the development more attractive to buyers. The builder absorbs those extra costs, but then when the community is completed and control is passed to the residents, they are hit with more realistic higher monthly maintenance fees. The term also means an unrealistically low first bid to purchase a piece of property.

m

manufactured housing. Homes that are built in a factory, then shipped to the building site where components are assembled.

market value. Generally accepted as the highest price that a ready, willing, and able buyer will pay and the lowest price a ready, willing, and able seller will accept for the property in question.

maturity date. The date on which principal and interest on a mortgage or other loan must be paid in full.

mortgage. A legal document that creates a lien on a piece of property.

mortgagee. The party or institution that lends the money.

mortgagor. The party or person that borrows the money, giving a lien on the property as security for the loan.

multiple listing. An agreement that allows real-estate brokers to distribute information on the properties that they have listed for sale to other members of a local real-estate organization in order to provide the widest possible marketing of those properties. Commissions are split by mutual agreement between the listing broker and the selling broker.

Multiple Listing Service (MLS). The office that supervises the printing and distribution of listings shared by members of the local board of realtors.

n

negative. A condition created when a loan payment does not cover all the interest due.

o

offering plan. See *prospectus*.

option. The exclusive right to purchase or lease a property at a stipulated price or rent within a specified period of time.

origination fee. A charge by a lender for granting a mortgage.

p

pilaster. A reinforced projection of the foundation wall that gives additional support to a floor girder or strengthens a length of wall.

PITI. Principal, interest, taxes, and insurance—the four components that can be included in a monthly mortgage payment.

plat book. Planning volume that shows location, size, and name(s) of owner(s) of every piece of land within a specific development or for an entire neighborhood or town.

point. Sometimes called discount. A fee that a lending institution charges for granting a mortgage. One point is 1 percent of the face value of the loan.

potability test. A test done on the water to determine if it is suitable for drinking.

power of attorney. Instrument in writing that gives one person the right to act as agent for another in signing papers, deeds, and so on.

prepayment. Paying back of a loan before it has reached its maturity date.

principal. The amount of money borrowed; the amount of money still owed.

private mortgage insurance. Insurance required by lenders when a buyer borrows more than 90 percent of a home's value. The insurance guarantees that the lender will be repaid in full if the buyer defaults on his or her payments.

probate court. A special court in each state that is set up to handle managing wills, estates of those dying without a will, and other functions.

probate estate. All property and assets of the deceased that are distributed under the direction of the probate court. (There can also be some property and assets in an estate exempt from probate court.)

prospectus. A document, also known as an offering plan, offered by condominium and cooperative sponsors, detailing ownership of the development, location, prices and layouts of the units, procedures to purchase, and numerous aspects of how the project will be run.

punch list. A list of items that the builder is contractually obligated to fix before closing.

r

real-estate broker. A person who has passed a state broker's test and represents others in realty transactions. Anyone having his or her own office must be a broker.

real-estate salesperson. A man or woman who has passed a state examination for that position and must work under the supervision of a broker.

real-estate taxes. Levies on land and buildings charged to owners by local governing agencies. Those charges, sometimes known as property taxes, are a primary source of local government revenues.

real property. Land and buildings and anything permanently attached to them. Houses and con-

dominiums are real property; cooperative apartments are personal property.

Realtor. A real-estate broker who is a member of the National Association of Realtors, a professional group. Not everyone who sells real estate is a Realtor. The word is a registered trademark and is capitalized.

recreation lease. A legal agreement that allows condo buyers to use that complex's pool, tennis courts, and other amenities. The owner of those facilities is usually the developer, and there is often a charge for that use. It is preferable that the condo own its recreational facilities.

redlining. Alleged practice of some lending institutions involving their refusal to make loans on properties they deem to be bad risks, sometimes entire blocks or neighborhoods.

refinance. To pay off one loan by taking out another on the same property.

rent control. Regulation by a local government agency of rental charges, usually according to set formulas for increase.

report of title. Document required before title insurance can be issued. It states the name of the owner, a legal description of the property, and the status of taxes, liens, and anything else that might affect the marketability of the title.

right of survivorship. Granted to two joint owners who purchase property under that buying style. Stipulates that one gets full rights and becomes sole owner of the property on the death of the other. Right of survivorship is the basic difference between buying property as joint tenants and as tenants in common.

riparian rights. The right of a property owner whose land abuts a body of water to swim in that water, build a wharf, and so forth.

riser. The vertical part of a step.

s

sash. The framework in which panes of glass are set in a window.

second mortgage. A lien on a property that is subordinate to a first mortgage. In the event of default, the second mortgage is repaid after the first. Some second mortgages are home equity loans.

settlement costs. See *closing costs*.

sheetrock. Plasterboard or drywall.

soffit. The visible horizontal underside of an eave.

splashblock. Stone or concrete formations under the downspouts that take water away from the foundation.

square foot. Used to measure buildings in realty transactions. For example, if a two-story home has dimensions of 30 feet by 30 feet, the area is 900 square feet on each floor, for a total of 1,800 square feet.

subletting. A leasing of property by one tenant from another tenant, the one who holds the lease.

sump. A pit in the basement floor or crawl space that collects water to be pumped out.

t

tax shelter. A realty investment that produces income tax deductions.

tenancy in common. Style of ownership in which two or more persons purchase a property jointly but with no right of survivorship. Owners are free to will their share to anyone they choose, a principal difference between that form of ownership and joint tenancy.

testate. Having a valid will, with the deceased passing assets on to heirs.

title. Actual ownership; the right of possession; evidence of ownership.

title insurance. An insurance policy that protects against any losses incurred because of defective title.

title search. A professional examination of public records to determine the chain of ownership of a particular piece of property, noting any liens, mortgages, encumbrances, easements, restrictions, or other factors that might affect the title.

tongue and groove. A type of interlocking-boards construction.

town home. A (usually) two-story living unit often operating under the condominium form of ownership.

tread. The horizontal part of a stair that you step on.

trust deed. An instrument used in place of a mortgage in certain states; a third party trustee, not the lender, holds the title to the property until the loan is paid out or defaulted.

u

usury. Charging a higher rate of interest on a loan than is legally allowed.

v

VA loan. Veterans' Affairs-backed mortgage. Sometimes referred to as a "G.I. loan."

variance. An exception to a zoning ordinance granted to meet certain specified needs.

vent pipes. Pipes that allow gas to be vented outdoors from the plumbing system.

void. Canceled; not legally enforceable.

w

waiver. Renunciation, disclaiming, or surrender of some claim, right, or prerogative.

will. A basic document for transferring property to whomever one wishes through probate court.

window well. An excavation around a cellar window.

z

zoning. Procedure that classifies real property for a number of different uses—residential, commercial, industrial, and so forth—in accordance with a land-use plan. Ordinances are enforced by a governing body or locality.

Appendix B

Mortgage Tables

The following pages reflect changing interest rates ranging from 5.00% to 13.00%.

Interest Rate: 5.00%

Amount Borrowed	Length of Loan (in Years)					
	5	10	15	20	25	30
$50,000	$943.56	$530.33	$395.40	$329.98	$292.30	$268.41
$60,000	$1,132.27	$636.39	$474.48	$395.97	$350.75	$322.09
$70,000	$1,320.99	$742.46	$553.56	$461.97	$409.21	$375.78
$80,000	$1,509.70	$848.52	$632.63	$527.96	$467.67	$429.46
$90,000	$1,698.41	$954.59	$711.71	$593.96	$526.13	$483.14
$100,000	$1,887.12	$1,060.66	$790.79	$659.96	$584.59	$536.82
$110,000	$2,075.84	$1,166.72	$869.87	$725.95	$643.05	$590.50
$120,000	$2,264.55	$1,272.79	$948.95	$791.95	$701.51	$644.19
$130,000	$2,453.26	$1,378.85	$1,028.03	$857.94	$759.97	$697.87
$140,000	$2,641.97	$1,484.92	$1,107.11	$923.94	$818.43	$751.55
$150,000	$2,830.69	$1,590.98	$1,186.19	$989.93	$876.89	$805.23
$160,000	$3,019.40	$1,697.05	$1,265.27	$1,055.93	$935.34	$858.91
$170,000	$3,208.11	$1,803.11	$1,344.35	$1,121.92	$993.80	$912.60
$180,000	$3,396.82	$1,909.18	$1,423.43	$1,187.92	$1,052.26	$966.28
$190,000	$3,585.53	$2,015.24	$1,502.51	$1,253.92	$1,110.72	$1,019.96
$200,000	$3,774.25	$2,121.31	$1,581.59	$1,319.91	$1,169.18	$1,073.64
$210,000	$3,962.96	$2,227.38	$1,660.67	$1,385.91	$1,227.64	$1,127.33
$220,000	$4,151.67	$2,333.44	$1,739.75	$1,451.90	$1,286.10	$1,181.01
$230,000	$4,340.38	$2,439.51	$1,818.83	$1,517.90	$1,344.56	$1,234.69
$240,000	$4,529.10	$2,545.57	$1,897.90	$1,583.89	$1,403.02	$1,288.37
$250,000	$4,717.81	$2,651.64	$1,976.98	$1,649.89	$1,461.48	$1,342.05
$260,000	$4,906.52	$2,757.70	$2,056.06	$1,715.88	$1,519.93	$1,395.74
$270,000	$5,095.23	$2,863.77	$2,135.14	$1,781.88	$1,578.39	$1,449.42
$280,000	$5,283.95	$2,969.83	$2,214.22	$1,847.88	$1,636.85	$1,503.10
$290,000	$5,472.66	$3,075.90	$2,293.30	$1,913.87	$1,695.31	$1,556.78
$300,000	$5,661.37	$3,181.97	$2,372.38	$1,979.87	$1,753.77	$1,610.46
$310,000	$5,850.08	$3,288.03	$2,451.46	$2,045.86	$1,812.23	$1,664.15

Interest Rate: 5.50%

Amount Borrowed	Length of Loan (in Years)					
	5	10	15	20	25	30
$50,000	$955.06	$542.63	$408.54	$343.94	$307.04	$283.89
$60,000	$1,146.07	$651.16	$490.25	$412.73	$368.45	$340.67
$70,000	$1,337.08	$759.68	$571.96	$481.52	$429.86	$397.45
$80,000	$1,528.09	$868.21	$653.67	$550.31	$491.27	$454.23
$90,000	$1,719.10	$976.74	$735.38	$619.10	$552.68	$511.01
$100,000	$1,910.12	$1,085.26	$817.08	$687.89	$614.09	$567.79
$110,000	$2,101.13	$1,193.79	$898.79	$756.68	$675.50	$624.57
$120,000	$2,292.14	$1,302.32	$980.50	$825.46	$736.90	$681.35
$130,000	$2,483.15	$1,410.84	$1,062.21	$894.25	$798.31	$738.13
$140,000	$2,674.16	$1,519.37	$1,143.92	$963.04	$859.72	$794.90
$150,000	$2,865.17	$1,627.89	$1,225.63	$1,031.83	$921.13	$851.68
$160,000	$3,056.19	$1,736.42	$1,307.33	$1,100.62	$982.54	$908.46
$170,000	$3,247.20	$1,844.95	$1,389.04	$1,169.41	$1,043.95	$965.24
$180,000	$3,438.21	$1,953.47	$1,470.75	$1,238.20	$1,105.36	$1,022.02
$190,000	$3,629.22	$2,062.00	$1,552.46	$1,306.99	$1,166.77	$1,078.80
$200,000	$3,820.23	$2,170.53	$1,634.17	$1,375.77	$1,228.17	$1,135.58
$210,000	$4,011.24	$2,279.05	$1,715.88	$1,444.56	$1,289.58	$1,192.36
$220,000	$4,202.26	$2,387.58	$1,797.58	$1,513.35	$1,350.99	$1,249.14
$230,000	$4,393.27	$2,496.10	$1,879.29	$1,582.14	$1,412.40	$1,305.91
$240,000	$4,584.28	$2,604.63	$1,961.00	$1,650.93	$1,473.81	$1,362.69
$250,000	$4,775.29	$2,713.16	$2,042.71	$1,719.72	$1,535.22	$1,419.47
$260,000	$4,966.30	$2,821.68	$2,124.42	$1,788.51	$1,596.63	$1,476.25
$270,000	$5,157.31	$2,930.21	$2,206.13	$1,857.30	$1,658.04	$1,533.03
$280,000	$5,348.33	$3,038.74	$2,287.83	$1,926.08	$1,719.44	$1,589.81
$290,000	$5,539.34	$3,147.26	$2,369.54	$1,994.87	$1,780.85	$1,646.59
$300,000	$5,730.35	$3,255.79	$2,451.25	$2,063.66	$1,842.26	$1,703.37
$310,000	$5,921.36	$3,364.31	$2,532.96	$2,132.45	$1,903.67	$1,760.15

Interest Rate: 6.00%

Amount Borrowed	Length of Loan (in Years)					
	5	10	15	20	25	30
$50,000	$966.64	$555.10	$421.93	$358.22	$322.15	$299.78
$60,000	$1,159.97	$666.12	$506.31	$429.86	$386.58	$359.73
$70,000	$1,353.30	$777.14	$590.70	$501.50	$451.01	$419.69
$80,000	$1,546.62	$888.16	$675.09	$573.14	$515.44	$479.64
$90,000	$1,739.95	$999.18	$759.47	$644.79	$579.87	$539.60
$100,000	$1,933.28	$1,110.21	$843.86	$716.43	$644.30	$599.55
$110,000	$2,126.61	$1,221.23	$928.24	$788.07	$708.73	$659.51
$120,000	$2,319.94	$1,332.25	$1,012.63	$859.72	$773.16	$719.46
$130,000	$2,513.26	$1,443.27	$1,097.01	$931.36	$837.59	$779.42
$140,000	$2,706.59	$1,554.29	$1,181.40	$1,003.00	$902.02	$839.37
$150,000	$2,899.92	$1,665.31	$1,265.79	$1,074.65	$966.45	$899.33
$160,000	$3,093.25	$1,776.33	$1,350.17	$1,146.29	$1,030.88	$959.28
$170,000	$3,286.58	$1,887.35	$1,434.56	$1,217.93	$1,095.31	$1,019.24
$180,000	$3,479.90	$1,998.37	$1,518.94	$1,289.58	$1,159.74	$1,079.19
$190,000	$3,673.23	$2,109.39	$1,603.33	$1,361.22	$1,224.17	$1,139.15
$200,000	$3,866.56	$2,220.41	$1,687.71	$1,432.86	$1,288.60	$1,199.10
$210,000	$4,059.89	$2,331.43	$1,772.10	$1,504.51	$1,353.03	$1,259.06
$220,000	$4,253.22	$2,442.45	$1,856.49	$1,576.15	$1,417.46	$1,319.01
$230,000	$4,446.54	$2,553.47	$1,940.87	$1,647.79	$1,481.89	$1,378.97
$240,000	$4,639.87	$2,664.49	$2,025.26	$1,719.43	$1,546.32	$1,438.92
$250,000	$4,833.20	$2,775.51	$2,109.64	$1,791.08	$1,610.75	$1,498.88
$260,000	$5,026.53	$2,886.53	$2,194.03	$1,862.72	$1,675.18	$1,558.83
$270,000	$5,219.86	$2,997.55	$2,278.41	$1,934.36	$1,739.61	$1,618.79
$280,000	$5,413.18	$3,108.57	$2,362.80	$2,006.01	$1,804.04	$1,678.74
$290,000	$5,606.51	$3,219.59	$2,447.18	$2,077.65	$1,868.47	$1,738.70
$300,000	$5,799.84	$3,330.62	$2,531.57	$2,149.29	$1,932.90	$1,798.65
$310,000	$5,993.17	$3,441.64	$2,615.96	$2,220.94	$1,997.33	$1,858.61

Interest Rate: 6.50%

Amount Borrowed	Length of Loan (in Years)					
	5	10	15	20	25	30
$50,000	$978.31	$567.74	$435.55	$372.79	$337.60	$316.03
$60,000	$1,173.97	$681.29	$522.66	$447.34	$405.12	$379.24
$70,000	$1,369.63	$794.84	$609.78	$521.90	$472.65	$442.45
$80,000	$1,565.29	$908.38	$696.89	$596.46	$540.17	$505.65
$90,000	$1,760.95	$1,021.93	$784.00	$671.02	$607.69	$568.86
$100,000	$1,956.61	$1,135.48	$871.11	$745.57	$675.21	$632.07
$110,000	$2,152.28	$1,249.03	$958.22	$820.13	$742.73	$695.27
$120,000	$2,347.94	$1,362.58	$1,045.33	$894.69	$810.25	$758.48
$130,000	$2,543.60	$1,476.12	$1,132.44	$969.25	$877.77	$821.69
$140,000	$2,739.26	$1,589.67	$1,219.55	$1,043.80	$945.29	$884.90
$150,000	$2,934.92	$1,703.22	$1,306.66	$1,118.36	$1,012.81	$948.10
$160,000	$3,130.58	$1,816.77	$1,393.77	$1,192.92	$1,080.33	$1,011.31
$170,000	$3,326.25	$1,930.32	$1,480.88	$1,267.47	$1,147.85	$1,074.52
$180,000	$3,521.91	$2,043.86	$1,567.99	$1,342.03	$1,215.37	$1,137.72
$190,000	$3,717.57	$2,157.41	$1,655.10	$1,416.59	$1,282.89	$1,200.93
$200,000	$3,913.23	$2,270.96	$1,742.21	$1,491.15	$1,350.41	$1,264.14
$210,000	$4,108.89	$2,384.51	$1,829.33	$1,565.70	$1,417.94	$1,327.34
$220,000	$4,304.55	$2,498.06	$1,916.44	$1,640.26	$1,485.46	$1,390.55
$230,000	$4,500.21	$2,611.60	$2,003.55	$1,714.82	$1,552.98	$1,453.76
$240,000	$4,695.88	$2,725.15	$2,090.66	$1,789.38	$1,620.50	$1,516.96
$250,000	$4,891.54	$2,838.70	$2,177.77	$1,863.93	$1,688.02	$1,580.17
$260,000	$5,087.20	$2,952.25	$2,264.88	$1,938.49	$1,755.54	$1,643.38
$270,000	$5,282.86	$3,065.80	$2,351.99	$2,013.05	$1,823.06	$1,706.58
$280,000	$5,478.52	$3,179.34	$2,439.10	$2,087.60	$1,890.58	$1,769.79
$290,000	$5,674.18	$3,292.89	$2,526.21	$2,162.16	$1,958.10	$1,833.00
$300,000	$5,869.84	$3,406.44	$2,613.32	$2,236.72	$2,025.62	$1,896.20
$310,000	$6,065.51	$3,519.99	$2,700.43	$2,311.28	$2,093.14	$1,959.41

Interest Rate: 7.00%

Amount Borrowed	Length of Loan (in Years)					
	5	10	15	20	25	30
$50,000	$990.06	$580.54	$449.41	$387.65	$353.39	$332.65
$60,000	$1,188.07	$696.65	$539.30	$465.18	$424.07	$399.18
$70,000	$1,386.08	$812.76	$629.18	$542.71	$494.75	$465.71
$80,000	$1,584.10	$928.87	$719.06	$620.24	$565.42	$532.24
$90,000	$1,782.11	$1,044.98	$808.95	$697.77	$636.10	$598.77
$100,000	$1,980.12	$1,161.08	$898.83	$775.30	$706.78	$665.30
$110,000	$2,178.13	$1,277.19	$988.71	$852.83	$777.46	$731.83
$120,000	$2,376.14	$1,393.30	$1,078.59	$930.36	$848.14	$798.36
$130,000	$2,574.16	$1,509.41	$1,168.48	$1,007.89	$918.81	$864.89
$140,000	$2,772.17	$1,625.52	$1,258.36	$1,085.42	$989.49	$931.42
$150,000	$2,970.18	$1,741.63	$1,348.24	$1,162.95	$1,060.17	$997.95
$160,000	$3,168.19	$1,857.74	$1,438.13	$1,240.48	$1,130.85	$1,064.48
$170,000	$3,366.20	$1,973.84	$1,528.01	$1,318.01	$1,201.52	$1,131.01
$180,000	$3,564.22	$2,089.95	$1,617.89	$1,395.54	$1,272.20	$1,197.54
$190,000	$3,762.23	$2,206.06	$1,707.77	$1,473.07	$1,342.88	$1,264.07
$200,000	$3,960.24	$2,322.17	$1,797.66	$1,550.60	$1,413.56	$1,330.60
$210,000	$4,158.25	$2,438.28	$1,887.54	$1,628.13	$1,484.24	$1,397.14
$220,000	$4,356.26	$2,554.39	$1,977.42	$1,705.66	$1,554.91	$1,463.67
$230,000	$4,554.28	$2,670.50	$2,067.31	$1,783.19	$1,625.59	$1,530.20
$240,000	$4,752.29	$2,786.60	$2,157.19	$1,860.72	$1,696.27	$1,596.73
$250,000	$4,950.30	$2,902.71	$2,247.07	$1,938.25	$1,766.95	$1,663.26
$260,000	$5,148.31	$3,018.82	$2,336.95	$2,015.78	$1,837.63	$1,729.79
$270,000	$5,346.32	$3,134.93	$2,426.84	$2,093.31	$1,908.30	$1,796.32
$280,000	$5,544.34	$3,251.04	$2,516.72	$2,170.84	$1,978.98	$1,862.85
$290,000	$5,742.35	$3,367.15	$2,606.60	$2,248.37	$2,049.66	$1,929.38
$300,000	$5,940.36	$3,483.25	$2,696.48	$2,325.90	$2,120.34	$1,995.91
$310,000	$6,138.37	$3,599.36	$2,786.37	$2,403.43	$2,191.02	$2,062.44

Interest Rate: 7.50%

Amount Borrowed	Length of Loan (in Years)					
	5	10	15	20	25	30
$50,000	$1,001.90	$593.51	$463.51	$402.80	$369.50	$349.61
$60,000	$1,202.28	$712.21	$556.21	$483.36	$443.39	$419.53
$70,000	$1,402.66	$830.91	$648.91	$563.92	$517.29	$489.45
$80,000	$1,603.04	$949.61	$741.61	$644.47	$591.19	$559.37
$90,000	$1,803.42	$1,068.32	$834.31	$725.03	$665.09	$629.29
$100,000	$2,003.79	$1,187.02	$927.01	$805.59	$738.99	$699.21
$110,000	$2,204.17	$1,305.72	$1,019.71	$886.15	$812.89	$769.14
$120,000	$2,404.55	$1,424.42	$1,112.41	$966.71	$886.79	$839.06
$130,000	$2,604.93	$1,543.12	$1,205.12	$1,047.27	$960.69	$908.98
$140,000	$2,805.31	$1,661.82	$1,297.82	$1,127.83	$1,034.59	$978.90
$150,000	$3,005.69	$1,780.53	$1,390.52	$1,208.39	$1,108.49	$1,048.82
$160,000	$3,206.07	$1,899.23	$1,483.22	$1,288.95	$1,182.39	$1,118.74
$170,000	$3,406.45	$2,017.93	$1,575.92	$1,369.51	$1,256.29	$1,188.66
$180,000	$3,606.83	$2,136.63	$1,668.62	$1,450.07	$1,330.18	$1,258.59
$190,000	$3,807.21	$2,255.33	$1,761.32	$1,530.63	$1,404.08	$1,328.51
$200,000	$4,007.59	$2,374.04	$1,854.02	$1,611.19	$1,477.98	$1,398.43
$210,000	$4,207.97	$2,492.74	$1,946.73	$1,691.75	$1,551.88	$1,468.35
$220,000	$4,408.35	$2,611.44	$2,039.43	$1,772.31	$1,625.78	$1,538.27
$230,000	$4,608.73	$2,730.14	$2,132.13	$1,852.86	$1,699.68	$1,608.19
$240,000	$4,809.11	$2,848.84	$2,224.83	$1,933.42	$1,773.58	$1,678.11
$250,000	$5,009.49	$2,967.54	$2,317.53	$2,013.98	$1,847.48	$1,748.04
$260,000	$5,209.87	$3,086.25	$2,410.23	$2,094.54	$1,921.38	$1,817.96
$270,000	$5,410.25	$3,204.95	$2,502.93	$2,175.10	$1,995.28	$1,887.88
$280,000	$5,610.63	$3,323.65	$2,595.63	$2,255.66	$2,069.18	$1,957.80
$290,000	$5,811.01	$3,442.35	$2,688.34	$2,336.22	$2,143.07	$2,027.72
$300,000	$6,011.38	$3,561.05	$2,781.04	$2,416.78	$2,216.97	$2,097.64
$310,000	$6,211.76	$3,679.75	$2,873.74	$2,497.34	$2,290.87	$2,167.56

Interest Rate: 8.00%

Amount Borrowed	Length of Loan (in Years)					
	5	10	15	20	25	30
$50,000	$1,013.82	$606.64	$477.83	$418.22	$385.91	$366.88
$60,000	$1,216.58	$727.97	$573.39	$501.86	$463.09	$440.26
$70,000	$1,419.35	$849.29	$668.96	$585.51	$540.27	$513.64
$80,000	$1,622.11	$970.62	$764.52	$669.15	$617.45	$587.01
$90,000	$1,824.88	$1,091.95	$860.09	$752.80	$694.63	$660.39
$100,000	$2,027.64	$1,213.28	$955.65	$836.44	$771.82	$733.76
$110,000	$2,230.40	$1,334.60	$1,051.22	$920.08	$849.00	$807.14
$120,000	$2,433.17	$1,455.93	$1,146.78	$1,003.73	$926.18	$880.52
$130,000	$2,635.93	$1,577.26	$1,242.35	$1,087.37	$1,003.36	$953.89
$140,000	$2,838.70	$1,698.59	$1,337.91	$1,171.02	$1,080.54	$1,027.27
$150,000	$3,041.46	$1,819.91	$1,433.48	$1,254.66	$1,157.72	$1,100.65
$160,000	$3,244.22	$1,941.24	$1,529.04	$1,338.30	$1,234.91	$1,174.02
$170,000	$3,446.99	$2,062.57	$1,624.61	$1,421.95	$1,312.09	$1,247.40
$180,000	$3,649.75	$2,183.90	$1,720.17	$1,505.59	$1,389.27	$1,320.78
$190,000	$3,852.51	$2,305.22	$1,815.74	$1,589.24	$1,466.45	$1,394.15
$200,000	$4,055.28	$2,426.55	$1,911.30	$1,672.88	$1,543.63	$1,467.53
$210,000	$4,258.04	$2,547.88	$2,006.87	$1,756.52	$1,620.81	$1,540.91
$220,000	$4,460.81	$2,669.21	$2,102.43	$1,840.17	$1,698.00	$1,614.28
$230,000	$4,663.57	$2,790.53	$2,198.00	$1,923.81	$1,775.18	$1,687.66
$240,000	$4,866.33	$2,911.86	$2,293.57	$2,007.46	$1,852.36	$1,761.03
$250,000	$5,069.10	$3,033.19	$2,389.13	$2,091.10	$1,929.54	$1,834.41
$260,000	$5,271.86	$3,154.52	$2,484.70	$2,174.74	$2,006.72	$1,907.79
$270,000	$5,474.63	$3,275.85	$2,580.26	$2,258.39	$2,083.90	$1,981.16
$280,000	$5,677.39	$3,397.17	$2,675.83	$2,342.03	$2,161.09	$2,054.54
$290,000	$5,880.15	$3,518.50	$2,771.39	$2,425.68	$2,238.27	$2,127.92
$300,000	$6,082.92	$3,639.83	$2,866.96	$2,509.32	$2,315.45	$2,201.29
$310,000	$6,285.68	$3,761.16	$2,962.52	$2,592.96	$2,392.63	$2,274.67

Interest Rate: 8.50%

Amount Borrowed	Length of Loan (in Years)					
	5	10	15	20	25	30
$50,000	$1,025.83	$619.93	$492.37	$433.91	$402.61	$384.46
$60,000	$1,230.99	$743.91	$590.84	$520.69	$483.14	$461.35
$70,000	$1,436.16	$867.90	$689.32	$607.48	$563.66	$538.24
$80,000	$1,641.32	$991.89	$787.79	$694.26	$644.18	$615.13
$90,000	$1,846.49	$1,115.87	$886.27	$781.04	$724.70	$692.02
$100,000	$2,051.65	$1,239.86	$984.74	$867.82	$805.23	$768.91
$110,000	$2,256.82	$1,363.84	$1,083.21	$954.61	$885.75	$845.80
$120,000	$2,461.98	$1,487.83	$1,181.69	$1,041.39	$966.27	$922.70
$130,000	$2,667.15	$1,611.81	$1,280.16	$1,128.17	$1,046.80	$999.59
$140,000	$2,872.31	$1,735.80	$1,378.64	$1,214.95	$1,127.32	$1,076.48
$150,000	$3,077.48	$1,859.79	$1,477.11	$1,301.73	$1,207.84	$1,153.37
$160,000	$3,282.65	$1,983.77	$1,575.58	$1,388.52	$1,288.36	$1,230.26
$170,000	$3,487.81	$2,107.76	$1,674.06	$1,475.30	$1,368.89	$1,307.15
$180,000	$3,692.98	$2,231.74	$1,772.53	$1,562.08	$1,449.41	$1,384.04
$190,000	$3,898.14	$2,355.73	$1,871.01	$1,648.86	$1,529.93	$1,460.94
$200,000	$4,103.31	$2,479.71	$1,969.48	$1,735.65	$1,610.45	$1,537.83
$210,000	$4,308.47	$2,603.70	$2,067.95	$1,822.43	$1,690.98	$1,614.72
$220,000	$4,513.64	$2,727.69	$2,166.43	$1,909.21	$1,771.50	$1,691.61
$230,000	$4,718.80	$2,851.67	$2,264.90	$1,995.99	$1,852.02	$1,768.50
$240,000	$4,923.97	$2,975.66	$2,363.37	$2,082.78	$1,932.55	$1,845.39
$250,000	$5,129.13	$3,099.64	$2,461.85	$2,169.56	$2,013.07	$1,922.28
$260,000	$5,334.30	$3,223.63	$2,560.32	$2,256.34	$2,093.59	$1,999.18
$270,000	$5,539.46	$3,347.61	$2,658.80	$2,343.12	$2,174.11	$2,076.07
$280,000	$5,744.63	$3,471.60	$2,757.27	$2,429.91	$2,254.64	$2,152.96
$290,000	$5,949.79	$3,595.58	$2,855.74	$2,516.69	$2,335.16	$2,229.85
$300,000	$6,154.96	$3,719.57	$2,954.22	$2,603.47	$2,415.68	$2,306.74
$310,000	$6,360.12	$3,843.56	$3,052.69	$2,690.25	$2,496.20	$2,383.63

Interest Rate: 9.00%

Amount Borrowed	Length of Loan (in Years)					
	5	10	15	20	25	30
$50,000	$1,037.92	$633.38	$507.13	$449.86	$419.60	$402.31
$60,000	$1,245.50	$760.05	$608.56	$539.84	$503.52	$482.77
$70,000	$1,453.08	$886.73	$709.99	$629.81	$587.44	$563.24
$80,000	$1,660.67	$1,013.41	$811.41	$719.78	$671.36	$643.70
$90,000	$1,868.25	$1,140.08	$912.84	$809.75	$755.28	$724.16
$100,000	$2,075.84	$1,266.76	$1,014.27	$899.73	$839.20	$804.62
$110,000	$2,283.42	$1,393.43	$1,115.69	$989.70	$923.12	$885.08
$120,000	$2,491.00	$1,520.11	$1,217.12	$1,079.67	$1,007.04	$965.55
$130,000	$2,698.59	$1,646.79	$1,318.55	$1,169.64	$1,090.96	$1,046.01
$140,000	$2,906.17	$1,773.46	$1,419.97	$1,259.62	$1,174.87	$1,126.47
$150,000	$3,113.75	$1,900.14	$1,521.40	$1,349.59	$1,258.79	$1,206.93
$160,000	$3,321.34	$2,026.81	$1,622.83	$1,439.56	$1,342.71	$1,287.40
$170,000	$3,528.92	$2,153.49	$1,724.25	$1,529.53	$1,426.63	$1,367.86
$180,000	$3,736.50	$2,280.16	$1,825.68	$1,619.51	$1,510.55	$1,448.32
$190,000	$3,944.09	$2,406.84	$1,927.11	$1,709.48	$1,594.47	$1,528.78
$200,000	$4,151.67	$2,533.52	$2,028.53	$1,799.45	$1,678.39	$1,609.25
$210,000	$4,359.25	$2,660.19	$2,129.96	$1,889.42	$1,762.31	$1,689.71
$220,000	$4,566.84	$2,786.87	$2,231.39	$1,979.40	$1,846.23	$1,770.17
$230,000	$4,774.42	$2,913.54	$2,332.81	$2,069.37	$1,930.15	$1,850.63
$240,000	$4,982.01	$3,040.22	$2,434.24	$2,159.34	$2,014.07	$1,931.09
$250,000	$5,189.59	$3,166.89	$2,535.67	$2,249.31	$2,097.99	$2,011.56
$260,000	$5,397.17	$3,293.57	$2,637.09	$2,339.29	$2,181.91	$2,092.02
$270,000	$5,604.76	$3,420.25	$2,738.52	$2,429.26	$2,265.83	$2,172.48
$280,000	$5,812.34	$3,546.92	$2,839.95	$2,519.23	$2,349.75	$2,252.94
$290,000	$6,019.92	$3,673.60	$2,941.37	$2,609.21	$2,433.67	$2,333.41
$300,000	$6,227.51	$3,800.27	$3,042.80	$2,699.18	$2,517.59	$2,413.87
$310,000	$6,435.09	$3,926.95	$3,144.23	$2,789.15	$2,601.51	$2,494.33

Interest Rate: 9.50%

Amount Borrowed	Length of Loan (in Years)					
	5	10	15	20	25	30
$50,000	$1,050.09	$646.99	$522.11	$466.07	$436.85	$420.43
$60,000	$1,260.11	$776.39	$626.53	$559.28	$524.22	$504.51
$70,000	$1,470.13	$905.78	$730.96	$652.49	$611.59	$588.60
$80,000	$1,680.15	$1,035.18	$835.38	$745.70	$698.96	$672.68
$90,000	$1,890.17	$1,164.58	$939.80	$838.92	$786.33	$756.77
$100,000	$2,100.19	$1,293.98	$1,044.22	$932.13	$873.70	$840.85
$110,000	$2,310.20	$1,423.37	$1,148.65	$1,025.34	$961.07	$924.94
$120,000	$2,520.22	$1,552.77	$1,253.07	$1,118.56	$1,048.44	$1,009.03
$130,000	$2,730.24	$1,682.17	$1,357.49	$1,211.77	$1,135.81	$1,093.11
$140,000	$2,940.26	$1,811.57	$1,461.91	$1,304.98	$1,223.18	$1,177.20
$150,000	$3,150.28	$1,940.96	$1,566.34	$1,398.20	$1,310.54	$1,261.28
$160,000	$3,360.30	$2,070.36	$1,670.76	$1,491.41	$1,397.91	$1,345.37
$170,000	$3,570.32	$2,199.76	$1,775.18	$1,584.62	$1,485.28	$1,429.45
$180,000	$3,780.34	$2,329.16	$1,879.60	$1,677.84	$1,572.65	$1,513.54
$190,000	$3,990.35	$2,458.55	$1,984.03	$1,771.05	$1,660.02	$1,597.62
$200,000	$4,200.37	$2,587.95	$2,088.45	$1,864.26	$1,747.39	$1,681.71
$210,000	$4,410.39	$2,717.35	$2,192.87	$1,957.48	$1,834.76	$1,765.79
$220,000	$4,620.41	$2,846.75	$2,297.29	$2,050.69	$1,922.13	$1,849.88
$230,000	$4,830.43	$2,976.14	$2,401.72	$2,143.90	$2,009.50	$1,933.96
$240,000	$5,040.45	$3,105.54	$2,506.14	$2,237.11	$2,096.87	$2,018.05
$250,000	$5,250.47	$3,234.94	$2,610.56	$2,330.33	$2,184.24	$2,102.14
$260,000	$5,460.48	$3,364.34	$2,714.98	$2,423.54	$2,271.61	$2,186.22
$270,000	$5,670.50	$3,493.73	$2,819.41	$2,516.75	$2,358.98	$2,270.31
$280,000	$5,880.52	$3,623.13	$2,923.83	$2,609.97	$2,446.35	$2,354.39
$290,000	$6,090.54	$3,752.53	$3,028.25	$2,703.18	$2,533.72	$2,438.48
$300,000	$6,300.56	$3,881.93	$3,132.67	$2,796.39	$2,621.09	$2,522.56
$310,000	$6,510.58	$4,011.32	$3,237.10	$2,889.61	$2,708.46	$2,606.65

Interest Rate: 10.00%

Amount Borrowed	Length of Loan (in Years)					
	5	10	15	20	25	30
$50,000	$1,062.35	$660.75	$537.30	$482.51	$454.35	$438.79
$60,000	$1,274.82	$792.90	$644.76	$579.01	$545.22	$526.54
$70,000	$1,487.29	$925.06	$752.22	$675.52	$636.09	$614.30
$80,000	$1,699.76	$1,057.21	$859.68	$772.02	$726.96	$702.06
$90,000	$1,912.23	$1,189.36	$967.14	$868.52	$817.83	$789.81
$100,000	$2,124.70	$1,321.51	$1,074.61	$965.02	$908.70	$877.57
$110,000	$2,337.17	$1,453.66	$1,182.07	$1,061.52	$999.57	$965.33
$120,000	$2,549.65	$1,585.81	$1,289.53	$1,158.03	$1,090.44	$1,053.09
$130,000	$2,762.12	$1,717.96	$1,396.99	$1,254.53	$1,181.31	$1,140.84
$140,000	$2,974.59	$1,850.11	$1,504.45	$1,351.03	$1,272.18	$1,228.60
$150,000	$3,187.06	$1,982.26	$1,611.91	$1,447.53	$1,363.05	$1,316.36
$160,000	$3,399.53	$2,114.41	$1,719.37	$1,544.03	$1,453.92	$1,404.11
$170,000	$3,612.00	$2,246.56	$1,826.83	$1,640.54	$1,544.79	$1,491.87
$180,000	$3,824.47	$2,378.71	$1,934.29	$1,737.04	$1,635.66	$1,579.63
$190,000	$4,036.94	$2,510.86	$2,041.75	$1,833.54	$1,726.53	$1,667.39
$200,000	$4,249.41	$2,643.01	$2,149.21	$1,930.04	$1,817.40	$1,755.14
$210,000	$4,461.88	$2,775.17	$2,256.67	$2,026.55	$1,908.27	$1,842.90
$220,000	$4,674.35	$2,907.32	$2,364.13	$2,123.05	$1,999.14	$1,930.66
$230,000	$4,886.82	$3,039.47	$2,471.59	$2,219.55	$2,090.01	$2,018.41
$240,000	$5,099.29	$3,171.62	$2,579.05	$2,316.05	$2,180.88	$2,106.17
$250,000	$5,311.76	$3,303.77	$2,686.51	$2,412.55	$2,271.75	$2,193.93
$260,000	$5,524.23	$3,435.92	$2,793.97	$2,509.06	$2,362.62	$2,281.69
$270,000	$5,736.70	$3,568.07	$2,901.43	$2,605.56	$2,453.49	$2,369.44
$280,000	$5,949.17	$3,700.22	$3,008.89	$2,702.06	$2,544.36	$2,457.20
$290,000	$6,161.64	$3,832.37	$3,116.35	$2,798.56	$2,635.23	$2,544.96
$300,000	$6,374.11	$3,964.52	$3,223.82	$2,895.06	$2,726.10	$2,632.71
$310,000	$6,586.58	$4,096.67	$3,331.28	$2,991.57	$2,816.97	$2,720.47

Interest Rate: 10.50%

Amount Borrowed	Length of Loan (in Years)					
	5	10	15	20	25	30
$50,000	$1,074.70	$674.67	$552.70	$499.19	$472.09	$457.37
$60,000	$1,289.63	$809.61	$663.24	$599.03	$566.51	$548.84
$70,000	$1,504.57	$944.54	$773.78	$698.87	$660.93	$640.32
$80,000	$1,719.51	$1,079.48	$884.32	$798.70	$755.35	$731.79
$90,000	$1,934.45	$1,214.41	$994.86	$898.54	$849.76	$823.27
$100,000	$2,149.39	$1,349.35	$1,105.40	$998.38	$944.18	$914.74
$110,000	$2,364.33	$1,484.28	$1,215.94	$1,098.22	$1,038.60	$1,006.21
$120,000	$2,579.27	$1,619.22	$1,326.48	$1,198.06	$1,133.02	$1,097.69
$130,000	$2,794.21	$1,754.15	$1,437.02	$1,297.89	$1,227.44	$1,189.16
$140,000	$3,009.15	$1,889.09	$1,547.56	$1,397.73	$1,321.85	$1,280.64
$150,000	$3,224.09	$2,024.02	$1,658.10	$1,497.57	$1,416.27	$1,372.11
$160,000	$3,439.02	$2,158.96	$1,768.64	$1,597.41	$1,510.69	$1,463.58
$170,000	$3,653.96	$2,293.89	$1,879.18	$1,697.25	$1,605.11	$1,555.06
$180,000	$3,868.90	$2,428.83	$1,989.72	$1,797.08	$1,699.53	$1,646.53
$190,000	$4,083.84	$2,563.76	$2,100.26	$1,896.92	$1,793.95	$1,738.00
$200,000	$4,298.78	$2,698.70	$2,210.80	$1,996.76	$1,888.36	$1,829.48
$210,000	$4,513.72	$2,833.63	$2,321.34	$2,096.60	$1,982.78	$1,920.95
$220,000	$4,728.66	$2,968.57	$2,431.88	$2,196.44	$2,077.20	$2,012.43
$230,000	$4,943.60	$3,103.50	$2,542.42	$2,296.27	$2,171.62	$2,103.90
$240,000	$5,158.54	$3,238.44	$2,652.96	$2,396.11	$2,266.04	$2,195.37
$250,000	$5,373.48	$3,373.37	$2,763.50	$2,495.95	$2,360.45	$2,286.85
$260,000	$5,588.41	$3,508.31	$2,874.04	$2,595.79	$2,454.87	$2,378.32
$270,000	$5,803.35	$3,643.24	$2,984.58	$2,695.63	$2,549.29	$2,469.80
$280,000	$6,018.29	$3,778.18	$3,095.12	$2,795.46	$2,643.71	$2,561.27
$290,000	$6,233.23	$3,913.11	$3,205.66	$2,895.30	$2,738.13	$2,652.74
$300,000	$6,448.17	$4,048.05	$3,316.20	$2,995.14	$2,832.55	$2,744.22
$310,000	$6,663.11	$4,182.98	$3,426.74	$3,094.98	$2,926.96	$2,835.69

Interest Rate: 11.00%

Amount Borrowed	Length of Loan (in Years)					
	5	10	15	20	25	30
$50,000	$1,087.12	$688.75	$568.30	$516.09	$490.06	$476.16
$60,000	$1,304.55	$826.50	$681.96	$619.31	$588.07	$571.39
$70,000	$1,521.97	$964.25	$795.62	$722.53	$686.08	$666.63
$80,000	$1,739.39	$1,102.00	$909.28	$825.75	$784.09	$761.86
$90,000	$1,956.82	$1,239.75	$1,022.94	$928.97	$882.10	$857.09
$100,000	$2,174.24	$1,377.50	$1,136.60	$1,032.19	$980.11	$952.32
$110,000	$2,391.67	$1,515.25	$1,250.26	$1,135.41	$1,078.12	$1,047.56
$120,000	$2,609.09	$1,653.00	$1,363.92	$1,238.63	$1,176.14	$1,142.79
$130,000	$2,826.51	$1,790.75	$1,477.58	$1,341.84	$1,274.15	$1,238.02
$140,000	$3,043.94	$1,928.50	$1,591.24	$1,445.06	$1,372.16	$1,333.25
$150,000	$3,261.36	$2,066.25	$1,704.90	$1,548.28	$1,470.17	$1,428.49
$160,000	$3,478.79	$2,204.00	$1,818.56	$1,651.50	$1,568.18	$1,523.72
$170,000	$3,696.21	$2,341.75	$1,932.21	$1,754.72	$1,666.19	$1,618.95
$180,000	$3,913.64	$2,479.50	$2,045.87	$1,857.94	$1,764.20	$1,714.18
$190,000	$4,131.06	$2,617.25	$2,159.53	$1,961.16	$1,862.21	$1,809.41
$200,000	$4,348.48	$2,755.00	$2,273.19	$2,064.38	$1,960.23	$1,904.65
$210,000	$4,565.91	$2,892.75	$2,386.85	$2,167.60	$2,058.24	$1,999.88
$220,000	$4,783.33	$3,030.50	$2,500.51	$2,270.81	$2,156.25	$2,095.11
$230,000	$5,000.76	$3,168.25	$2,614.17	$2,374.03	$2,254.26	$2,190.34
$240,000	$5,218.18	$3,306.00	$2,727.83	$2,477.25	$2,352.27	$2,285.58
$250,000	$5,435.61	$3,443.75	$2,841.49	$2,580.47	$2,450.28	$2,380.81
$260,000	$5,653.03	$3,581.50	$2,955.15	$2,683.69	$2,548.29	$2,476.04
$270,000	$5,870.45	$3,719.25	$3,068.81	$2,786.91	$2,646.31	$2,571.27
$280,000	$6,087.88	$3,857.00	$3,182.47	$2,890.13	$2,744.32	$2,666.51
$290,000	$6,305.30	$3,994.75	$3,296.13	$2,993.35	$2,842.33	$2,761.74
$300,000	$6,522.73	$4,132.50	$3,409.79	$3,096.57	$2,940.34	$2,856.97
$310,000	$6,740.15	$4,270.25	$3,523.45	$3,199.78	$3,038.35	$2,952.20

Interest Rate: 11.50%

Amount Borrowed	Length of Loan (in Years)					
	5	10	15	20	25	30
$50,000	$1,099.63	$702.98	$584.09	$533.21	$508.23	$495.15
$60,000	$1,319.56	$843.57	$700.91	$639.86	$609.88	$594.17
$70,000	$1,539.48	$984.17	$817.73	$746.50	$711.53	$693.20
$80,000	$1,759.41	$1,124.76	$934.55	$853.14	$813.18	$792.23
$90,000	$1,979.33	$1,265.36	$1,051.37	$959.79	$914.82	$891.26
$100,000	$2,199.26	$1,405.95	$1,168.19	$1,066.43	$1,016.47	$990.29
$110,000	$2,419.19	$1,546.55	$1,285.01	$1,173.07	$1,118.12	$1,089.32
$120,000	$2,639.11	$1,687.15	$1,401.83	$1,279.72	$1,219.76	$1,188.35
$130,000	$2,859.04	$1,827.74	$1,518.65	$1,386.36	$1,321.41	$1,287.38
$140,000	$3,078.97	$1,968.34	$1,635.47	$1,493.00	$1,423.06	$1,386.41
$150,000	$3,298.89	$2,108.93	$1,752.28	$1,599.64	$1,524.70	$1,485.44
$160,000	$3,518.82	$2,249.53	$1,869.10	$1,706.29	$1,626.35	$1,584.47
$170,000	$3,738.74	$2,390.12	$1,985.92	$1,812.93	$1,728.00	$1,683.50
$180,000	$3,958.67	$2,530.72	$2,102.74	$1,919.57	$1,829.64	$1,782.52
$190,000	$4,178.60	$2,671.31	$2,219.56	$2,026.22	$1,931.29	$1,881.55
$200,000	$4,398.52	$2,811.91	$2,336.38	$2,132.86	$2,032.94	$1,980.58
$210,000	$4,618.45	$2,952.50	$2,453.20	$2,239.50	$2,134.58	$2,079.61
$220,000	$4,838.37	$3,093.10	$2,570.02	$2,346.15	$2,236.23	$2,178.64
$230,000	$5,058.30	$3,233.70	$2,686.84	$2,452.79	$2,337.88	$2,277.67
$240,000	$5,278.23	$3,374.29	$2,803.66	$2,559.43	$2,439.53	$2,376.70
$250,000	$5,498.15	$3,514.89	$2,920.47	$2,666.07	$2,541.17	$2,475.73
$260,000	$5,718.08	$3,655.48	$3,037.29	$2,772.72	$2,642.82	$2,574.76
$270,000	$5,938.00	$3,796.08	$3,154.11	$2,879.36	$2,744.47	$2,673.79
$280,000	$6,157.93	$3,936.67	$3,270.93	$2,986.00	$2,846.11	$2,772.82
$290,000	$6,377.86	$4,077.27	$3,387.75	$3,092.65	$2,947.76	$2,871.85
$300,000	$6,597.78	$4,217.86	$3,504.57	$3,199.29	$3,049.41	$2,970.87
$310,000	$6,817.71	$4,358.46	$3,621.39	$3,305.93	$3,151.05	$3,069.90

Interest Rate: 12.00%

Amount Borrowed	Length of Loan (in Years)					
	5	10	15	20	25	30
$50,000	$1,112.22	$717.35	$600.08	$550.54	$526.61	$514.31
$60,000	$1,334.67	$860.83	$720.10	$660.65	$631.93	$617.17
$70,000	$1,557.11	$1,004.30	$840.12	$770.76	$737.26	$720.03
$80,000	$1,779.56	$1,147.77	$960.13	$880.87	$842.58	$822.89
$90,000	$2,002.00	$1,291.24	$1,080.15	$990.98	$947.90	$925.75
$100,000	$2,224.44	$1,434.71	$1,200.17	$1,101.09	$1,053.22	$1,028.61
$110,000	$2,446.89	$1,578.18	$1,320.18	$1,211.19	$1,158.55	$1,131.47
$120,000	$2,669.33	$1,721.65	$1,440.20	$1,321.30	$1,263.87	$1,234.34
$130,000	$2,891.78	$1,865.12	$1,560.22	$1,431.41	$1,369.19	$1,337.20
$140,000	$3,114.22	$2,008.59	$1,680.24	$1,541.52	$1,474.51	$1,440.06
$150,000	$3,336.67	$2,152.06	$1,800.25	$1,651.63	$1,579.84	$1,542.92
$160,000	$3,559.11	$2,295.54	$1,920.27	$1,761.74	$1,685.16	$1,645.78
$170,000	$3,781.56	$2,439.01	$2,040.29	$1,871.85	$1,790.48	$1,748.64
$180,000	$4,004.00	$2,582.48	$2,160.30	$1,981.96	$1,895.80	$1,851.50
$190,000	$4,226.45	$2,725.95	$2,280.32	$2,092.06	$2,001.13	$1,954.36
$200,000	$4,448.89	$2,869.42	$2,400.34	$2,202.17	$2,106.45	$2,057.23
$210,000	$4,671.33	$3,012.89	$2,520.35	$2,312.28	$2,211.77	$2,160.09
$220,000	$4,893.78	$3,156.36	$2,640.37	$2,422.39	$2,317.09	$2,262.95
$230,000	$5,116.22	$3,299.83	$2,760.39	$2,532.50	$2,422.42	$2,365.81
$240,000	$5,338.67	$3,443.30	$2,880.40	$2,642.61	$2,527.74	$2,468.67
$250,000	$5,561.11	$3,586.77	$3,000.42	$2,752.72	$2,633.06	$2,571.53
$260,000	$5,783.56	$3,730.24	$3,120.44	$2,862.82	$2,738.38	$2,674.39
$270,000	$6,006.00	$3,873.72	$3,240.45	$2,972.93	$2,843.71	$2,777.25
$280,000	$6,228.45	$4,017.19	$3,360.47	$3,083.04	$2,949.03	$2,880.12
$290,000	$6,450.89	$4,160.66	$3,480.49	$3,193.15	$3,054.35	$2,982.98
$300,000	$6,673.33	$4,304.13	$3,600.50	$3,303.26	$3,159.67	$3,085.84
$310,000	$6,895.78	$4,447.60	$3,720.52	$3,413.37	$3,264.99	$3,188.70

Interest Rate: 12.50%

Amount Borrowed	Length of Loan (in Years)					
	5	10	15	20	25	30
$50,000	$1,124.90	$731.88	$616.26	$568.07	$545.18	$533.63
$60,000	$1,349.88	$878.26	$739.51	$681.68	$654.21	$640.35
$70,000	$1,574.86	$1,024.63	$862.77	$795.30	$763.25	$747.08
$80,000	$1,799.84	$1,171.01	$986.02	$908.91	$872.28	$853.81
$90,000	$2,024.81	$1,317.39	$1,109.27	$1,022.53	$981.32	$960.53
$100,000	$2,249.79	$1,463.76	$1,232.52	$1,136.14	$1,090.35	$1,067.26
$110,000	$2,474.77	$1,610.14	$1,355.77	$1,249.75	$1,199.39	$1,173.98
$120,000	$2,699.75	$1,756.51	$1,479.03	$1,363.37	$1,308.42	$1,280.71
$130,000	$2,924.73	$1,902.89	$1,602.28	$1,476.98	$1,417.46	$1,387.44
$140,000	$3,149.71	$2,049.27	$1,725.53	$1,590.60	$1,526.50	$1,494.16
$150,000	$3,374.69	$2,195.64	$1,848.78	$1,704.21	$1,635.53	$1,600.89
$160,000	$3,599.67	$2,342.02	$1,972.04	$1,817.82	$1,744.57	$1,707.61
$170,000	$3,824.65	$2,488.39	$2,095.29	$1,931.44	$1,853.60	$1,814.34
$180,000	$4,049.63	$2,634.77	$2,218.54	$2,045.05	$1,962.64	$1,921.06
$190,000	$4,274.61	$2,781.15	$2,341.79	$2,158.67	$2,071.67	$2,027.79
$200,000	$4,499.59	$2,927.52	$2,465.04	$2,272.28	$2,180.71	$2,134.52
$210,000	$4,724.57	$3,073.90	$2,588.30	$2,385.90	$2,289.74	$2,241.24
$220,000	$4,949.55	$3,220.28	$2,711.55	$2,499.51	$2,398.78	$2,347.97
$230,000	$5,174.53	$3,366.65	$2,834.80	$2,613.12	$2,507.81	$2,454.69
$240,000	$5,399.51	$3,513.03	$2,958.05	$2,726.74	$2,616.85	$2,561.42
$250,000	$5,624.48	$3,659.40	$3,081.31	$2,840.35	$2,725.89	$2,668.14
$260,000	$5,849.46	$3,805.78	$3,204.56	$2,953.97	$2,834.92	$2,774.87
$270,000	$6,074.44	$3,952.16	$3,327.81	$3,067.58	$2,943.96	$2,881.60
$280,000	$6,299.42	$4,098.53	$3,451.06	$3,181.19	$3,052.99	$2,988.32
$290,000	$6,524.40	$4,244.91	$3,574.31	$3,294.81	$3,162.03	$3,095.05
$300,000	$6,749.38	$4,391.29	$3,697.57	$3,408.42	$3,271.06	$3,201.77
$310,000	$6,974.36	$4,537.66	$3,820.82	$3,522.04	$3,380.10	$3,308.50

Interest Rate: 13.00%

Amount Borrowed	Length of Loan (in Years)					
	5	10	15	20	25	30
$50,000	$1,137.65	$746.55	$632.62	$585.79	$563.92	$553.10
$60,000	$1,365.18	$895.86	$759.15	$702.95	$676.70	$663.72
$70,000	$1,592.72	$1,045.18	$885.67	$820.10	$789.48	$774.34
$80,000	$1,820.25	$1,194.49	$1,012.19	$937.26	$902.27	$884.96
$90,000	$2,047.78	$1,343.80	$1,138.72	$1,054.42	$1,015.05	$995.58
$100,000	$2,275.31	$1,493.11	$1,265.24	$1,171.58	$1,127.84	$1,106.20
$110,000	$2,502.84	$1,642.42	$1,391.77	$1,288.73	$1,240.62	$1,216.82
$120,000	$2,730.37	$1,791.73	$1,518.29	$1,405.89	$1,353.40	$1,327.44
$130,000	$2,957.90	$1,941.04	$1,644.81	$1,523.05	$1,466.19	$1,438.06
$140,000	$3,185.43	$2,090.35	$1,771.34	$1,640.21	$1,578.97	$1,548.68
$150,000	$3,412.96	$2,239.66	$1,897.86	$1,757.36	$1,691.75	$1,659.30
$160,000	$3,640.49	$2,388.97	$2,024.39	$1,874.52	$1,804.54	$1,769.92
$170,000	$3,868.02	$2,538.28	$2,150.91	$1,991.68	$1,917.32	$1,880.54
$180,000	$4,095.55	$2,687.59	$2,277.44	$2,108.84	$2,030.10	$1,991.16
$190,000	$4,323.08	$2,836.90	$2,403.96	$2,225.99	$2,142.89	$2,101.78
$200,000	$4,550.61	$2,986.21	$2,530.48	$2,343.15	$2,255.67	$2,212.40
$210,000	$4,778.15	$3,135.53	$2,657.01	$2,460.31	$2,368.45	$2,323.02
$220,000	$5,005.68	$3,284.84	$2,783.53	$2,577.47	$2,481.24	$2,433.64
$230,000	$5,233.21	$3,434.15	$2,910.06	$2,694.62	$2,594.02	$2,544.26
$240,000	$5,460.74	$3,583.46	$3,036.58	$2,811.78	$2,706.80	$2,654.88
$250,000	$5,688.27	$3,732.77	$3,163.11	$2,928.94	$2,819.59	$2,765.50
$260,000	$5,915.80	$3,882.08	$3,289.63	$3,046.10	$2,932.37	$2,876.12
$270,000	$6,143.33	$4,031.39	$3,416.15	$3,163.25	$3,045.16	$2,986.74
$280,000	$6,370.86	$4,180.70	$3,542.68	$3,280.41	$3,157.94	$3,097.36
$290,000	$6,598.39	$4,330.01	$3,669.20	$3,397.57	$3,270.72	$3,207.98
$300,000	$6,825.92	$4,479.32	$3,795.73	$3,514.73	$3,383.51	$3,318.60
$310,000	$7,053.45	$4,628.63	$3,922.25	$3,631.88	$3,496.29	$3,429.22

Appendix C

Resources

HUD OFFICES

Headquarters

U.S. Department of Housing and
Urban Development
451 Seventh Street, SW
Washington, DC, 20410
☎ (202) 708-1112

New England

Connecticut State Office
330 Main Street, 1st Floor
Hartford, CT 06106-1860
☎ (203) 240-4522

Maine State Office
99 Franklin Street
Bangor, ME 04401-4925
☎ (207) 945-0467

Massachusetts State Office
Thomas P. O'Neill Jr. Federal Building
10 Causeway Street, Room 375
Boston, MA 02222-1095
☎ (617) 565-5234

New Hampshire State Office
Norris Cotton Federal Building
275 Chestnut Street
Manchester, NH 03101-2487
☎ (603) 666-7681

Rhode Island State Office
10 Weybosset Street, 6th Floor
Providence, RI 02903-2808
☎ (401) 528-5230

Vermont State Office
Federal Building
11 Elmwood Avenue, Room 237
PO Box 879
Burlington, VT 05402-0879
☎ (802) 951-6290

New York/New Jersey

New Jersey State Office
1 Newark Center, 13th Floor
Newark, NJ 07102-5260
☎ (201) 622-7900

New York State Office
26 Federal Plaza
New York, NY 10278-0068
☎ (212) 264-6500

Albany Area Office
52 Corporate Circle
Albany, NY 12203-5121
☎ (518) 464-4200

Buffalo Area Office
Lafayette Court, 5th Floor
465 Main Street
Buffalo, NY 14203-1780
☎ (716) 551-5755

Camden Area Office
Hudson Building
800 Hudson Square, 2nd Floor
Camden, NJ 08102-1156
☎ (609) 757-5081

Mid-Atlantic

Delaware State Office
824 Market Street, Suite 850
Wilmington, DE 19801-3016
☎ (302) 573-6300

District of Columbia Office
820 First Street, NE, Suite 450
Washington, DC 20002-4205
☎ (202) 275-9200

Maryland State Office
City Crescent Building, 5th Floor
10 South Howard Street
Baltimore, MD 21201-2505
☎ (410) 962-2520

Pennsylvania State Office
The Wanamaker Building
100 Penn Square East
Philadelphia, PA 19107-3380
☎ (215) 656-0600

Virginia State Office
The 3600 Centre
3600 West Broad Street
Richmond, VA 23230-4920
☎ (804) 278-4539

West Virginia State Office
405 Capitol Street, Suite 708
Charleston, WV 25301-1795
📞 (304) 347-7000

Pittsburgh Area Office
339 Sixth Avenue, 6th Floor
Pittsburgh, PA 15222-2525
📞 (412) 644-6428

South/Caribbean

Alabama State Office
Beacon Ridge Tower
600 Beacon Parkway West,
    Suite 300
Birmingham, AL 35209-3144
📞 (205) 290-7617

Caribbean Office
New San Juan Office Building
159 Carlos E. Chardon Avenue
San Juan, PR 00918-1804
📞 (787) 766-6121

Florida State Office
Gable 1 Tower
1320 South Dixie Highway
Coral Gables, FL 33146-2926
📞 (305) 662-4500

Georgia State Office
Richard B. Russell Federal Building
75 Spring Street, SW
Atlanta, GA 30303-3388
📞 (404) 331-5136

Kentucky State Office
601 West Broadway
PO Box 1044
Louisville, KY 40201-1044
📞 (502) 582-5251

Mississippi State Office
Doctor A. H. McCoy Federal Building
100 West Capitol Street, Suite 910
Jackson, MS 39269-1018
📞 (601) 965-4738

North Carolina State Office
Kroger Building
2306 West Meadowview Road
Greensboro, NC 27407-3707
📞 (919) 547-4000

South Carolina State Office
Strom Thurmond Federal Building
1835 Assembly Street
Columbia, SC 29201-2480
📞 (803) 765-5592

Tennessee State Office
251 Cumberland Bend Drive,
    Suite 200
Nashville, TN 37228-1803
📞 (615) 736-5213

Arkansas State Office
TCBY Tower
425 West Capitol Avenue, Suite 900
Little Rock, AR 72201-3488
📞 (501) 324-5931

Louisiana State Office
Hale Boggs Federal Building
501 Magazine Street, 9th Floor
New Orleans, LA 70130-3099
📞 (504) 589-7201

Jacksonville Area Office
Southern Bell Tower
301 West Bay Street, Suite 2200
Jacksonville, FL 32202-5121
📞 (904) 232-2626

Knoxville Area Office
John J. Duncan Federal Building
710 Locust Street, 3rd Floor
Knoxville, TN 37902-2526
📞 (423) 545-4384

Memphis Area Office
One Memphis Place
200 Jefferson Avenue, Suite 1200
Memphis, TN 38103
📞 (901) 544-3367

Orlando Area Office
Langley Building
3751 Maguire Boulevard, Suite 270
Orlando, FL 32803-3032
📞 (407) 648-6441

Tampa Area Office
Timberlake Federal Building Annex
501 East Polk Street, Suite 700
Tampa, FL 33602-3945
📞 (813) 228-2501

Shreveport Area Office
401 Edwards Street, Suite 1510
Shreveport, LA 71101-3289
📞 (318) 676-3385

Tulsa Area Office
50 E. 15th Street
Tulsa, OK 74119-4030
📞 (918) 581-7434

Midwest

Illinois State Office
Ralph H. Metcalfe Federal Building
77 West Jackson Boulevard
Chicago, IL 60604-3507
📞 (312) 353-5680

Indiana State Office
151 North Delaware Street
Indianapolis, IN 46204-2526
📞 (317) 226-6303

Michigan State Office
Patrick V. McNamara Federal
    Building
477 Michigan Avenue
Detroit, MI 48226-2592
📞 (313) 226-7900

Minnesota State Office
220 Second Street, South
Minneapolis, MN 55401-2195
📞 (612) 370-3000

Ohio State Office
200 North High Street
Columbus, OH 43215-2499
☏ (614) 469-5737

Oklahoma State Office
500 Main Plaza
500 West Main Street
Oklahoma City, OK 73102-2233
☏ (405) 553-7401

Iowa State Office
Federal Building
210 Walnut Street, Room 239
Des Moines, IA 50309-2155
☏ (515) 284-4512

Kansas/Missouri State Office
Gateway Tower II
400 State Avenue, Room 200
Kansas City, KS 66101-2406
☏ (913) 551-5462

Nebraska State Office
Executive Tower Centre
10909 Mill Valley Road
Omaha, NE 68154-3955
☏ (402) 492-3100

St. Louis Area Office
Robert A. Young Federal Building
1222 Spruce Street, 3rd Floor
St. Louis, MO 63103-2836
☏ (314) 539-6583

Wisconsin State Office
Henry S. Reuss Federal Plaza
310 West Wisconsin Avenue,
    Suite 1380
Milwaukee, WI 53203-2289
☏ (414) 297-3214

Cincinnati Area Office
525 Vine Street, 7th Floor
Cincinnati, OH 45202-3188
☏ (513) 684-3451

Cleveland Area Office
Renaissance Building
1350 Euclid Avenue, 5th Floor
Cleveland, OH 44115-1815
☏ (216) 522-4065

Flint Area Office
605 N. Saginaw Street, Room 200
Flint, MI 48502-2043
☏ (810) 766-5108

Grand Rapids Area Office
Trade Center Building
50 Louis Street, NW, 3rd Floor
Grand Rapids, MI 49503-2648
☏ (616) 456-2100

Texas and Southwest

Arizona State Office
2 Arizona Center
400 North 5th Street, Suite 1600
Phoenix, AZ 85004-2361
☏ (602) 379-4434

Tucson Area Office
Security Pacific Bank Plaza
33 North Stone Avenue, Suite 700
Tucson, AZ 85701-1467
☏ (520) 670-6237

New Mexico State Office
625 Truman Street, NE
Albuquerque, NM 87110-6472
☏ (505) 262-6463

Texas State Office
1600 Throckmorton
PO Box 2905
Fort Worth, TX 76113-2905
☏ (817) 978-9000

Dallas Area Office
525 Griffin Street, Room 860
Dallas, TX 75202-5007
☏ (214) 767-8359

Houston Area Office
Norfolk Tower
2211 Norfolk, Suite 200
Houston, TX 77098-4096
☏ (713) 313-2274

Lubbock Area Office
Federal Office Building
1205 Texas Avenue
Lubbock, TX 79401-4093
☏ (806) 472-7265

San Antonio Area Office
Washington Square
800 Dolorosa Street
San Antonio, TX 78207-4563
☏ (210) 472-6806

Rocky Mountains

Colorado State Office
633 17th Street
Denver, CO 80202-3607
☏ (303) 672-5440

Montana State Office
Federal Office Building, Drawer
    10095
301 S. Park, Room 340
Helena, MT 59626-0095
☏ (406) 441-1298

North Dakota State Office
Federal Building
653 2nd Avenue North, Room 366
PO Box 2483
Fargo, ND 58108-2483
☏ (701) 239-5136

South Dakota State Office
2400 West 49th Street, Suite I-201
Sioux Falls, SD 57105-6558
☏ (605) 330-4223

Utah State Office
257 Tower
257 East 200 South, Suite 550
Salt Lake City, UT 84111-2048
☎ (801) 524-3323

Wyoming State Office
Federal Office Building
100 East B Street, Room 4229
Casper, WY 82601-1918
☎ (307) 261-6250

Pacific/Hawaii

California State Office
Phillip Burton Federal Building and
    U.S. Courthouse
450 Golden Gate Avenue
PO Box 36003
San Francisco, CA 94102-3448
☎ (415) 436-6550

Fresno Area Office
2135 Fresno Street, Suite 100
Fresno, CA 93721-1718
☎ (209) 487-5032

Los Angeles Area Office
611 West 6th Street, Suite 800
Los Angeles, CA 90017-3127
☎ (213) 894-8000

Sacramento Area Office
777 12th Street, Suite 200
Sacramento, CA 95814-1997
☎ (916) 498-5220

San Diego Area Office
Mission City Corporate Center
2365 Northside Drive, Suite 300
San Diego, CA 92108-2712
☎ (619) 557-5310

Santa Ana Area Office
3 Hutton Centre, Suite 500
Santa Ana, CA 92707-5764
☎ (714) 957-7333

Hawaii State Office
Seven Waterfront Plaza
500 Ala Moana Boulevard, Suite 500
Honolulu, HI 96813-4918
☎ (808) 522-8175

Nevada State Office
Atrium Building
333 N. Rancho Drive, Suite 700
Las Vegas, NV 89106-3714
☎ (702) 388-6525

Reno Area Office
1575 Delucchi Lane, Suite 114
Reno, NV 89502-6581
☎ (702) 784-5066

Northwest/Alaska

Alaska State Office
University Plaza Building
949 East 36th Avenue, Suite 401
Anchorage, AK 99508-4135
☎ (907) 271-4170

Idaho State Office
Plaza IV
800 Park Boulevard, Suite 200
Boise, ID 83712-7743
☎ (208) 334-1990

Oregon State Office
400 Southwest Sixth Avenue,
    Suite 700
Portland, OR 97204-1632
☎ (503) 326-2561

Washington State Office
Seattle Federal Office Building
909 1st Avenue, Suite 200
Seattle, WA 98104-1000
☎ (206) 220-5101

Spokane Area Office
Farm Credit Bank Building
601 West First Avenue, 8th Floor East
Spokane, WA 99204-0317
☎ (509) 353-2510

BOOKS, MAGAZINES, AND PAMPHLETS

Buying or Selling a Home: Top Tips from NAR
The National Association of Realtors
430 N. Michigan Avenue
Chicago, IL 60611-4087
✆(800) 847-6500
✍*www.realtor.org*
This booklet offers more than 300 tips and sells for $8.95 per copy.

Everyone's Money Book, by Jordan Goodman (Dearborn Trade; ✍*www.dearborntrade.com*)

Booklets from HSH Associates that cover a variety of topics:
- *What Every Consumer Needs to Know*
- *A Homeowner's Guide to Private Mortgage Insurance (PMI)*
- *The Homebuyer's Mortgage Kit*
- *A Homeowner's Guide to Refinancing*
- *A Homeowner's Guide to Home Equity Loans and Lines of Credit*
- *A Homeowner's Guide to Prepaying Your Mortgage*

HSH Associates
1200 Route 23
Butler, NJ 07405
(800) UPDATES
✍*www.hsh.com*

National Trust for Historic Preservation
Preservation Magazine
1785 Massachusetts Ave., NW
Washington, DC 20036
✆(202) 588-6000
✍*www.nationaltrust.org*
This glossy bimonthly magazine is a benefit of membership in the National Trust; membership costs $20 annually.

Streetwise® Landlording and Property Management, by Mark B. Weiss and Dan Baldwin (Adams Media; ✍*www.adamsmedia.com*)

The Everything® Homeselling Book, by Ruth Rejnis (Adams Media Corporation; ✍*www.adamsmedia.com*)

The Old House Interiors
108 E. Main Street
Gloucester, MA 01930
✆(978) 283-3200
This bimonthly publication is filled with interior design tips; a subscription is $26 a year.

ORGANIZATIONS

American Institute of Architects
1735 New York Ave., NW
Washington, DC, 20006
✆(800) AIA-3837
✍*www.aia.org*
The AIA can refer you to members in your area.

American Society of Home Inspectors, Inc. (ASHI)
932 Lee Street, Suite 101
Des Plaines, IL 60016
✆(847) 759-2820, (800) 743-ASHI
✍*www.ashi.com*
They can provide you with the name of a home inspector in your area.

Buyer's Homefinding Network, at (800) 500-3569
✍*www.finderhome.com*
Provides a free service to match consumers with buyer agents.

The Council of Better Business Bureaus
c/o Publications Department
4200 Wilson Boulevard,
      Arlington, VA 22203
☎ (703) 276-0100

They offer tips on home inspection.

The Consumer Information Center
PO Box 100
Pueblo, CO 81002

The Consumer Information Center offers a free catalog (available at most libraries) as well as many good government pamphlets covering settlement costs, manufactured homes, and G.I. loans.

Employee Relocation Council
1717 Pennsylvania Ave., NW, Suite 800
Washington, DC, 20006
☎ (202) 857-0857
✍ www.erc.org

Federal National Mortgage Association
3900 Wisconsin Ave., NW
Washington, DC, 20016
☎ (202) 752-7000
✍ www.fanniemae.com

Provides home-buying information for single-family and multifamily houses, guidelines for mortgage qualification and application, information about what's new in lending, dates and locations of home-buying and home-financing seminars, and listings of Fannie Mae–owned properties for sale or auction.

Federal Reserve Board
20th St. and C St., NW
Washington, DC, 20551
☎ (202) 452-3946
✍ www.federalreserve.gov

The Federal Reserve offers many free brochures about real estate.

Mortgage Bankers Association of America
1919 Pennsylvania Ave., NW
Washington, DC, 20006-3438
☎ (202) 557-2700
✍ www.mbaa.org

Mortgage Bankers of America offers a section for consumers on homebuying, as well as overall home-buying tips and a glossary.

National Association of Home Builders
1201 15th St., NW
Washington, DC 20005
☎ (202) 822-0200
✍ www.nahb.com

This association represents builders, remodelers, and others involved in the home building industry.

National Association of Realtors
430 N. Michigan Avenue
Chicago, IL 60611
☎ (312) 329-8200, (800) 874-6500
✍ www.realtor.com

This association provides information to both consumers and real-estate agents, including homes for sale and tons of educational materials.

The National Association of the Remodeling Industry (NARI)
780 Lee Street, Suite 200
Des Plaines, IL 60016
☎ (847) 298-9200
✍ www.nari.org

NARI offers a wealth of material that ranges from design ideas to remodeling plans, a library of resources, and consumer tips to help avoid scams in this industry.

National Flood Insurance Program, administered by the
Federal Emergency Management Agency (FEMA)
500 C Street, SW
Washington, DC 20472
☎ (202) 566-1600
✐ www.fema.gov

FEMA offers information on flood insurance.

National Trust for Historic Preservation
1785 Massachusetts Ave., NW
Washington, DC, 20036
☎ (202) 588-6000
✐ www.nationaltrust.org

The National Trust for Historic Preservation works to
preserve and protect historical property through a variety
of educational, technical, political, and financial means.

CREDIT REPORTS

You can obtain a copy of your credit report by contacting
one of the following agencies.

Equifax
P.O. Box 740241
Atlanta, GA 30348
☎ (888) 685-1111
✐ www.equifax.com

Experian
P.O. Box 2104
Allen, TX 75013
☎ (888) 397-3742
✐ www.experian.com

Trans Union
P.O. Box 1000
Chester, PA 19022
☎ (800) 888-4213
✐ www.transunion.com

Index

THE EVERYTHING HOMESELLING BOOK

By Ruth Rejnis

THE EVERYTHING HOMESELLING BOOK
From open house to closing the deal, everything you need to know to get the most money for your house
Ruth Rejnis

Trade paperback,
$12.95 ($19.95 CAN)
1-58062-304-2, 304 pages

I f you are getting ready to sell your house, or are thinking about putting it on the market, *The Everything® Homeselling Book* is the perfect introduction. It walks you through every step of the process, from your first open house to closing the deal. There are literally dozens of homeselling strategies, and real-estate expert Ruth Rejnis shows you which one is right for you. *The Everything® Homeselling Book* details the many steps that need to be taken, including preparing the house, dealing with brokers, hiring an attorney, and more.

OTHER *EVERYTHING®* BOOKS BY ADAMS MEDIA CORPORATION

BUSINESS

Everything® **Business Planning Book**
Everything® **Coaching & Mentoring Book**
Everything® **Home-Based Business Book**
Everything® **Leadership Book**
Everything® **Managing People Book**
Everything® **Network Marketing Book**
Everything® **Online Business Book**
Everything® **Project Management Book**
Everything® **Selling Book**
Everything® **Start Your Own Business Book**
Everything® **Time Management Book**

COMPUTERS

Everything® **Build Your Own Home Page Book**
Everything® **Computer Book**

Everything® **Internet Book**
Everything® **Microsoft® Word 2000 Book**

COOKING

Everything® **Bartender's Book, $9.95**
Everything® **Barbecue Cookbook**
Everything® **Chocolate Cookbook**
Everything® **Cookbook**
Everything® **Dessert Cookbook**
Everything® **Diabetes Cookbook**
Everything® **Low-Carb Cookbook**
Everything® **Low-Fat High-Flavor Cookbook**
Everything® **Mediterranean Cookbook**
Everything® **One-Pot Cookbook**
Everything® **Pasta Book**
Everything® **Quick Meals Cookbook**
Everything® **Slow Cooker Cookbook**

Everything® **Soup Cookbook**
Everything® **Thai Cookbook**
Everything® **Vegetarian Cookbook**
Everything® **Wine Book**

HEALTH

Everything® **Anti-Aging Book**
Everything® **Dieting Book**
Everything® **Herbal Remedies Book**
Everything® **Hypnosis Book**
Everything® **Menopause Book**
Everything® **Stress Management Book**
Everything® **Vitamins, Minerals, and Nutritional Supplements Book**
Everything® **Nutrition Book**

HISTORY

Everything® **American History Book**

All Everything® books are priced at $12.95 or $14.95, unless otherwise stated. Prices subject to change without notice.
Canadian prices range from $11.95–$22.95 and are subject to change without notice.

Everything® **Civil War Book**
Everything® **World War II Book**

HOBBIES

Everything® **Bridge Book**
Everything® **Candlemaking Book**
Everything® **Casino Gambling Book**
Everything® **Chess Basics Book**
Everything® **Collectibles Book**
Everything® **Crossword and Puzzle Book**
Everything® **Digital Photography Book**
Everything® **Drums Book (with CD),** $19.95, ($31.95 CAN)
Everything® **Family Tree Book**
Everything® **Games Book**
Everything® **Guitar Book**
Everything® **Knitting Book**
Everything® **Magic Book**
Everything® **Motorcycle Book**
Everything® **Online Genealogy Book**
Everything® **Playing Piano and Keyboards Book**
Everything® **Rock & Blues Guitar Book (with CD),** $19.95, ($31.95 CAN)
Everything® **Scrapbooking Book**

HOME IMPROVEMENT

Everything® **Feng Shui Book**
Everything® **Gardening Book**
Everything® **Home Decorating Book**
Everything® **Landscaping Book**
Everything® **Lawn Care Book**
Everything® **Organize Your Home Book**

KIDS' STORY BOOKS

Everything® **Bedtime Story Book**
Everything® **Bible Stories Book**
Everything® **Fairy Tales Book**
Everything® **Mother Goose Book**

NEW AGE

Everything® **Astrology Book**

Everything® **Divining the Future Book**
Everything® **Dreams Book**
Everything® **Ghost Book**
Everything® **Meditation Book**
Everything® **Numerology Book**
Everything® **Palmistry Book**
Everything® **Spells and Charms Book**
Everything® **Tarot Book**
Everything® **Wicca and Witchcraft Book**

PARENTING

Everything® **Baby Names Book**
Everything® **Baby Shower Book**
Everything® **Baby's First Food Book**
Everything® **Baby's First Year Book**
Everything® **Breastfeeding Book**
Everything® **Get Ready for Baby Book**
Everything® **Homeschooling Book**
Everything® **Potty Training Book,** $9.95, ($15.95 CAN)
Everything® **Pregnancy Book**
Everything® **Pregnancy Organizer,** $15.00, ($22.95 CAN)
Everything® **Toddler Book**
Everything® **Tween Book**

PERSONAL FINANCE

Everything® **Budgeting Book**
Everything® **Get Out of Debt Book**
Everything® **Get Rich Book**
Everything® **Investing Book**
Everything® **Homebuying Book, 2nd Ed.**
Everything® **Homeselling Book**
Everything® **Money Book**
Everything® **Mutual Funds Book**
Everything® **Online Investing Book**
Everything® **Personal Finance Book**

PETS

Everything® **Cat Book**
Everything® **Dog Book**
Everything® **Dog Training and Tricks**
Everything® **Horse Book**
Everything® **Puppy Book**
Everything® **Tropical Fish Book**

REFERENCE

Everything® **Astronomy Book**
Everything® **Car Care Book**
Everything® **Christmas Book,** $15.00, ($21.95 CAN)
Everything® **Classical Mythology Book**
Everything® **Divorce Book**
Everything® **Etiquette Book**
Everything® **Great Thinkers Book**
Everything® **Learning French Book**
Everything® **Learning German Book**
Everything® **Learning Italian Book**
Everything® **Learning Latin Book**
Everything® **Learning Spanish Book**
Everything® **Mafia Book**
Everything® **Philosophy Book**
Everything® **Shakespeare Book**
Everything® **Tall Tales, Legends, & Other Outrageous Lies Book**
Everything® **Toasts Book**
Everything® **Trivia Book**
Everything® **Weather Book**
Everything® **Wills & Estate Planning Book**

RELIGION

Everything® **Angels Book**
Everything® **Buddhism Book**
Everything® **Catholicism Book**
Everything® **Judaism Book**
Everything® **Saints Book**
Everything® **World's Religions Book**
Everything® **Understanding Islam Book**

SCHOOL & CAREERS

Everything® **After College Book**
Everything® **College Survival Book**
Everything® **Cover Letter Book**
Everything® **Get-a-Job Book**
Everything® **Hot Careers Book**
Everything® **Job Interview Book**
Everything® **Online Job Search Book**
Everything® **Resume Book, 2nd Ed.**
Everything® **Study Book**

All Everything® books are priced at $12.95 or $14.95, unless otherwise stated. Prices subject to change without notice.
Canadian prices range from $11.95–$22.95 and are subject to change without notice.

WE HAVE EVERYTHING . . . .

SPORTS/FITNESS

Everything® **Bicycle Book**
Everything® **Fishing Book**
Everything® **Fly-Fishing Book**
Everything® **Golf Book**
Everything® **Golf Instruction Book**
Everything® **Pilates Book**
Everything® **Running Book**
Everything® **Sailing Book, 2nd Ed.**
Everything® **T'ai Chi and QiGong Book**
Everything® **Total Fitness Book**
Everything® **Weight Training Book**
Everything® **Yoga Book**

TRAVEL

Everything® **Guide to Las Vegas**
Everything® **Guide to New England**
Everything® **Guide to New York City**
Everything® **Guide to Washington D.C.**

Everything® **Travel Guide to The Disneyland Resort®, California Adventure®, Universal Studios®, and the Anaheim Area**
Everything® **Travel Guide to the Walt Disney World® Resort, Universal Studios®, and Greater Orlando, 3rd Ed.**

WEDDINGS & ROMANCE

Everything® **Creative Wedding Ideas Book**
Everything® **Dating Book**
Everything® **Jewish Wedding Book**
Everything® **Romance Book**
Everything® **Wedding Book, 2nd Ed.**
Everything® **Wedding Organizer, $15.00** ($22.95 CAN)

Everything® **Wedding Checklist,** $7.95 ($11.95 CAN)
Everything® **Wedding Etiquette Book,** $7.95 ($11.95 CAN)
Everything® **Wedding Shower Book,** $7.95 ($12.95 CAN)
Everything® **Wedding Vows Book,** $7.95 ($11.95 CAN)
Everything® **Weddings on a Budget Book, $9.95** ($15.95 CAN)

WRITING

Everything® **Creative Writing Book**
Everything® **Get Published Book**
Everything® **Grammar and Style Book**
Everything® **Grant Writing Book**
Everything® **Guide to Writing Children's Books**
Everything® **Writing Well Book**

ALSO AVAILABLE:
THE EVERYTHING® KIDS' SERIES!

Each book is 8" x 9¼", 144 pages, and two-color throughout.

Everything® **Kids' Baseball Book, 2nd Edition, $6.95** ($11.95 CAN)
Everything® **Kids' Bugs Book, $6.95** ($10.95 CAN)
Everything® **Kids' Cookbook, $6.95** ($10.95 CAN)
Everything® **Kids' Joke Book, $6.95** ($10.95 CAN)
Everything® **Kids' Math Puzzles Book, $6.95** ($10.95 CAN)
Everything® **Kids' Mazes Book, $6.95** ($10.95 CAN)
Everything® **Kids' Money Book, $6.95** ($11.95 CAN)

Everything® **Kids' Monsters Book, $6.95** ($10.95 CAN)
Everything® **Kids' Nature Book, $6.95** ($11.95 CAN)
Everything® **Kids' Puzzle Book $6.95,** ($10.95 CAN)
Everything® **Kids' Science Experiments Book, $6.95** ($10.95 CAN)
Everything® **Kids' Soccer Book, $6.95** ($11.95 CAN)
Everything® **Kids' Travel Activity Book, $6.95** ($10.95 CAN)

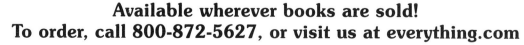

Available wherever books are sold!
To order, call 800-872-5627, or visit us at everything.com

Everything® is a registered trademark of Adams Media Corporation.